MINDFULNESS-BASED INTERVENTION RESEARCH

This book provides an outline and critical discussion of the characteristics of mindfulness-based interventions (MBIs) research. Since the first reports on the use of mindfulness practices in health interventions, a large body of research literature has emerged to document the effectiveness of MBIs for reducing psychological distress and for increasing well-being. The integration of mindfulness into very diverse psychological theories makes it a unique concept in psychology that has generated a large amount of interest both in academic research but also the broader media. With this growing literature, mindfulness researchers have also recognised the need to be more critical of its developments, such as how MBIs are presented to the public or what types of research methods are used to test claims of an MBI's effectiveness. This book examines the large variety of approaches in which MBIs have been studied, including an outline of the philosophical underpinnings of MBI research, definition and measurement of mindfulness, the use of qualitative and quantitative research methods, research design, and research that addresses cultural and religious factors. The book contributes to increased awareness of the current direction of MBI research and thus seeks to contribute to further methodological refinement and sophistication of the research field. This book on the characteristics of research on MBIs is a must read for any researcher or practitioner interested in this fascinating topic.

Christian U. Krägeloh, PhD, is Associate Professor in the Discipline of Psychology at Auckland University of Technology, New Zealand. His research interests include psychometrics, quality of life research, and mindfulness. Chris is a founding member of the New Zealand World Health Organisation Quality of Life Group. He is an author on nearly 100 book chapters and articles in international journals, co-author of a popular research methods textbook, and co-editor of two books on student well-being. Chris is currently Associate Editor for the journal *Mindfulness*.

Marcus A. Henning, PhD, is Associate Professor and Post-Graduate Academic Advisor at the Centre for Medical and Health Sciences Education at the University of Auckland. He is actively engaged in research, and his specific interests include: quality of life, the motivation to teach and learn, organisational behaviour, conflict management, and professional integrity. His background is in psychology, education, and mathematics teaching. His PhD was in the area of educational psychology.

Oleg N. Medvedev, PhD, is Lecturer/Assistant Professor at the University of Waikato School of Psychology and Associate Editor of the *Journal of Child and Family Studies*. He is teaching advanced research methods and is actively involved in research covering areas of health psychology, mindfulness-based interventions, well-being, health-related quality of life, psychophysiology of stress, dynamic and enduring symptoms of psychopathology, healthy aging, and surgical safety. A substantial amount of Oleg's work focuses on application of advanced statistical and psychometric methods such as Generalisability Theory and Rasch analysis to evaluate and enhance measurement of health-related outcomes.

Xuan Joanna Feng, PhD, completed her doctoral thesis at Auckland University of Technology in 2016 with the title "Differences and similarities between Buddhism and psychology in the conceptualisation of mindfulness".

Fiona Moir, PhD, is Senior Lecturer and Co-Director of Medical Student Affairs at the University of Auckland. She has integrated mindfulness into the medical programme as part of the "SAFE-DRS" well-being curriculum. Fiona has created comprehensive pastoral care policies and pathways for medical students, and mental health strategies for the wider university. She is a director of two companies: Connect Communications, providing well-being, supervision and communication skills training, and First Response, specialising in peer-interventions for identifying and responding to distress in the workplace. In 2018, she won the University of Auckland Vice-Chancellor's Excellence Award for Health, Safety and Wellbeing.

Rex Billington, PhD, has held academic posts in medical schools in USA and Scotland before joining the World Health Organisation in 1982 where he worked for 18 years in a career appointment. He held senior posts in Educational Development, and Directorships in the Global Programme on AIDS and Mental Health. In recent years, he has been Adjunct Professor and Professorial Fellow at Auckland University of Technology. Special interests are in public health, psychometrics, positive psychology, and quality of life assessment. Now in semi-retirement, he enjoys contributing to mental health community development programmes, particularly outcomes assessment, supporting research, and mentoring.

Richard J. Siegert, PhD, is Professor of Psychology and Rehabilitation at the Auckland University of Technology. His research interests include psychometrics, outcomes in mental health and rehabilitation, goal setting, and applying mind-fulness techniques for people with chronic health conditions. Richard is on the editorial committee of the journals *Disability and Rehabilitation* and *Mindfulness*. He is an author on over 140 articles in international journals and an author of two popular textbooks on rehabilitation. His most recent book is *Rehabilitation Goal Setting: Theory, Practice and Evidence* published recently by CRC Press/Taylor and Francis.

MINDFULNESS-BASED INTERVENTION RESEARCH

Characteristics, Approaches, and Developments

Christian U. Krägeloh, Marcus A. Henning,
Oleg N. Medvedev, Xuan Joanna Feng,
Fiona Moir, Rex Billington and Richard J. Siegert

Routledge
Taylor & Francis Group

LONDON AND NEW YORK

First published 2019
by Routledge
2 Park Square, Milton Park, Abingdon, Oxon OX14 4RN

and by Routledge
52 Vanderbilt Avenue, New York, NY 10017

Routledge is an imprint of the Taylor & Francis Group, an informa business

British Library Cataloguing in Publication Data
A catalogue record for this book is available from the British Library

Library of Congress Cataloging-in-Publication Data
Names: Krägeloh, Christian U., author.
Title: Mindfulness-based intervention research : characteristics, approaches, and developments / Christian U. Krägeloh, Marcus A. Henning, Oleg N. Medvedev, Xuan Joanna Feng, Fiona Moir, Rex Billington, Richard J. Siegert.
Description: Abingdon, Oxon ; New York, NY : Routledge, 2019. | Includes bibliographical references and index.
Identifiers: LCCN 2018054421| ISBN 9781138681385 (hardback) | ISBN 9781138681392 (pbk.) | ISBN 9781315545875 (e-book)
Subjects: | MESH: Mind-Body Therapies--methods | Mindfulness | Research
Classification: LCC RC480.5 | NLM WB 880 | DDC 616.89/1--dc23
LC record available at https://lccn.loc.gov/2018054421

ISBN: 978-1-138-68138-5 (hbk)
ISBN: 978-1-138-68139-2 (pbk)
ISBN: 978-1-315-54587-5 (ebk)

Typeset in Bembo
by Taylor & Francis Books
Printed by CPI Group (UK) Ltd, Croydon CR0 4YY

CONTENTS

TABLES

FOREWORD

Mindfulness has become a term that one is increasingly likely to encounter in a variety of contexts – inside and outside academia. Mindfulness provides a connecting thread between ancient practices and philosophies on one hand and modern science and everyday life on the other. The wide-spread fascination with mindfulness may be related to the fact that it resonates with experiences that we all have quite naturally at times and that we identify as healthy, meaningful, and profound. Some of us may interpret experiences of mindfulness from a framework of spirituality, religiousness, or personal beliefs, or we may just see these experiences as moments of contentment that are worth reflecting on and cherishing.

Even though mindfulness is commonly associated with clarity, purity, calmness, and simplicity, the discourse around it is often complex and contradictory. Of course, one must not confuse discussions and theories of mindfulness with mindfulness itself, which involves personal experiences and the attitudes one fosters to contextualise emotions and thoughts. It is precisely this multitude of functions of mindfulness that has triggered this enormous amount of literature. Depending on where, when, and why it is applied, the mindfulness practitioner needs to unlearn different habits and learn new ones. Discussions are also not being helped by the fact that we are using the term mindfulness in diverse ways – ranging from mindfulness as a practice or skill, to mindfulness as a disposition and habit, to mindfulness as a state or experience. With any emerging field of research and inquiry, a suitable vocabulary is necessary to express various nuances, which can be observed as already having started to occur.

While much of the mindfulness literature is situated in psychology, the topic has gained the attention of many allied disciplines, particularly in its application to the promotion of health. Mindfulness has been studied extensively in clinical contexts, such as in mindfulness-based interventions (MBIs) to address stress, depression, and anxiety, but is now also increasingly investigated as an intervention for general health and well-being. With the rapid growth of the field, the designs and procedures used in studies on mindfulness are gradually evolving. As mindfulness concerns experiential aspects of consciousness, mindfulness research inevitably makes contact with philosophy, thus also stimulating debates on wider theoretical issues in psychology.

In what might be interpreted as a sign of maturity, mindfulness research has also increasingly become self-critical of its own developments. Connecting to this trend to look inwards, the present book aims to outline current directions in research on MBIs, which will hopefully serve as a platform for self-reflection and a stimulus for further sophistication of research approaches. While this endeavour inevitably involves some coverage of the outcomes of particular studies, the main purpose of the book is not on the specific findings of these studies or the history of the development of this research field. Instead, the discussion will be structured by the context in which certain research methods have been applied and the theoretical debates that those studies have generated. For anyone planning to conduct research in the area, this book will be a resource to identify a suitable theoretical framework as well as appropriate research designs and measures. The book makes the assumption that the reader already possesses at least an introductory understanding of mindfulness practice as well as its effects and perceived purpose.

The book is structured into five chapters. Chapter 1 provides an outline of the literature that the increased popularity of MBIs generated, such as multidisciplinary and critical discussion, its links to spirituality, and conceptual work on appropriate operational definitions. Chapter 2 outlines the range of philosophical assumptions that underpin such research as well as how mindfulness has been studied using qualitative methods, and Chapter 3 presents an analysis of how mindfulness has been measured and assessed. Chapter 4 provides a critical overview of the quantitative research that directly investigated the effectiveness of MBIs, and Chapter 5 discusses the role of culture and belief systems in relation to MBI research.

1

THE CHARACTERISTICS OF RESEARCH ON MINDFULNESS-BASED INTERVENTIONS

When reading about mindfulness in the academic literature, it is not uncommon to encounter phrases such as "exponential" (Williams & Kabat-Zinn, 2011) or "explosion of interest" (Crane, Barnhofer, Hargus, Amarasinghe, & Winder, 2017) to describe its rapid rise in popularity. A common way to emphasise this trend is to present a diagram of the number of publications per year that are more or less directly related to mindfulness such as by mentioning mindfulness in the abstract or list of article keywords (Williams & Kabat-Zinn, 2011; & Jennings, 2016; Kabat-Zinn, 2017). Of course, one needs to be aware that such diagrams will always need to be interpreted with the knowledge that publication numbers in fields such as psychology have been growing steadily overall (Krampen, von Eye, & Schui, 2011). However, mindfulness is also increasingly covered in the news media, with one estimate showing that for each scientific article about mindfulness, around 30 appeared in the media (Van Dam et al., 2018).

Another indicator of the increased interest in mindfulness research is the launch of the journal *Mindfulness* (Singh, 2010), which has now become the flagship journal of the area, followed later by the appearance of another journal specifically devoted to mindfulness, namely *Mindfulness & Compassion* (García-Campayo & Demarzo, 2016). Regular in-depth discussions of specific mindfulness topics also appear within the book series *Mindfulness in Behavioral Health*, which recently published work on mindful parenting (Bögels & Restifo, 2014), mindfulness interventions for children with autism spectrum disorders (Hwang & Kearney, 2015), mindfulness in education (Schonert-Reichl & Roeser, 2016), mindfulness and Zen (Masuda & O'Donohue, 2017), and the ethical foundations of mindfulness (Stanley, Purser, & Singh, 2018), to name a few examples. The increasingly large number of mindfulness-related publications also prompted the creation of a regularly updated database to which readers can subscribe (Black, 2010).

The present book focuses on research about mindfulness as taught and conceptualised within the literature emerging from so-called mindfulness-based interventions (MBIs) such as Mindfulness-Based Stress Reduction (MBSR; Kabat-Zinn, 1990) and Mindfulness-Based Cognitive Therapy (MBCT; Segal, Williams, & Teasdale, 2013), which emphasise the practice of mindfulness-based meditation as a central component of their intervention (Crane et al., 2017). Such programmes are referred to as *mindfulness-based* as they share distinctive features such a systematic and sustained training in mindfulness and meditation for both course participants as well as teachers. Mindfulness is also regarded as central in theoretical models explaining the therapeutic benefits of such interventions. These approaches to mindfulness are thus in contrast with those that Crane et al. (2017) described as *mindfulness-informed*, such as Acceptance and Commitment Therapy (ACT; Hayes, Strosahl, & Wilson, 2011) or Dialectical Behavioural Therapy (DBT; Linehan, 1993) where mindfulness plays a less central role. Another way to classify these approaches is through the description of MBSR and MBCT as exemplifying neo-traditional mindfulness and ACT as well as DBT as cognitive-behavioural mindfulness (Hartelius, 2015). Additionally, the present book does not cover the research belonging to the literature of the purely socio-cognitive conceptualisation of mindfulness by Ellen Langer, which defines the concept in contrast to *mindlessness*, or the default mode of cognitive functioning in an automatic and inflexible manner (Khoury et al., 2017).

The present chapter outlines the literature around the increased acceptance of MBIs into mainstream psychological treatment approaches, including the discussion that this generated about mindfulness as multidisciplinary, transparadigmatic, and transdiagnostic. Increased critical discussion can also be noticed about this development, such as criticism of commercialisation of mindfulness practice and the ambiguous role of MBIs in regard to spirituality. Lastly, an overview is provided in this chapter of the various ways in which researchers and theorists have attempted to define mindfulness.

Bringing mindfulness into mainstream clinical applications

While mentioning mindfulness and meditation in academic settings may have previously conjured up stereotypes and hippie images, such connotations are no longer triggered (Bahl, 2017). Early psychological and psychophysical exploration of mindfulness practices tended to be related to transcendental meditation (e.g. Wallace, 1970) but have now shifted to more structured secular applications, which in turn has transformed how mindfulness is commonly perceived. The systematic integration of mindfulness into modern-day health interventions started with the pioneering work by Jon Kabat-Zinn. In 1979, Kabat-Zinn started MBSR at the University of Massachusetts Medical School. Unlike other Westerners who had already promoted the inclusion of Eastern philosophy into Western psychotherapy at that time, such as Carl Gustav Jung and Erich Fromm, Kabat-Zinn did not have a psychology or psychotherapy background but instead was a recent PhD graduate in molecular biology (Harrington & Dunne, 2015). He had also received extensive training in various Buddhist traditions, meaning that Kabat-Zinn can be considered a teacher of the so-called *dharma* – which can be translated as Buddhist teachings or even more broadly as the natural law of the world.

The first applications of mindfulness training by Kabat-Zinn at the medical school were in the form of an onsite self-care training programme for patients with a chronic pain condition, which eventually carried the name MBSR (Harrington & Dunne, 2015). This programme was particularly suited for patients with this condition as the programme taught them to develop a new attitude to their condition, shifting away from excessive self-criticism, anxiety, and catastrophising of pain to recognising their pain with acceptance and without judgment and habitual reactivity. The current model of MBSR is a structured programme that teaches meditation and mindfulness practices adapted from Buddhism but taught in a nonreligious manner. Participants are taught to develop sustained awareness of the present moment and stop worrying about the future or ruminating about the past. MBSR participants typically meet in evening groups for around two hours over a period of at least eight weeks as well as a full-day workshop around half way through the programme (Carmody & Baer, 2009). The mindfulness techniques taught during the programme include insight meditation, hatha yoga, breathing exercises, body scan exercises, mindful walking, and mindful eating. A major goal is for participants to apply these techniques to their everyday life routines, reinforced through daily home practice and the keeping of a diary.

Although it was originally intended to help patients who did not respond well to traditional medical and psychological treatments (Kabat-Zinn, 2003), MBSR has now been used to remediate a wide range of health issues (Didonna, 2009), and courses are offered in many places around the world (Cullen, 2011). Following a very similar format, MBCT (Segal et al., 2013) is more specifically focused on how participants respond to their cognitions as the programme was designed for individuals who have previously recovered from depression but who are still vulnerable to relapse. As a result of completing the course, participants will learn to process their cognitions differently, such as not getting caught up in their literal content and observing them nonjudgmentally. Apart from these two MBIs, mindfulness practice has since then been integrated into many other types of therapies and found a firm place in mainstream psychology (Shapiro, 2009; Harrington & Dunne, 2015). This position has been strengthened by the well-documented health benefits of MBIs. This includes effectiveness of mindfulness for reducing stress, anxiety, depression, chronic pain, or substance abuse (Chiesa & Serretti, 2009, 2010; Hofmann, Sawyer, Witt, & Oh, 2010; Khoury et al., 2013; Reiner, Tibi, & Lipsitz, 2013), increased coping with symptoms from chronic illness (Grossman, Niemann, Schmidt, & Walach, 2004) as well as improvement in regulation of emotions and well-being (Chambers, Gullone, & Allen, 2009; Eberth & Sedlmeir, 2012).

Further evidence for the increased acceptance of mindfulness as a mainstream therapeutic approach is the fact that it is now taught very widely. In a systematic search of website content, Barnes, Hattan, Black, and Schuman-Olivier (2018) found that, in 2014, mindfulness-related activities were present at 79% of medical schools in the United States. Universities increasingly recognise the importance of mindfulness as a tool to foster resilience in future health professionals such as medical students. There is a growing understanding that mindfulness not only fosters resilience to prevent burnout but also "improve[s] students' capacity for nonjudgmental presence and attention, so crucial in the doctor-patient relationship" (Wong, Chen, & Chan, 2018, p.97). The importance of personal mindfulness practice is thus not only recognised by mindfulness teachers and facilitators of MBIs (Fjorback & Walach, 2012; Shonin & Van Gordon, 2015) but also by primary care physicians (Krasner et al., 2009). In general psychotherapeutic practice, personal meditation practice of the therapist has also been reported to be associated with increased empathy and other interpersonal skills (Keane, 2014).

Mindfulness as a conduit for multidisciplinary and transdiagnostic approaches

The rapid rise of mindfulness research was fuelled by repeated reports of the benefits of MBIs, which subsequently attracted the interest of researchers in many different fields. As a result, mindfulness research has become multidisciplinary, including a wide range of both clinical and nonclinical applications as well as fundamental research into psychological and physiological functioning. This multidisciplinary expansion of mindfulness research has inevitably contributed to its increased complexity and diversity, thus opening up new opportunities for research and therapeutic applications. Nevertheless, it has also resulted in unique new challenges, particularly the question to what extent studies that refer to mindfulness can be described as investigating the same concept.

In the clinical context, reports of the beneficial effects from diverse applications of mindfulness are encouraging but raise some important theoretical considerations. Apart from the early original clinical applications of mindfulness to chronic pain as well as anxiety and depression, mindfulness has since been applied to a range of other psychological conditions including borderline personality disorder, posttraumatic stress disorder, eating disorders, and psychosis (Didonna, 2009) – to such an extent that mindfulness has been regularly referred to as having *transdiagnostic* applicability (Hanley, Abell, Osborn, Roehrig, & Canto, 2016; , Williams, van Mawijk, Armitage, & Sheffield, 2018). While some researchers have offered some hypotheses about what might be the transdiagnostic elements in mindfulness practice – for example the practitioner's ability to tolerate distressing qualia (Lomas, Edginton, Cartwright, & Ridge, 2015) – such transdiagnostic conceptualisations of mindfulness tend to lead to the conclusion that there will be one primary mechanism of function for mindfulness that can be proposed and studied scientifically. Although various such mechanisms have been proposed (Cebolla et al., 2018; Chiesa, Anselmi, & Serretti, 2014), the field is still far from being close to a consensus about this matter.

In addition to being transdiagnostic, arguments could be made that mindfulness is transparadigmatic as several psychological paradigms and approaches have found ways to incorporate mindfulness into their theoretical frameworks. Teasdale et al. (2000) successfully merged MBSR with principles of cognitive behavioural therapy (CBT), resulting in the popular MBCT programme. Common aspects between

CBT and MBCT, for example, are techniques used to facilitate a decentred view according to which clients learn not to identify themselves with their thoughts. Even though psychodynamic therapy is very different to CBT, mindfulness is also seen to function well within this paradigm. As Martin (1997) illustrated, mindfulness resonates well with psychodynamic psychology and is considered as something that therapists see as important to develop during the psychodynamic therapy process, such as through free association and interpretation as well as transference and countertransference. Within the humanistic paradigm, the recognition of the utility of mindfulness is also seen as pre-dating the more recent emergence of MBIs in the late 1970s. An example of a humanistic therapeutic approach that gives mindfulness a prominent role is the Hakomi method (Bageant, 2012).

A further psychological paradigm that has found a way to integrate mindfulness is that of behavioural psychology, particularly via contextual behavioural science (Hayes, Barnes-Holmes, & Wilson, 2012). This development in behavioural psychology acknowledges the role of thoughts and feelings, which radical behaviourism refers to as private events – and might be in contrast with the common perception that all forms of behaviourism endorse some form of a black box understanding of the brain and mind (Arntzen, Lokke, Lokke, & Eilertsen, 2010; Delprato & Midgley, 1992). Aligned with the philosophy of contextual behavioural science is ACT that may use some mindfulness exercises in its therapy (Hayes et al., 2011). While most classifications consider ACT to be distinct from MBIs such as MBSR and MBCT due to the less central role of mindfulness practice in ACT (Crane et al., 2017; Hartelius, 2015), another way to classify ACT is by grouping it with DBT and MBCT under the term *third wave of behavioural and cognitive therapies* (Hayes, 2004; Kahl, Winter, & Schweiger, 2012). What characterises such third wave therapies is a focus on awareness and one's responses to thoughts, unlike in CBT, for example, where the emphasis is placed on changing the content of cognitions. Because of this common understanding of the role of mindfulness to develop this awareness, there is a sense that traditional paradigm distinctions may become less noticeable. For instance, the behavioural approach of ACT could be considered to have more in common with MBCT than MBCT has in common with CBT, from which MBCT originated (Hayes, 2004).

Researchers in some areas of psychology or psychotherapy that have not entered mainstream explicitly admit that the rapid growth in popularity of mindfulness could arouse feelings of envy (Yapko, 2014). Additionally, Yapko (2014) noted how there does not appear to be the same kind of deep division in the professional mindfulness community as you tend to find with hypnosis, which may be related to the fact that acceptance and compassion is at the core of mindfulness practice. Part of the popularity of mindfulness may also be its flexibility to be adapted and applied together with a variety of therapy approaches. This includes hypnosis, which has been combined with mindfulness to develop Mindfulness-Based Cognitive Hypnotherapy (Alladin, 2014). Such integrations of mindfulness are facilitated by the fact that mindfulness is starting to be perceived as evidence-based and thus an example how mind-body approaches have been investigated using rigorous scientific methods.

Apart from repeated systematic literature reviews and meta-analyses of MBIs (e.g. Bohlmeijer, Prenger, Taal, & Cuijpers, 2010; Ledesma & Kumano, 2009; Lauche, Cramer, Dobos, Langhorst, & Schmidt, 2013; Smith, Richardson, Hoffman, & Pilkington, 2005), the evidence base for the benefits of mindfulness has been strengthened by brain imaging studies that are able to link meditative practices to specific brain regions. For example, one functional magnetic resonance imaging study (Pagnoni, Cekic, & Guo, 2008) reported that experienced Zen practitioners exhibit decreased duration of neural activity associated with conceptual automatic thinking compared to controls. The authors suggested that higher levels of experience in meditation may facilitate voluntary regulation of the flow of so-called *mentations*. Additionally, evidence obtained using magnetic resonance imaging (Pagnoni & Cekic, 2007) showed that the typically found age-related decline in brain grey matter volume and attention-task performance in the normal, nonmeditative population was not observed in experienced Zen practitioners. These findings suggest that meditation practice may prevent age-related cognitive deterioration by inhibiting reduction of grey matter volume. Consistent with these findings, Hölzel et al. (2011) reported increased grey matter density in the brain regions involved in emotion regulation, learning, memory, perspective taking, and self-related cognitions after an MBI. These areas include the hippocampus, posterior cingulate cortex, cerebellum, and temporo-parietal junction. Similarly, Grant, Courtemanche, Duerden, Duncan, and Rainville (2010) found regular long-term meditators to have a thicker cortex in areas of the brain related to affect and pain.

The evidence base from clinical applications and fundamental neuroscience work was no doubt a contributing factor to the expansion of mindfulness to increasingly diverse contexts. Mindfulness has now also been the topic of considerable investigation in areas including parenting and developing interpersonal relationships (Block-Lerner, Adair, Plumb, Rhatigan, & Orsillo, 2007; Bögels & Restifo, 2014; Moll, Frolic, & Key, 2015), fostering well-being of teachers and students in educational settings (Felver & Jennings, 2016), reducing stress and burnout in the workplace (Hyland, Lee, & Mills, 2015), promoting task-related performance and resilience in military personnel (Johnson et al., 2014; et al., 2015), improving sports performance (Birrer, Röthlin, & Morgan, 2012), or enhancing coach–athlete interactions (Longshore & Sachs, 2015). Other areas of novel explorations are the role of mindfulness to address wider social issues such as mindfulness and sustainability through pro-environmental attitudes and sustainable consumption (Ericson, Kjønstad, & Barstad, 2014; Barbaro & Pickett, 2016; Fischer, Stanszus, Geiger, Grossman, & Schrader, 2017), fostering positive emotions and generating support for political compromise in regional conflicts (Alkoby, Halperin, Tarrasch, & Levit-Binnun, 2017), or promoting increased self-awareness and contemplative practice in education (Zajonc, 2016).

Mindfulness has also been recognised as a dispositional variable (as opposed to a temporary state) and has been studied increasingly using cross-sectional research designs, particularly for the prediction of psychological health in those with and without mindfulness and meditation practice (Tomlinson, Yousaf, Vittersø, &

Jones, 2018). While such research often includes samples from university students, the associations between mindfulness and psychological well-being have been found to be similar in individuals sampled from the general population (Medvedev, Norden, Krägeloh, & Siegert, 2018). Lastly, such cross-sectional investigations have not only been limited to psychological health indicators but also include the relationship between mindfulness and factors such as authenticity and meaningfulness (Allan, Bott, & Suh, 2015).

Critical discussion of the development of mindfulness applications

So numerous have been the applications of mindfulness and the dissemination of the evidence for their effectiveness, that this may have created a climate of social pressure to expect benefits from mindfulness and could lead to wide-spread noncritical beliefs that mindfulness is a panacea (Hanley et al., 2016). Some of the words and phrases used to describe the unrestrained growth of mindfulness have been *hype* (Van Dam et al., 2018), *buzzword* (Sun, 2014), and "divulged in a sensationalist way" (Farias & Wikholm, 2016, p.329). While there have been increasing numbers of systematic and qualitative literature reviews that explored the methods and methodologies of studies on MBIs and presented points for critical discussions about alternative explanations and methodological concerns (e.g. Eby, Allen, Conley, Williamson, Henderson, & Mancini, 2018; Shaw, Sekelja, Frasca, Dhillon, & Price, 2018), most of the critical discussion of the development of mindfulness research has been in the form of opinion pieces or commentaries.

One review article that received significant media attention (e.g. Bergland, 2017; Stetka, 2017) when it appeared in early in print online during October 2017 and has been cited more than 50 times (according to Google Scholar) within the first 11 months is a publication by Van Dam et al. (2018) with the title "Mind the Hype: A Critical Evaluation and Prescriptive Agenda for Research on Mindfulness and Meditation". After sketching out the rapid growth of mindfulness in the academic literature and the media, the authors discussed the ambiguity of the concept and inconsistencies in which it had been defined and assessed. Based on this discussion, the authors proposed several items for a future research agenda, including: a move away from the use of a single term to refer to a variety of different aspects of mindfulness; using a larger variety of techniques to assess mindfulness such as neurobiological or behavioural measures; using more rigorous methods to test the effectiveness of clinical interventions; increasing efforts to monitor any adverse effects more systematically; and evaluating results from contemplative neuroscience studies more rigorously so that the links between mindfulness practice and brain states and function are not overstated.

In direct response to the article by Van Dam et al. (2018), Davidson and Dahl (2018) argued that most of the above-mentioned concerns are not specific issues pertaining to mindfulness research but also to psychology in general. Another main argument of rebuttal by Davidson and Dahl (2018) was that mindfulness was originally contextualised within contemplative practice and has only recently been applied in clinical situations. Attempts to evaluate mindfulness should therefore consider its primary role in fostering human flourishing rather than eliminating immediate suffering. The last point also echoes criticism that has been raised repeatedly about the recent mindfulness movement and its over-application for short-term benefits. Purser and Loy (2013) used the expression *McMindfulness* to lament the trend of commercialisation of mindfulness training – away from its original liberative and transformative purposes – and Hyland (2017) referred to this phenomenon as *McDonaldising* and called for increased awareness of the role of social transformation and ethics in mindfulness.

Other perspectives were offered through a Foucauldian lens, focusing on the way that mindfulness can be seen as having been medicalised and being in line with neo-liberal ideology (Reveley, 2016). Similar arguments were presented by Arthington (2016), according to whom mindfulness has been utilised to perpetuate a neo-liberal ideology by promoting the idea that individuals are responsible for their own well-being and not societal systems, and that well-being can be achieved through a lifelong project of self-improvement. As highlighted by Purser and Milillo (2015), separating mindfulness in that way from its original ethical context makes it easy to misappropriate the practice to pacify employees and thus function as a pretext not to address toxic organisational cultures. Further critical discussion has appeared in a book by Purser, Forbes, and Burke (2016), where a series of chapters debated the above-mentioned arguments. Notable here is also a reply by Repetti (2016) that provides a commentary to the common sentiment expressed in these critical chapters, which Repetti described as the *Anti-McMindfulness Bandwagon*. Another, more neutral, perspective has been offered by Schmidt (2014a), who argued that the mindfulness boom could be regarded as a reaction to increased functionalisation, individualisation, globalisation, and rationalisation. From this point of view, mindfulness represents a way of collective self-regulation of culture.

Secularity and spirituality in mindfulness-based interventions

Considerable debate has taken place about how MBIs should be presented to the public in relation to the role it assigns to spirituality and personal transformation. While MBIs such as MBSR are clearly aimed at more than just immediate health benefits by fostering development of meaningful reflective practice (Kabat-Zinn, 2011), their associations with Buddhism have been rather ambiguous. Although the Buddhist training and background of Jon Kabat-Zinn is well-known (Harrington & Dunne, 2015), Kabat-Zinn often distances himself from the perception of being a Buddhist (Williams & Kabat-Zinn, 2011) and presents MBIs as involving "relatively intensive training in Buddhist meditation without the Buddhism" (Kabat-Zinn, 2011, p.294). Some confusion, however, about the relationship between MBSR and Buddhism may be related to the fact that Kabat-Zinn regularly uses the term *dharma*, although he indirectly distinguishes between *dharma* as a general universal principle and *dharma* as the Buddhist teaching through the way in which he explicitly states when the latter meaning is intended (e.g. Kabat-Zinn, 2011). Cullen (2011) discusses this use of the term *dharma* more specifically and distinguishes between the Buddhist *dharma*, a universal nonreligious *dharma*, and even an American *dharma*. Nevertheless, the use of the term in this way can still be regarded as Kabat-Zinn interpreting phenomena through an inherent Buddhist perspective. Other examples of such universalist interpretations of Buddhist concepts is the view that the Buddhist Noble Eightfold Path (the so-called fourth Noble Truth taught by the Buddha that outlines how suffering can be eliminated) can be understood as a description of naturally occurring causality or as a law of nature (Monteiro, Musten, & Compson, 2015).

Obviously, the views of individual practitioners and MBI teachers will vary, but there are numerous other examples of mixed messages regarding MBIs documented in interviews of MBSR teachers and in observations from course participants to the extent that Purser (2015a) described MBSR as having a "chameleon and shape-shifting nature" (p.25) or dual identity. Some of this discourse may appear less ambiguous if seen as coming from a fundamental assumption that Buddhism has a universal essence that can be extracted and presented in a secular package (Purser, 2015a). However, unless it is explicitly stated that this is what is meant when it is argued that MBIs are *grounded* in Buddhist philosophy, the spiritually-laden language used in such contexts appear incongruent with the way in which MBIs are presented to the public (Shonin, Van Gordon, & Griffiths, 2013). To avoid the perception that MBIs are unethical in their self-portrayal, Van Gordon, Shonin, and Griffiths (2016) recommended that the primary intention of MBIs is presented more clearly as either an intervention that transmits Buddhist teachings or as an attention-based intervention that is fundamentally different from the way Buddhism teaches mindfulness.

In an attempt to position MBIs more clearly in their relationship to spirituality and religion, Van Gordon, Shonin, and Griffiths (2015) encouraged making the distinction between so-called first- and second-generation MBIs. First-generation MBIs (FG-MBIs) refer to approaches such as MBSR, MBCT, and various directly related derivatives such as Mindfulness-Based Eating Awareness Training (Kristeller, Wolever, & Sheets, 2014) or Mindfulness-Based Relapse Prevention (Witkiewitz, Marlatt, & Walker, 2005). Such approaches may be summarised by their primary clinical focus that teaches course participants mindfulness techniques most beneficial for that context, namely to develop attentional regulation and a nonjudgmental attitude towards dysfunctional thoughts and feelings (Van Gordon et al., 2015). Second-generation MBIs (SG-MBIs), in contrast, are those that extend beyond immediate therapeutic settings by promoting a broader application of mindfulness in everyday life. Additionally, SG-MBIs are explicit about their spiritual orientation, which also leads such programmes to utilise a larger variety of meditative techniques, including those related to ethical awareness and compassion for others (Van Gordon et al., 2015). Apart from the proposed distinction between FG-MBIs and SG-MBIs, other researchers have stressed the importance of presenting MBIs clearly in terms of their secularity by publishing best practice guidelines (Jennings, 2016).

How is mindfulness defined?

One could argue that a fairly accurate picture of the characteristics of a research area can be gathered by analysing the definitions used for its main concepts of interest – in this case mindfulness as a central variable in the mechanism of therapeutic action of MBIs. Such understanding will also assist in attempts to delineate any differences between MBIs and other psychological approaches or even differences among MBIs themselves (such as in the distinction between FG-MBIs and SG-MBIs). In the literature on MBIs, a commonly cited definition of mindfulness has been one that was provided by Kabat-Zinn (1994): "paying attention in a particular way: on purpose, in the present moment, and non-judgmentally" (p. 4). The essential aspects of this definition remained unchanged, and in a later operational working definition Kabat-Zinn (2003) described mindfulness as "the awareness that emerges through paying attention on purpose, in the present moment, and nonjudgmentally to the unfolding of experience moment by moment" (p.145). When reflecting on the development of MBSR, Kabat-Zinn (2011) outlined the purpose of these operational definitions in the context of early MBI research and stated that he:

> felt that the details concerning the use of the word *mindfulness* in the various contexts in which we were deploying it could be worked out later by scholars and researchers who were knowledgeable in this area, and interested in making such distinctions and resolving important issues that may have been confounded and compounded by the early but intentional ignoring or glossing over of potentially important historical, philosophical, and cultural nuances.
>
> *(p. 290)*

In a further commentary on the development of MBSR and the working definitions of mindfulness that have been used in this context, Kabat-Zinn (2017) clarified that mindfulness is intended as a synonym for awareness or pure awareness. Such understanding of mindfulness is very related to that taught in insight meditation, where the emphasis is also placed on bare attention (Sun, 2014). Given the intensive training Kabat-Zinn obtained in the practices of insight meditation (Gilpin, 2008), the parallels in his definition with those used in such approaches are unlikely to be a coincidence. Particularly influential Western insight meditation teachers have been Joseph Goldstein, Jack Kornfield, and Sharon Salzberg, who founded the *Insight Meditation Society* in the United States in 1975 after having received training from Theravāda teachers in Asia (Seager, 1999). Another important figure in the insight meditation movement is Sylvia Boorstein. Her books, *It's Easier Than You Think: The Buddhist Way to Happiness* and *Don't Just Do Something, Sit There*, are some of the most widely known introductory classics of insight meditation (Seager, 1999).

Some of the definitions of mindfulness used by these insight meditation teachers are listed in Table 1.1. For example, Goldstein (1987) referred to observing the flow of inner experiences as part of being mindful. This characteristic of simply noticing resembles the description of bare attention in the literature of modern

TABLE 1.1 Selected mindfulness definitions by insight meditation teachers Joseph Goldstein, Jack Kornfield, Sharon Salzberg, and Sylvia Boorstein.

Author	Book, Year	Definition of mindfulness
Boorstein	Don't Just Do Something, Sit There, 1996	The principal meditative practice the Buddha taught is called mindfulness: relaxed, nonclinging, nonaversive awareness of present experience (p.8).
	It's Easier Than You Think: The Buddhist Way to Happiness, 1997	Mindfulness is the aware, balanced acceptance of present experience. It isn't more complicated than that. It is opening to or receiving the present moment, pleasant or unpleasant, just as it is, without either clinging to it or rejecting it (p.60).
Goldstein	The Experience of Insight, 1987	Mindfulness ... means being aware of what is happening in the present moment. It means noticing the flow of things ..... Whatever the object is, to notice it, to be aware of it, without grasping, which is greed, without condemning, which is hatred, without forgetting, which is delusion, just observing the flow, is observing the process (p.13).
Goldstein & Kornfield	Seeking the Heart of Wisdom, 2001	Mindfulness is that quality of attention which notices without choosing, without preference; it is a choiceless awareness that, like the sun, shines on all things equally (p.19).
	Seeking the Heart of Wisdom, 2001	The first factor for our enlightenment, ... is the quality of mindfulness, a clear awareness of what is happening each moment .... Mindfulness means seeing how things are, directly and immediately seeing for oneself that which is present and true. It has a quality of fullness and impeccability to it, a bringing of our whole heart and mind, our full attention, to each moment (p.76).
Kornfield	Modern Buddhist Masters, 2007	In the development of wisdom, one quality of mind above all others is the key to practice. This quality is mindfulness, attention or self-recollection. The most direct way to understand our life situation, who we are and how our mind and body operate, is to observe with a mind that simply notices all events equally. This attitude of non-judgmental, direct observation allows all events to occur in a natural way (p.14).
	Modern Buddhist Masters, 2007	Mindfulness focuses on the moment of the process rather than on the reflection of it in concepts. Awareness is directed at the present moment, to the process itself, the only place where the understanding of reality's true nature can be gained (p.14).
Salzberg	Real Happiness: The Power of Meditation, 2011	Mindfulness refines our attention so that we can connect fully and directly with whatever life brings (p.12).
	Real Happiness: The Power of Meditation, 2011	Mindfulness, also called wise attention, helps us see what we're adding to our experiences, not only during meditation sessions but also elsewhere (p.78–79).

Burmese *Vipassana*/insight meditation such as by the German-born monk Nyanaponika Thera (Gilpin, 2008; Sun, 2014). Mark Epstein, who also became a well-known insight meditation teacher, even explicitly referred to bare attention when he described mindfulness as "bare attention, in which moment-to-moment awareness of changing objects of perception is cultivated" (Epstein, 1995, p.96). Boorstein (1996, 1997) described mindfulness as a practice that involves open awareness to the present moment with acceptance, and other definitions also referred to aspects of attention and awareness. For instance, Kornfield (2007) described mindfulness as a form of attention, and Salzberg (2011) named mindfulness *wise attention*. When mindfulness is defined as awareness, it is sometimes understood as a transformative way of perception: "seeing how things are, directly and immediately seeing for oneself that which is present and true" (Goldstein & Kornfield, 2001, p.76). What is also common to these definitions within the insight meditation literature is references to awareness qualities such as nonjudgmental, present-centred, and insight-oriented.

The discussion in the earlier part of the chapter outlined how the content and delivery format of MBIs had resulted in inconsistent perceptions of MBIs in relation to Buddhism such that it is unclear whether the MBIs emerging in the West can genuinely be described as secular or whether they are *de facto* Buddhist. In the literature about suitable definitions of mindfulness, similar debates can be detected. Here, the issue is not so much about the explicit mentioning of religious themes and content, as the wording in Buddhist descriptions of mindfulness is also very much focused on mental processes and techniques. Instead, distinctions have typically been made regarding emphasis placed on various characteristics or the purpose of practice that might be implied by such practice. For example, Rapgay and Bystrisky (2009) compared the conceptualisation of mindfulness from so-called modern approaches such as MBIs with those of so-called classical mindfulness, and Otani (2016) distinguished between pure mindfulness versus clinical mindfulness. On the other hand, it is arguable whether the necessary generalisations for such classifications can be justified, as detailed analyses typically reveal that the conceptualisations of mindfulness within different Buddhist schools are just as diverse as the presumed differences with secular MBIs (Dorjee, 2010; Dunne, 2011). Therefore, instead of describing one approach in a particular way and contrasting it with another (thus potentially amplifying any differences), Dorjee (2010) recognised that Buddhist and MBI approaches may instead differ in terms of the emphasis placed on various aspects of mindfulness, which they depicted in a schematic diagram.

A common theme when comparing mindfulness in MBIs with that of Buddhism relates to the supposedly excessive focus of the former on present-moment awareness. Mindfulness in MBIs has been criticised for being regarded as something that is primarily palliative and focused on relieving short-term stress. This alleged fixation on present-moment awareness in order to achieve these therapeutic goals has been described as *here-and-now-ism* (Brazier, 2013; Purser, 2015b). Both theoretical (e.g. Dreyfus, 2011; Shonin, Van Gordon, & Singh, 2015) as well as empirical work (e.g. Christopher, Woodrich, & Tiernan, 2014; Feng, Krägeloh, Billington, & Siegert, 2018) highlighted the role of ethical considerations in Buddhist mindfulness practice, which appears incongruent with instructions not to evaluate one's thoughts and feelings. Buddhist practitioners, in contrast, are encouraged to develop so-called right or wholesome mindfulness that involves elements of ethics as well as wisdom developed from continued practice (Feng et al., 2018). Krägeloh (2016) hypothesised that ethics may still play an implicit role in MBIs despite their tendency not to give it any explicit focus due to the need to present value- and belief-neutral content.

Possibly in response to continued criticism about the lack of ethical considerations, Kabat-Zinn (2017) specifically clarified his interpretation of nonjudgmental awareness, namely as "to be aware of how judgmental the mind can be, and as best we can, not getting caught in it or recognizing when we are and not compounding our suffering by judging the judging" (p.1127). The significance of this statement may be lost due to its subtle argument and the fact that it was not followed up with further elaboration. The idea expressed here appears reminiscent of more advanced Buddhist teachings such as *no thought* and *emptiness* (Krägeloh, 2016) or the concept of so-called wise judging (Feng et al., 2018). Conceptual discussions about the similarities and differences between implicit and explicit understandings of mindfulness in MBIs and in Buddhism thus continue. The issue of nonjudgmental awareness has also been identified as a point of distinction of SG-MBIs. Unlike the standard FG-MBIs found in secular and clinical contexts, SG-MBIs tend to have an explicitly spiritual and self-transformative orientation that extends beyond immediate therapeutic settings and promotes a broader application of mindfulness in everyday life (Van Gordon et al., 2015). This approach thus emphasises a more active and discriminative form of awareness that involves discernment to determine adaptive action while at the same time being able to observe stimuli in a nonattached fashion. This aspect is essential to avoid the scenario that one misunderstands nonjudgmental as encouraging inaction in situations where action is necessary to prevent harm.

Within the MBIs literature, the lack of consensus or clarity about operational definitions of mindfulness has regularly been noted (e.g. Chiesa, 2013; Hanley et al., 2016; Malinowski, 2008), and therefore conceptual work has often been concerned with the question of what range of characteristics are most appropriate to include. Table 1.2 shows a selection of definitions to illustrate this variety. While nonjudgmental awareness remains a common aspect in these definitions, other definitions emphasise acceptance, acquisition of insight, or the quality of attention. Some researchers implied that mindfulness is a relatively stable disposition or capacity (Brown & Ryan, 2003, 2004), while others described mindfulness as a state-like style of attention (Lau et al., 2006), a skill (Erisman & Roemer, 2012), or even as the behavioural process of observing (e.g. Baer, 2003). Some of these definitions are located in publications reporting on the development or the testing of psychometric properties of a self-report mindfulness questionnaire, and the dimensionality implied by such definitions can be identified most unambiguously by regarding the factor structure of these instruments. Given the increasing complexity and variety of ways to define and measure mindfulness, some work has identified the need to summarise patterns of characteristics found in the literature.

TABLE 1.2 Selected definitions of mindfulness in the literature related to MBIs (presented in alphabetical order by author name)

Author	Definition	Salient characteristics
Baer (2003)	"mindfulness is the nonjudgmental observation of the ongoing stream of internal and external stimuli as they arise" (p.125)	Nonjudgmental observation
Bishop et al. (2004)	We see mindfulness as a process of regulating attention in order to bring a quality of nonelaborative awareness to current experience and a quality of relating to one's experience within an orientation of curiosity, experiential openness, and acceptance. We further see mindfulness as a process of gaining *insight* into the nature of one's mind and the adoption of a de-centered perspective ... on thoughts and feelings so that they can be experienced in terms of their subjectivity (versus their necessary validity) and transient nature (versus their permanence) (p.234).	Process of self-regulation of attention; openness and acceptance; process of gaining insight
Brown & Ryan (2003)	"naturally occurring characteristic" (p.822) "capacity to attend and to be aware" (p.822) "mindfulness can be considered an enhanced attention to and awareness of current experience or present reality" (p.822) "Mindfulness is inherently a state of consciousness. Although awareness and attention to the present events and experiences are given features of the human organism, these qualities can vary considerably...This suggests (a) that because of inherent capability, discipline, or inclination, individuals may differ in the frequency with which they deploy attention and awareness and also (b) that there are intraindividual variations in mindfulness" (p.824).	Capacity for attention and awareness (primarily seen as a trait)
Brown & Ryan (2004)	"We have operationally defined mindfulness as an *open* and *receptive* awareness to and awareness of ongoing events and experience" (p.245). "mindfulness, as we define it here, subsumes an acceptance of what occurs. Specifically, embedded within the capacity to sustain attention to and awareness of what is occurring is an openness to and acceptance of it" (p.245)	Capacity for open and receptive awareness

Author	Definition	Salient characteristics
Brown, Ryan, & Creswell (2007)	"receptive attention to and awareness of present events and experience" (p.212)	Attention and awareness of present moment
Cardaciotto, Herbert, Forman, Moitra, & Farrow (2008)	"the tendency to be highly aware of one's internal and external experiences in the context of an accepting, nonjudgmental stance toward those experiences" (p.205)	Nonjudgmental awareness
Erisman & Roemer (2012)	"Mindfulness is a way of relating to oneself and the world that is characterized by curiosity, openness, and acceptance. Mindfulness is a skill that can be cultivated through repeated practice, such as through mindfulness meditation, in which individuals continually bring attention to their breath while maintaining an open and gentle awareness of the present moment" (p.31)	Curiosity, openness, and acceptance (primarily seen as a skill)
Grossman et al. (2004)	"characterized by dispassionate, nonevaluative and sustained moment-to-moment awareness of perceptible mental states and processes .... Mindfulness is non-deliberative: It merely implies sustained paying attention to ongoing mental content without thinking about, comparing or in other ways evaluating the ongoing mental phenomena that arise during periods of practice. Thus, mindfulness may be seen as a form of naturalistic observation, or participant-observation, in which the objects of observation are the perceptible mental phenomena that normally arise during waking consciousness" (p.36)	Nondeliberative awareness
Kabat-Zinn (1990)	"Mindfulness is basically just a particular way of paying attention. It is a way of looking deeply into oneself in the spirit of self-inquiry and self-understanding. For this reason it can be learned and practiced" (p.12).	A way of paying attention
Kabat-Zinn (1994)	"paying attention in a particular way: on purpose, in the present moment, and non-judgmentally" (p.4)	Paying attention
Kabat-Zinn (2003)	"the awareness that emerges through paying attention on purpose, in the present moment, and nonjudgmentally to the unfolding of experience moment by moment" (p.145) "includes an affectionate, compassionate quality within the attending, a sense of openhearted friendly presence and interest" (p. 145).	Nonjudgmental awareness
Kabat-Zinn (2005)	"open-hearted moment-to-moment, nonjudgmental awareness" (p.24)	Nonjudgmental awareness

(Continued)

TABLE 1.2 (cont.)

Author	Definition	Salient characteristics
Lau et al. (2006)	"a mode, or state-like quality, that is maintained only when attention to experience is intentionally cultivated with an open, nonjudgmental orientation to experience" (p.1147) "intentional, reflective style of introspection or self-observation" (p.1148) "Mindfulness is further defined by the style of self-focused, nonelaborative attention characterized by experiential openness, curiosity, and acceptance. Mindfulness thus appears to be related more to the intentional states of self-reflectiveness (a curious, decentered style of introspection) than to involuntary states of rumination ... or self-consciousness ..., which are distinct styles of self-focused attention" (p.1149)	State-like quality of attention with open and nonjudgmental orientation
Marlatt and Kristeller (1999)	"bringing one's complete attention to the present experience on a moment to moment basis" (p.68)	Complete attention to present moment
Shapiro (2009)	"the awareness that arises out of intentionally attending in an open and discerning way to whatever is arising in the present moment" (p.1149)	Present-moment awareness

This includes a study by Bergomi, Tschacher, and Kupper (2013) to inform the development of a more comprehensive questionnaire. Additionally, Nilsson and Kazemi (2016) conducted a thematic analysis of 33 mindfulness definitions identified in the academic mindfulness literature and extracted the themes of attention and awareness, nonjudgmental attitude, external events, and cultivation of mindfulness. However, their analysis was based on a wide range of articles including many sources beyond the MBI literature, such as Buddhist sources, ACT, and DBT.

A unique case in the development of a suitable operational definition is the work by Bishop et al. (2004) who convened a series of consensus meetings. In their definition, mindfulness consists of two components (Table 1.2). Firstly, mindfulness involves self-regulation of attention in order to bring about nonelaborative awareness. The second component concerns one's orientation towards these experiences, namely the encouragement to foster an attitude of curiosity, acceptance, and experiential openness. Brown and Ryan (2004), on the other hand, argued that it is not necessary to make explicit references to acceptance, as this follows directly from giving full attention to the moment, as opposed to re-directing attention to alter, avoid, or escape a certain event. For that reason, the authors had not included characteristics such as acceptance, empathy, and gratitude into the items of their unidimensional Mindful Attention Awareness Scale (Brown & Ryan, 2003) as they considered those to be *outcomes* of present-centred attention awareness and thus conceptually redundant (Brown & Ryan, 2004). Further discussion about dimensionality in relation to self-report instruments will be discussed in a subsequent chapter on measurement in mindfulness.

As can be seen in the range of definitions shown in Table 1.2, the concepts of attention and awareness play a central role in characterising mindfulness. As Brown and Ryan (2003) discussed, *awareness* refers to background monitoring of stimuli in one's internal and external environment, while *attention* is the process of focusing one's conscious awareness. Although these are intertwined, they are nevertheless distinct concepts, and Rapgay and Bystrisky (2009) argued that these are not sufficiently differentiated in definitions of mindfulness. Additionally, as the authors argued, there is a lack of clarity about the differences in the functions that these may have in mindfulness practice, which challenges our understanding of what exactly is being practised in MBIs. The inconsistency of the use of these terms can be illustrated by referring to another example: Blanke and Brose (2017) conceptualised acting with awareness as referring to one's own actions while they viewed present-moment attention as covering attention to aspects happening in the present moment that extend beyond one's own activities.

Lack of sufficient differentiation between awareness and attention is also found in the Buddhist literature (Nilsson & Kazemi, 2016). Additionally, there is a lack of agreement in terms of whether attention and awareness *characterises* mindfulness or whether they are the *precondition* of it. Given the long history of Buddhist traditions and the fact that the primary purpose of discourse and scriptures on mindfulness has been as a teaching device, such inconsistencies are to be expected. For the scientific study of mindfulness within the context of MBIs, in contrast, more precision is certainly required. Within the increasingly abundant mindfulness literature, beginning researchers may be forgiven for failing to appreciate the more detailed aspects of mindfulness as a concept and practice. The increased volume in the mindfulness literature also appears to have increased the need to communicate the core concepts of the research field in a concise way. One example would be an article by Nagy and Baer (2017) who outlined mindfulness in a relatively jargon-free review article for teachers of psychology courses.

An area of inconsistency in working up mindfulness definitions is the way in which mindfulness has been referred to as state, trait, or practice. Hanley, Garland, and Black (2014) clarified the differences in meaning when mindfulness is described using these different terms. As a state of awareness, mindfulness is "a naturalistic mindset characterized by an attentive and nonjudgmental metacognitive monitoring of moment-by-moment cognition, emotion, perception, and sensation without fixation on thoughts of past and future" (Hanley et al., 2014, p.294). Mindfulness as a trait, in contrast, can be defined as the general tendency to exhibit in one's everyday life such as nonjudgmental awareness of present-moment experience. Lastly, mindfulness as practice is intended to develop trait mindfulness by repeatedly engaging mindfulness states.

A similar understanding is expressed in the view that mindfulness is a skill to be developed or cultivated with systematic meditation practice (Malinowski, 2008). Such a conceptualisation is also recognised in two commonly used mindfulness questionnaires, the Kentucky Inventory of Mindfulness Skills (KIMS; Baer, Smith, & Allen, 2004) and Five Facet Mindfulness Questionnaire (FFMQ; Baer, Smith, Hopkins, Krietemeyer, & Toney, 2006). The KIMS was specifically developed to measure skills taught in DBT, while this approach is still reflected within the FFMQ as it proposes a similar multidimensional structure and contains many of the KIMS items. Some empirical evidence confirms the tenability of conceptualising mindfulness in terms of specific skills. For example, in a nine-month longitudinal study by Hildebrandt, McCall, and Singer (2017), the effects of three different specific mental training programmes had different effects on the FFMQ facets, indicating that these may indeed represent separately learnable skills. Other evidence that these FFMQ facets are tapping into separate processes comes from an experience-sampling study where participants answered questionnaires using a smartphone at several time points during the day (Blanke, Riediger, & Brose, 2018). When participants were attentive to the present moment, they tended to experience more positive affect, and they had higher levels of nonjudgmental awareness, they tended to experience less negative affect.

Lack of consensus in defining mindfulness has obviously not stalled the application and continual development of MBIs, and one might argue that a more fruitful starting point for developing a suitable definition of mindfulness may be from regarding the actual practice instructions provided in mindfulness and meditation exercises. Schmidt (2014b) published a tentative classification system for the different types of meditation techniques using a psychological vocabulary, which may assist in operationalising meditation practice. According to this classification system, meditation practices can be described a) in terms of the aspects of attention regulation related to the particular meditation exercise, b) in terms of the specific short- and long-term motivation underlying the practice, c) according to whether a particular attitudes such as joy or curiosity is being explicitly adopted or fostered during meditation, and lastly d) in terms of their practical context such as posture, location, timing, or whether practised in the presence of others. In a similar way, Isbel and Summers (2017) listed a variety of sitting exercise instructions in order to assist in the development of appropriate longitudinal randomised controlled trials that investigate the underlying cognitive processes of mindfulness. For that purpose, the authors distinguished between the cognitive faculty of mindfulness and the process of cultivating it. In order to define the former, the authors adopted the two-component definition by Bishop et al. (2004) of attentional processes and nonelaborative attitudinal factors. However, in order to gain more specificity about the latter, Isbel and Summers (2017) proposed to use equanimity as a concept to capture the nonjudgmental, nonelaborative, and nonreactive aspects of mindfulness. Derived directly from Buddhist ideas, Desbordes et al. (2015) defined equanimity as "an even-minded mental state or dispositional tendency toward all experiences or objects, regardless of their affective valence (pleasant, unpleasant or neutral) or source" (p.357). The two-component conceptualisation of mindfulness (Bishop et al., 2004) also informed other efforts to form a theoretical basis to explain mechanisms of mindfulness, such as Monitor and Acceptance Theory (Lindsay & Creswell, 2017).

In their attempt to systematise practice instructions, Isbel and Summers (2017) were also aware of the importance of informal mindfulness practice and therefore also presented exemplars to summarise different types of informal practice instructions. While this is a necessary step towards quantifying informal practice and could eventually enable assessment of its role as an additional variable related to between-subject responsiveness to the effects of MBIs, its function is also likely to be complex. As illustrated by a cross-sectional survey of individuals with experience in mindfulness practice (Birtwell et al., 2018), opportunities for exposure to mindfulness practice extend beyond formal MBIs. Participants are therefore likely to present with a variety of personal histories in both informal and formal mindfulness experience before participating in a course. Additionally, as Kabat-Zinn (2003) pointed out, the use of the term *practice* when referring to the so-called practice of meditation is not to be understood as some kind of rehearsal or technique but instead as a launching platform or a scaffolding mechanism for further practice to be applied in informal contexts as much as during formal practice occasions. Mindfulness is thus to be embodied (Kabat-Zinn, 2003) and becomes a way of life (Segal et al., 2013, p.320). Additionally, as pointed out by some conceptual work (e.g. Sauer, Lynch, Walach, & Kohls, 2011; Shapiro, Siegel, & Neff, 2018), mindfulness inevitably involves some underlying paradoxes that can only be disentangled experientially with committed practice. These paradoxes include apparent contradiction such that change is possible through acceptance or nonstriving effort in meditation practice.

Compared to the view of mindfulness as a skill, trait mindfulness has connotations of even more stable characteristics. While the trait mindfulness definition of Brown and Ryan (2003) acknowledges the role of disciplined practice (Table 1.2), it refers to broader reasons for individual differences beyond those related to deliberate or formal mindfulness practice. Also referred to as dispositional mindfulness, trait mindfulness is generally seen as a separate construct from learned or cultivated mindfulness (Rau & Williams, 2016). The capacity for mindfulness has been hypothesised to have a social foundation such as through the process of socialisation and culture (Brown et al., 2007) or more specifically the result from attachment security (Shaver, Lavy, Saron, & Mikulincer, 2007). Support for such hypotheses is difficult to obtain as it relies on converging evidence from cross-sectional studies that cannot fully rule out alternative explanations. For example, in a repeated-measures survey study using the Danish MAAS with a general community sample outside a mindfulness training context, Jensen et al. (2016) found mindfulness scores to be stable over a period of six months. This relationship was not dependent on demographic factors, and individuals with lower socioeconomic status (SES) tended to have higher levels of inattentiveness. However, given the complexity of SES as a variable, future research is necessary to investigate the important aspects of SES-related factors that might be linked to levels of mindfulness. Research has shown that mindfulness can be induced or developed in an incidental manner in a variety of ways where mindfulness may not be explicitly mentioned. This includes, for example, mind-body practices such as those displayed in Tai Chi or the martial arts (Lothes, Hakan, & Mochrie, 2015; Henning, Krägeloh, & Webster, 2017) or recreational activities such a choir singing (Lynch & Wilson, 2018).

Given the fact that the characteristics of dispositional mindfulness are potentially very distinct from those of explicitly cultivated mindfulness, extrapolations of findings from cross-sectional studies about dispositional mindfulness to derive implications for clinical practice (e.g. Crane, Barnhofer, Hargus, Amarasinghe, & Winder, 2010; Bränström, Duncan, & Moskowitz, 2011; Klainin-Yobas et al., 2016) need to be made with caution.

One avenue towards resolving the complexity of the construct of mindfulness is to examine empirical data to test the predictions derived from the various mindfulness definitions about the relationships between mindfulness and relevant behavioural, cognitive, or neurophysiological indicators. Correlations between mindfulness and measures of psychological well-being or between mindfulness and related constructs such as self-compassion (Neff, 2003) have limited informational value in this case as it could lead to a circular argument: correlations with such constructs are often used as discriminant or convergent validity requirements during the development of mind-fulness scales or vice versa (Baer et al., 2006; Pinto-Gouveia, Gregório, Dinis, & Xavier, 2012). Instead, research needs to consider evidence from other types of assessment, such as the prediction of cognitive functioning and evidence of the long-term effects of meditation and mindfulness practice on brain structure and function. Research on cognitive functioning relevant to mindfulness includes studies on implicit learning, or the learning that takes place outside one's awareness. Whitmarsh, Uddén, Barendregt, and Petersson (2013) argued that implicit learning benefits from one's disposition to respond to stimuli in a habitual and reactive manner, which would thus predict that individuals with high levels of mindfulness (and thus with the ability and perhaps tendency to inhibit reactive responding) perform worse on implicit memory tasks. To test this prediction, Whitmarsh et al. (2013) recruited university students for an artificial grammar learning task, which is a common paradigm to investigate implicit learning. Performance on this task is thought to depend on subcortical structures and thus relies on habitual responding and unconsciously acquired preferences during the task. In this experiment, dispositional mindfulness as assessed through the FFMQ (Baer et al., 2006) was negatively associated with task performance, thus in accordance with the prediction derived from the definition of mindfulness. This finding was later confirmed by Stillman, Feldman, Wambach, Howard, and Howard (2014) who used a sequence-learning task to test implicit learning and the MAAS (Brown & Ryan, 2003) to assess mindfulness. Further research will be discussed in a subsequent chapter covering the evidence for the effectiveness of MBIs.

Summary and conclusion

Mindfulness as a practice has been taught either explicitly or indirectly in various religious and spiritual traditions throughout the ages. However, the *systematic* application of mindfulness as a modern-day health intervention did not occur until the 1970s with the development of MBSR. The subsequent rapid and wide-spread adoption of mindfulness techniques in a wide range of clinical and nonclinical contexts were prompted by regular reports of the benefits of mindfulness, which eventually resulted in the acceptance of such approaches within mainstream psychology and clinical practice. Mindfulness has been applied to such a wide range of health conditions as a therapeutic or preventive intervention and has thus been labelled transdiagnostic. Its integration into a range of different therapeutic approaches has promoted efforts to identify previously unrecognised commonalities among the various psychological paradigms.

If one can speak of mindfulness as a *research field*, it has now become a noticeable sign of maturity of this research field that literature is increasingly self-critical of its developments. Some of the debates that have taken place addressed the challenges of uncontrolled over-application to the extent that there may be a tendency of uncritical acceptance of the universal utility of mindfulness. Additional arguments related to the ambiguous role of mindfulness and the boundaries between personal transformation and meaningfulness with spiritual and religious beliefs, particularly how MBIs are presented in terms of their association with Buddhism. Related to these debates is the question of suitable operational definitions of mindfulness. While the range of available definitions of mindfulness has not slowed down MBI research in any way, more sophisticated theoretical understanding of the benefits of mindfulness can only be developed with better consensus on suitable definitions. This includes clearer distinctions between mindfulness as a state, trait, skill, or practice.

The enormous growth of the mindfulness literature particularly since the 2010s increases the need for researchers to become critically aware of the direction in which research on MBIs is heading. Additionally, examining the nature of mindfulness research and current trends allows the field to identify areas that require further methodological refinement and sophistication. This will enable researchers to address the concerns voiced in some of the recent critical comments that, if not taken seriously, have the potential to devalue mindfulness in the long run.

References

Alkoby, A., Halperin, E., Tarrasch, R., & Levit-Binnun, N. (2017). Increased support for political compromise in the Israeli-Palestinian conflict following an 8-week mindfulness workshop. *Mindfulness*, 8(5), 1345–1353. doi:10.1007/s12671-017-0710-5

Alladin, A. (2014). Mindfulness-Based Hypnosis: blending science, beliefs, and wisdoms to catalyze healing. *American Journal of Clinical Hypnosis*, 56(3), 285–302. doi:10.1080/00029157.2013.857290

Allan, B. A., Bott, E. M., & Suh, H. (2015). Connecting mindfulness and meaning in life: exploring the role of authenticity. *Mindfulness*, 6(5), 996–1003. doi:10.1007/s12671-014-0341-z

Arntzen, E., Lokke, J., Lokke, G., & Eilertsen, D.-E. (2010). On misconceptions about behavior analysis among university students and teachers. *Psychological Record*, 60(2), 325–336. doi:10.1007/BF03395710

Arthington, P. (2016). Mindfulness: a critical perspective. *Community Psychology in Global Perspective*, 2(1), 87–104. doi:10.1285/i24212113v2i1p87

Baer, R. A. (2003). Mindfulness training as a clinical intervention: a conceptual and empirical review. *Clinical Psychology: Science and Practice*, 10(2), 125–143. doi:10.1093/clipsy/bpg015

Baer, R. A., Smith, G. T., & Allen, K. B. (2004). Assessment of mindfulness by self-report – the Kentucky Inventory of Mindfulness Skills. *Assessment*, 11(3), 191–206. doi:10.1177/1073191104268029

Baer, R. A., Smith, G. T., Hopkins, J., Krietemeyer, J., & Toney, L. (2006). Using self-report assessment methods to explore facets of mindfulness. *Assessment*, 13(1), 27–45. doi:10.1177/1073191105283504

Bageant, R. (2012). The Hakomi method: defining its place within the humanistic psychology tradition. *Journal of Humanistic Psychology*, 52(2), 178–189. doi:10.1177/0022167811423313

Bahl, S. (2017). Paradoxes of teaching mindfulness in business. In L. M. Monteiro, J. F. Compson, & F. Musten (Eds.), *Practitioner's guide to ethics and mindfulness-based interventions* (pp. 345–371). Cham, Switzerland: Springer Nature.

Barbaro, N., & Pickett, S. M. (2016). Mindfully green: examining the effect of connectedness to nature on the relationship between mindfulness and engagement in pro-environmental behavior. *Personality and Individual Differences*, 93, 137–142. doi:10.1016/j.paid.2015. 05. 02doi:6

Barnes, N., Hattan, P., Black, D. S., Schuman-Olivier, Z. (2018). An examination of mindfulness-based programs in US medical schools. *Mindfulness*. Online First. doi:10.1007/s12671-016-0623-8

Bergland, C. (2017, October 10). Is mindfulness being mindlessly overhyped? Experts say "yes". Retrieved from http://www.psychologytoday.com/us/blog/the-athletes-way/201710/is-mindfulness-being-mindlessly-overhyped-experts-say-yes

Bergomi, C., Tschacher, W., & Kupper, Z. (2013). Measuring mindfulness: first steps towards the development of a comprehensive mindfulness scale. *Mindfulness*, 4(1), 18–32. doi:10.1007/s12671-012-0102-9

Birrer, D., Röthlin, P., & Morgan, G. (2012). Mindfulness to enhance athletic performance: theoretical considerations and possible impact mechanisms. *Mindfulness*, 3(3), 235–246. doi:10.1007/s12671-012-0109-2

Birtwell, K., Williams, K., van Marwijk, H., Armitage, C. J., & Sheffield, D. (2018). An exploration of formal and informal mindfulness practice and associations with wellbeing. *Mindfulness*. Online First. doi:10.1007/s12671-018-0951-y

Bishop, S. R., Lau, M., Shapiro, S., Carlson, L., Anderson, N. D., Carmody, J., … Devins, G. (2004). Mindfulness: a proposed operational definition. *Clinical Psychology: Science and Practice*, 11(3), 230–241. doi:10.1093/clipsy/bph077

Black, D. S. (2010). Mindfulness Research Guide: a new paradigm for managing empirical health information. *Mindfulness*, 1(3), 174–176. doi:10.1007/s12671-010-0019-0

Blanke, E. S., & Brose, A. (2017). Mindfulness in daily life: a multidimensional approach. *Mindfulness*, 8(3), 737–750. doi:10.1007/s12671-016-0651-4 [Erratum. Blanke, E. S., & Brose (2017). *Mindfulness*, 8(6), 1727–1731. doi:10.1007/s12671-017-0769-z]

Blanke, E. S., Riediger, M., & Brose, A. (2018). Pathways to happiness are multidirectional: associations between state mindfulness and everyday affective experience. *Emotion, 18*(2), 202–211. doi:10.1037/emo0000323

Block-Lerner, J., Adair, C., Plumb, J. C., Rhatigan, D. L., & Orsillo, S. M. (2007). The case for mindfulness-based approaches in the cultivation of empathy: does nonjudgmental, present-moment awareness increase capacity for perspective-taking and empathic concern?. *Journal of Marital and Family Therapy*, 33(4), 501–516. doi:10.1111/j.1752-0606.2007.00034.x

Bögels, S., & Restifo, K. (Eds.) (2014). *Mindful parenting – a guide for mental health practitioners*. New York, USA: Springer.

Bohlmeijer, E., Prenger, R., Taal, E., & Cuijpers, P. (2010). The effects of mindfulness-based stress reduction therapy on mental health of adults with a chronic medical disease: a meta-analysis. *Journal of Psychosomatic Research*, 68(6), 539–544. doi:10.1016/j.jpsychores.2009. 10. 005

Boorstein, S. (1996). *Don't just do something, sit there.* New York, USA: HarperOne.

Boorstein, S. (1997). *It's easier than you think: the Buddhist way to happiness.* New York, USA: HarperOne.

Bränström, R., Duncan, L. G., & Moskowitz, J. T. (2011). The association between dispositional mindfulness, psychological well-being, and perceived health in a Swedish population-based sample. *British Journal of Health Psychology,* 16(Pt 2), 300–316. doi:10.1348/135910710X501683

Brazier, D. (2013). Mindfulness reconsidered. *European Journal of Psychotherapy & Counselling,* 15(2), 116–126. doi:10.1080/13642537.2013.795335

Brown, K. W., & Ryan, R. M. (2003). The benefits of being present: mindfulness and its role in psychological well-being. *Journal of Personality and Social Psychology, 84*(4), 822–848. doi:10.1037/0022-3514.84.4.822

Brown, K. W., & Ryan, R. M. (2004). Perils and promise in defining and measuring mindfulness: observations from experience. *Clinical Psychology: Science and Practice,* 11(3), 242–248. doi:10.1093/clipsy/bph078

Brown, K. W., Ryan, R. M., & Creswell, J. D. (2007). Mindfulness: theoretical foundations and evidence for its salutary effects. *Psychological Inquiry,* 18(4), 211–237. doi:10.1080/10478400701598298

Cardaciotto, L., Herbert, J. D., Forman, E. M., Moitra, E., & Farrow, V. (2008). The assessment of present-moment awareness and acceptance: the Philadelphia Mindfulness Scale. *Assessment,* 15(2), 204–223. doi:10.1177/1073191107311467

Carmody, J., & Baer, R. A. (2009). How long does a mindfulness-based stress reduction program need to be? A review of class contact hours and effects sizes for psychological distress. *Journal of Clinical Psychology,* 65(6), 627–638. doi:10.1002/jclp.20555

Cebolla, A., Galiana, L., Campos, D., Oliver, A., Soler, J., Demarzo, M., …, & García-Campayo, J. (2018). How does mindfulness work? Exploring a theoretical model using samples of meditators and non-meditators. *Mindfulness,* 9(3), 860–870. doi:10.1007/s12671-017-0826-7

Chambers, R., Gullone, E., & Allen, N. B. (2009). Mindful emotion regulation: nn integrative review. *Clinical Psychology Review,* 29(6), 560–572. doi:10.1016/j.cpr.2009.06.0doi:05

Chiesa, A., & Serretti, A. (2009). Mindfulness-based stress reduction for stress management in healthy people: a review and meta-analysis. *Journal of Alternative and Complementary Medicine,* 15(5), 593–600. doi:10.1089/acm.2008.0495

Chiesa, A., & Serretti, A. (2010). A systematic review of neurobiological and clinical features of mindfulness meditations. *Psychological Medicine,* 40(8), 1239–1252. doi:10.1017/S0033291709991747

Chiesa, A. (2013). The difficulty of defining mindfulness: current thought and critical issues. *Mindfulness,* 4(3), 255–268. doi:10.1007/s12671-012-0123-4

Chiesa, A., Anselmi, R., & Serretti, A. (2014). Psychological mechanisms of mindfulness-based interventions. *Holistic Nursing Practice,* 28(2), 124–148. doi:10.1097/HNP.0000000000000017

Christopher, M. S., Woodrich, L. E., & Tiernan, K. A. (2014). Using cognitive interviews to assess the cultural validity of state and trait measures of mindfulness among Zen Buddhists. *Mindfulness,* 5(2), 145–160. doi:10.1007/s12671-012-0160-z

Crane, C., Barnhofer, T., Hargus, E., Amarasinghe, M., & Winder, R. (2010). The relationship between dispositional mindfulness and conditional goal setting in depressed patients. *British Journal of Clinical Psychology,* 49(3), 281–290. doi:10.1348/014466509X455209

Crane, R. S., Brewer, J., Feldman, C., Kabat-Zinn, J., Santorelli, S., Williams, J. M. G., & Kuyken, W. (2017). What defines mindfulness-based programs? The warp and the weft. *Psychological Medicine,* 47(6), 990–999. doi:10.1017/S0033291716003317

Cullen, M. (2011). Mindfulness-based interventions: an emerging phenomenon. *Mindfulness,* 2(3), 186–193. doi:10.1007/s12671-011-0058-1

Davidson, R. J., & Dahl, C. J. (2018). Outstanding challenges in scientific research on mindfulness and meditation. *Perspectives on Psychological Science*, 13(1), 62–65. doi:10.1177/1745691617718358

Delprato, D. J., & Midgley, B. D. (1992). Some fundamentals of B.F. Skinner's behaviorism. *American Psychologist*, 47(11), 1507–1520. doi:10.1037/0003-066X.47. 11. 1507

Desbordes, G., Gard, T., Hoge, E. A., Hölzel, B. K., Kerr, C., Lazar, S. W., …, & Vago, D. R. (2015). Moving beyond mindfulness: defining equanimity as an outcome measure in meditation and contemplative research. *Mindfulness*, 6(2), 356–372. doi:10.1007/s12671-013-0269-8

Didonna, F. (2009). *Clinical handbook of mindfulness*. New York, NY: Springer.

Dorjee, D. (2010). Kinds and dimensions of mindfulness: why it is important to distinguish them. *Mindfulness*, 1(3), 152–160. doi:10.1007/s12671-010-0016-3

Dreyfus, G. (2011). Is mindfulness present-centred and non-judgmental? A discussion of the cognitive dimensions of mindfulness. *Contemporary Buddhism*, 12(1), 41–54. doi:10.1080/14639947.2011.564815

Dunne, J. (2011). Toward an understanding of non-dual mindfulness. *Contemporary Buddhism*, 12(1), 71–88. doi:10.1080/14639947.2011.564820

Eberth, J., & Sedlmeier, P. (2012). The effects of mindfulness meditation: a meta-analysis. *Mindfulness*, 3(3), 174–189. doi:10.1007/s12671-012-0101-x

Eby, L. T., Allen, T. D., Conley, K. M., Williamson, R. L., Henderson, T. G., & Mancini, V. S. (2018). Mindfulness-based training interventions for employees: a qualitative review of the literature. *Human Resource Management Review*. Online First. doi:10.1016/j.hrmr.2017. 03. 00doi:4

Epstein, M. (1995). *Thoughts without a thinker: psychotherapy from a Buddhist perspective*. New York: Basic Books.

Ericson, T., Kjønstad, B. G., & Barstad, A. (2014). Mindfulness and sustainability. *Ecological Economics*, 104, 73–79. doi:10.1016/j.ecolecon.2014. 04. 00doi:7

Erisman, S. M., & Roemer, L. (2012). A preliminary investigation of the process of mindfulness. *Mindfulness*, 3(1), 30–43. doi:10.1007/s12671-011-0078-x

Farias, M., & Wikholm, C. (2016). Has the science of mindfulness lost its mind?. *BJPsych Bulletin*, 40(6), 329–332. doi:10.1192/pb.bp.116.053686

Felver, J. C., & Jennings, P. A. (2016). Applications of mindfulness-based interventions in school settings: an introduction. *Mindfulness*, 7(1), 1–4. doi:10.1007/s12671-015-0478-4

Feng, X. J., Krägeloh, C. U., Billington, D. R., & Siegert, R. J. (2018). To what extent is mindfulness as presented in commonly used mindfulness questionnaires different from how it is conceptualized by senior ordained Buddhists?. *Mindfulness*, 9(2), 441–460. doi:10.1007/s12671-017-0788-9

Fischer, D., Stanszus, L., Geiger, S., Grossman, P., & Schrader, U. (2017). Mindfulness and sustainable consumption: a systematic literature review of research approaches and findings. *Journal of Cleaner Production*, 162, 544–558. doi:10.1016/j.jclepro.2017.06.doi:007

Fjorback, L. O., & Walach, H. (2012). Meditation based therapies – a systematic review and some critical observations. *Religions*, 3(1), 1–18. doi:10.3390/rel3010001

García-Campayo, J., & Demarzo, M. (2016). Mindfulness and compassion: a Latin American perspective [Spanish]. *Mindfulness & Compassion*, 1(1), 1. doi:10.1016/j.mincom.2016. 09. 001

Gilpin, R. (2008). The use of Theravāda Buddhist practices and perspectives in mindfulness-based cognitive therapy. *Contemporary Buddhism*, 9(2), 227–251. doi:10.1080/14639940802556560

Goldstein, J. (1987). *The experience of insight: a simple and direct guide to Buddhist meditation*. Boston, USA: Shambhala.

Goldstein, J., & Kornfield, J. (2001). *Seeking the heart of wisdom: the path of insight meditation*. Boston, USA: Shambhala.

Grant, J. A., Courtemanche, J., Duerden, E. G., Duncan, G. H., & Rainville, P. (2010). Cortical thickness and pain sensitivity in Zen meditators. *Emotion*, 10(1), 43–53. doi:10.1016/j.psycychresns.2010. 08. 006

Grossman, P., Niemann, L., Schmidt, S., & Walach, H. (2004). Mindfulness-based stress reduction and health benefits: a meta-analysis. *Journal of Psychosomatic Research*, 57(1), 35–43. doi:10.1016/S0022-3999(03)00573-7

Hanley, A., Garland, E. L., & Black, D. S. (2014). Use of mindful reappraisal coping among meditation practitioners. *Journal of Clinical Psychology*, 70(3), 294–301. doi:10.1002/jclp.22023

Hanley, A. W., Abell, N., Osborn, D. S., Roehrig, A. D., & Canto, A. I. (2016). Mind the gaps: Are conclusions about mindfulness entirely conclusive?. *Journal of Counseling & Development*, 94(1), 103–113. doi:10.1002/jcad.12066

Harrington, A., & Dunne, J. D. (2015). When mindfulness is therapy – ethical qualms, historical perspectives. *American Psychologist*, 70(7), 621–631. doi:10.1037/a0039460

Hartelius, G. (2015). Body maps of attention: phenomenal markers for two varieties of mindfulness. *Mindfulness*, 6(6), 1271–1281. doi:10.1007/s12671-015-0391-x

Hayes, S. C. (2004). Acceptance and commitment therapy, relational frame theory, and the third wave of behavioral and cognitive therapies. *Behavior Therapy*, 35(4), 639–665. doi:10.1016/S0005-7894(04)80013-3

Hayes, S. C., Strosahl, K. D., & Wilson, K. G. (2011). *Acceptance and Commitment Therapy: the process and practice of mindful change*. New York, USA: Guilford Press.

Hayes, S. C., Barnes-Holmes, D., & Wilson, K. G. (2012). Contextual Behavioral Science: creating a science more adequate to the challenge of the human condition. *Journal of Contextual Behavioral Science*, 1(1–2), 1–16. doi:10.1016/j.jcbs.2012. 09. 004

Henning, M. A., Krägeloh, C. U., & Webster, C. S. (2017). Mindfulness and Taijiquan. *The Annals of Cognitive Science*, 1(1), 1–6

Hildebrandt, L. K., McCall, C., & Singer, T. (2017). Differential effects of attention-, compassion-, and socio-cognitively based mental practices on self-reports of mindfulness and compassion. *Mindfulness*, 8(6), 1488–1512. doi:10.1007/s12671-017-0716-z

Hofmann, S. G., Sawyer, A. T., Witt, A. A., & Oh, D. (2010). The effect of mindfulness-based therapy on anxiety and depression: a meta-analytic review. *Journal of Consulting and Clinical Psychology*, 78(2), 169–183. doi:10.1037/a0018555

Hölzel, B. K., Carmody, J., Vangel, M., Congleton, C., Yerramsetti, S. M., Garda, T., & Lazara, S. W. (2011). Mindfulness practice leads to increases in regional brain gray matter density. *Psychiatry Research: Neuroimaging*, 191(1), 36–43. doi:10.1016/j.psycychresns.2010. 08. 006

Hwang, Y.-S., & Kearney, P. (Eds.) (2015). *A mindfulness intervention for children with autism spectrum disorders – new directions in research and practice*. New York, USA: Springer.

Hyland, P. K., Lee, R. A., & Mills, M. J. (2015). Mindfulness at work: a new approach to improving individual and organizational performance. *Industrial and Organizational Psychology*, 8(4), 576–602. doi:10.1017/iop.2015.41

Hyland, T. (2017). McDonaldizing spirituality: mindfulness, education, and consumerism. *Journal Transformative Education*, 15(4), 334–356. doi:10.1177/1541344617696972

Isbel, B., & Summers, M. J. (2017). Distinguishing the cognitive processes of mindfulness: developing a standardised mindfulness technique for use in longitudinal randomised control trials. *Consciousness and Cognition*, 52, 75–92. doi:10.1016/j.concog.2017.04.doi:019

Jennings, P. A. (2016). Mindfulness-based programs and the American public school system: recommendations for best practices to ensure secularity. *Mindfulness*, 7(1), 176–178. doi:10.1007/s12671-015-0477-5

Jensen, C. G., Niclasen, J., Vangkilde, S. A., Petersen, A., & Hasselbalch, S. G. (2016). General inattentiveness is a long-term reliable trait independently predictive of psychological health: Danish validation studies of the Mindful Attention Awareness Scale. *Psychological Assessment*, 28(5), e70–87. doi:10.1037/pas0000196

Jha, A. P., Morrison, A. B., Dainer-Best, J., Parker, S., Rostrup, N., & Stanley, E. A. (2015). Minds "at attention": Mindfulness training curbs attentional lapses in military cohorts. *PLoS One*, 10(2), e0116889. doi:10.1371/journal.pone.0116889

Johnson, D. C., Thom, N. J., Stanley, E. A., Haase, L., Simmons, A. N., Shih, P.-A., ..., & Paulus, M. P. (2014). Modifying resilience mechanisms in at-risk individuals: a controlled study of mindfulness training in marines preparing for deployment. *American Journal of Psychiatry*, 171(8), 844–853. doi:10.1176/appi.ajp.2014.13040502

Kabat-Zinn, J. (1990). *Full catastrophe living: using the wisdom of your body and mind to face stress, pain, and illness*. New York, USA: Delacourt.

Kabat-Zinn, J. (1994). *Wherever you go, there you are: mindfulness meditation in everyday life*. New York, USA: Hyperion.

Kabat-Zinn, J. (2003). Mindfulness-based interventions in context: past, present, and future. *Clinical Psychology: Science and Practice*, 10(2), 144–156. doi:10.1093/clipsy.bpg016

Kabat-ZinnJ. (2005). *Coming to our senses: healing ourselves and the world through mindfulness*. New York, USA: Hyperion.

Kabat-Zinn, J. (2011). Some reflections on the origins of MBSR, skillful means, and the trouble with maps. *Contemporary Buddhism*, 12(1), 281–306. doi:10.1080/14639947.2011.564844

Kabat-Zinn, J. (2017). Too early to tell: the potential impact and challenges—ethical and otherwise—inherent in the mainstreaming of Dharma in an increasingly dystopian world. *Mindfulness*, 8(5), 1125–1135. doi:10.1007/s12671-017-0758-2

Kahl, K. G., Winter, L., & Schweiger, U. (2012). The third wave of cognitive behavioural therapies: 2hat is new and what is effective?. *Current Opinion in Psychiatry*, 25(6), 522–528. doi:10.1097/YCO.0b013e328358e531

Keane, A. (2014). The influence of therapist mindfulness practice on psychotherapeutic work: a mixed methods study. *Mindfulness*, 5(6), 689–703. doi:10.1007/s12671-013-0223-9

Khoury, B., Lecomte, T., Fortin, G., Masse, M., Therien, P., Bouchard, V., ..., & Hofmann, S. G. (2013). Mindfulness-based therapy: a comprehensive meta-analysis. *Clinical Psychology Review*, 33(6), 763–771. doi:10.1016/j.cpr.2013.doi:05.005

Khoury, B., Knäuper, B., Pagnini, F., Trent, N., Chiesa, A., & Carrière, K. (2017). Embodied mindfulness. *Mindfulness*, 8(5), 1160–1171. doi:10.1007/s12671-017-0700-7

Klainin-Yobas, P., Ramirez, D., Fernandez, Z., Sarmiento, J., Thanoi, W., Ignacio, J., & Lau, Y. (2016). Examining the predicting effect of mindfulness on psychological well-being among undergraduate students: a structural equation modelling approach. *Personality and Individual Differences*, 91, 63–68. doi:10.1016/j.paid.2015.11.0doi:34

Kornfield, J. (2007). *Modern Buddhist masters*. Kandy, Sri Lanka: Buddhist Publication Society.

Krägeloh, C. U. (2016). Importance of morality in mindfulness practice. *Counseling and Values*, 61(1), 97–110. doi:10.1002/cvj.12028

Krampen, G., von Eye, A., & Schui, G. (2011). Forecasting trends of development of psychology from a bibliometric perspective. *Scientometrics*, 87(3), 687–694. doi:10.1007/s11192-011-0357-2

Krasner, M. S., Epstein, R. M., Backman, H., Suchman, A. L., Chapman, B., Mooney, C. J., & Quill, T. E. (2009). Association of an educational program in mindful communication with burnout, empathy, and attitudes among primary care physicians. *JAMA*, 302(12), 1284–1293. doi:10.1001/jama.2009.1384

Kristeller, J., Wolever, R. Q., & Sheets, V. (2014). Mindfulness-Based Eating Awareness Training (MBEAT) for binge eating: a randomized clinical trial. *Mindfulness*, 5(3), 282–297. doi:10.1007/s12671-012-0179-1

Lau, M. A., Bishop, S. R., Segal, Z. V., Buis, T., Anderson, N. D., Carlson, L., ..., & Carmody, J. (2006). The Toronto Mindfulness Scale: development and validation. *Journal of Clinical Psychology*, 62(12), 1445–1467. doi:10.1002/jclp.20326

Lauche, R., Cramer, H., Dobos, G., Langhorst, J., & Schmidt, S. (2013). A systematic review and meta-analysis of mindfulness-based stress reduction for the fibromyalgia syndrome. *Journal of Psychosomatic Research*, 75(6), 500–510. doi:10.1016/j.jpsychores.2013.1doi:0.010

Ledesma, D., & Kumano, H. (2009). Mindfulness-based stress reduction and cancer: a meta-analysis. *Psycho-Oncology*, 18(6), 571–579. doi:10.1002/pon.1400

Lindsay, E. K., & Creswell, J. D. (2017). Mechanisms of mindfulness training: Monitor and Acceptance Theory (MAT). *Clinical Psychology Review*, 51, 48–59. doi:10.1016/j.cpr.2016.10.01doi:1

Linehan, M. M. (1993). *Cognitive-behavioural treatment of borderline personality disorder*. New York, USA: Guilford Press.

Lomas, T., Edginton, T., Cartwright, T., & Ridge, D. (2015). Cultivating equanimity through mindfulness meditation: a mixed methods enquiry into the development of decentering capabilities in men. *International Journal of Wellbeing*, 5(3), 88–106. doi:10.5502/ijw.v5i3.7

Longshore, K., & Sachs, M. (2015). Mindfulness training for coaches: a mixed-method exploratory study. *Journal of Clinical Sport Psychology*, 9(2), 116–137. doi:10.1123/jcsp.2014-0038

Lothes, J., Hakan, R., & Mochrie, K. (2015). Differences of novice to black belt Aikido practitioners in mindfulness: a longitudinal study. *International Journal of Wellbeing*, 5(3), 63–71. doi:10.5502/ijw.v5i3.4

Lynch, J., & Wilson, C. E. (2018). Exploring the impact of choral singing on mindfulness. *Psychology of Music*. Online First. doi:10.1177/0305735617729452

Malinowski, P. (2008). Mindfulness as psychological dimension: concepts and applications. *Irish Journal of Psychology*, 29(1–2), 155–166. doi:10.1080/03033910.2008.10446281

Marlatt, G. A., & Kristeller, J. L. (1999). Mindfulness and meditation. In W. R. Miller (Ed.), *Integrating spirituality into treatment* (pp. 67–84). Washington, DC: American Psychological Association.

Martin, J. R. (1997). Mindfulness: a proposed common factor. *Journal of Psychotherapy Integration*, 7(4), 291–312. doi:10.1023/B:JOPI.0000010885.18025.bc

Masuda, A., & O'Donohue, W. T. (Eds.) (2017). *Handbook of Zen, mindfulness, and behavioural health*. New York, USA: Springer.

Medvedev, O. N., Norden, P. A., Krägeloh, C., & Siegert, R. J. (2018). Investigating unique contributions of dispositional mindfulness facets to depression, anxiety, and stress in general and student populations. *Mindfulness*. doi:10.1007/s12671-018-0917-0

Moll, S., Frolic, A., & Key, B. (2015). Investing in compassion: exploring mindfulness as a strategy to enhance interpersonal relationships in healthcare practice. *Journal of Hospital Administration*, 4(6), 36–45. doi:10.5430/jha.v4n6p36

Monteiro, L. M., Musten, R. F., & Compson, J. (2015). Traditional and contemporary mindfulness: finding the middle path in the tangle of concerns. *Mindfulness*, 6(1), 1–13. doi:10.1007/s12671-014-0301-7

Nagy, L. M., & Baer, R. A. (2017). Mindfulness: what should teachers of psychology know?. *Teaching of Psychology*, 44(4), 353–359. doi:10.1177/0098628317727913

Neff, K. D. (2003). The development and validation of a scale to measure self-compassion. *Self and Identity*, 2(3), 223–250. doi:10.1080/15298860390209035

Nilsson, H., & Kazemi, A. (2016). Reconciling and thematizing definitions of mindfulness: the Big Five of mindfulness. *Review of General Psychology*, 20(2), 183–193. doi:10.1037/gpr0000074

Otani, A. (2016). Hypnosis and mindfulness: the twain finally meet. *American Journal of Clinical Hypnosis*, 58(4), 383–398. doi:10.1080/00029157.2015.1085364

Pagnoni, G., & Cekic, M. (2007). Age effects on gray matter volume and attentional performance in Zen meditation. *Neurobiology of Aging*, 28, 1623–1627. doi:10.1016/j.neurobiolaging.2007. 06. 008

Pagnoni, G., Cekic, M., & Guo, Y. (2008). 'Thinking about not-thinking': neural correlates of conceptual processing during Zen meditation. *PLoS One*, 3(9), e3083. doi:10.1371/journal.pone.0003083

Pinto-Gouveia, J., Gregório, S., Dinis, A., & Xavier, A. (2012). Experiential avoidance in clinical and non-clinical samples: AAQ-II Portuguese version . *International Journal of Psychology & Psychological Therapy*, 12(2), 139–156.

Purser, R., & Loy, D. (2013). Beyond McMindfulness. *The Huffington Post*. Retrieved from www.huffingtonpost.com/ron-purser/beyond-mcmindfulness_b_3519289.html

Purser, R. E. (2015a). Clearing the muddled path of traditional and contemporary mindfulness: a response to Monteiro, Musten, and Compson. *Mindfulness*, 6(1), 23–45. doi:10.1007/s12671-014-0373-4

Purser, R. (2015b). The myth of the present moment. *Mindfulness*, 6(3), 680–686. doi:10.1007/s12671-014-0333-z

Purser, R. E., & Milillo, J. (2015). Mindfulness revisited: a Buddhist-based conceptualization. *Journal of Management Inquiry*, 24(1), 3–24. doi:10.1177/1056492614532315

Purser, R. E., Forbes, D., & Burke, A. (Eds.) (2016). *Handbook of mindfulness – culture, context, and social engagement*. Switzerland: Springer Nature.

Rapgay, L., & Bystrisky, A. (2009). Classical mindfulness – an introduction to its theory and practice for clinical application. *Annals of the New York Academy of Sciences*, 1172, 148–162. doi:10.1111/j.1749-6632.2009.04405.x

Rau, H. K., & Williams, P. G. (2016). Dispositional mindfulness: a critical review of construct validation research. *Personality and Individual Differences*, 93, 32–43. doi:10.1016/j.paid.2015. 09. 035

Repetti, R. (2016). Meditation matters: replies to the Anti-McMindfulness Bandwagon. In R. E. Purser, D. Forbes, & A. Burke (Eds.), *Handbook of mindfulness: culture, context, and social engagement* (pp. 473–494). Switzerland: Springer Nature.

Reveley, J. (2016). Neoliberal meditations: how mindfulness training medicalizes education and responsibilizes young people. *Policy Futures in Education*, 14(4), 497–511. doi:10.1177/1478210316637972

Reiner, K., Tibi, L., & Lipsitz, J. D. (2013). Do mindfulness-based interventions reduce pain intensity? A critical review of the literature. *Pain Medicine*, 14(2), 230–242. doi:10.1111/pme.12006

Salzberg, S. (2011). *Real happiness: The power of meditation*. New York, USA: Workman Publishing Company.

Sauer, S., Lynch, S., Walach, H., & Kohls, N. (2011). Dialectics of mindfulness: implications for western medicine. *Philosophy, Ethics, and Humanities in Medicine*, 6, 10. doi:10.1186/1747-5341-6-10

Schmidt, S. (2014a). Mindfulness – origin, practice and conception [German]. *Sucht*, 60(1), 13–19. doi:10.1024/0939-5911.a000287

Schmidt, S. (2014b). Opening up meditation for science: the development of a meditation classification system. In S. Schmidt & H. Walach (Eds.), *Meditation – neuroscientific approaches and philosophical implications* (pp. 137–152). Switzerland: Springer. doi:10.1007/978-3-319-01634-4_8

Schonert-Reichl, K. A., & Roeser, R. W. (Eds.) (2016). *Handbook of mindfulness in education*. New York, USA: Springer.

Seager, R. H. (1999). *Buddhism in America*. New York, USA: Columbia University Press.

Segal, Z. V., Williams, J. M. G., & Teasdale, J. D. (2013). *Mindfulness-based cognitive therapy for depression: a new approach to preventing relapse* (2nd ed.). New York, USA: The Guilford Press.

Shapiro, S. L. (2009). The integration of mindfulness and psychology. *Journal of Clinical Psychology*, 65(6), 555–560. doi:10.1002/jclp.20602

Shapiro, S., Siegel, R., & Neff, K. D. (2018). Paradoxes of mindfulness. *Mindfulness*. Online First. doi:10.1007/s12671-018-0957-5

Shaver, P. R., Lavy, S., Saron, C. D., & Mikulincer, M. (2007). Social foundations of the capacity for mindfulness: an attachment perspective. *Psychological Inquiry*, 18(4), 264–271. doi:10.1080/10478400701598389

Shaw, J. M., Sekelja, N., Frasca, D., Dhillon, H. M., & Price, M. A. (2018). Being mindful of mindfulness interventions in cancer: a systematic review of intervention reporting and study methodology. *Psycho-Oncology*, 27(4), 1161–1171. doi:10.1002/pon.4651

Shonin, E., Van Gordon, W., & Griffiths, M. D. (2013). Mindfulness-based interventions: towards mindful clinical integration. *Frontiers in Psychology*, 4, 194. doi:10.3389/fpsyg.2013.00194

Shonin, E., & Van Gordon, W. (2015). Practical recommendations for teaching mindfulness effectively. *Mindfulness*, 6(4), 952–955. doi:10.1007/s12671–12014–0342-y

Shonin, E., Van Gordon, W., & Singh, N. N. (2015). Buddhist foundations of mindfulness. New York, USA: Springer.

Singh, N. S. (2010). Mindfulness: a finger pointing to the moon. *Mindfulness*, 1(1), 1–3. doi:10.1007/s12671-010-0009-2

Smith, J. E., Richardson, J., Hoffman, C., & Pilkington, K. (2005). Mindfulness-Based Stress Reduction as supportive therapy in cancer care: systematic review. *Journal of Advanced Nursing*, 52(3), 315–327. doi:10.1111/j.1365-2648.2005.03592.x

Stanley, S., Purser, R. E. & Singh, N. N. (Eds.) (2018). *Handbook of ethical foundations of mindfulness*. New York, USA: Springer.

Stetka, B. (2017, October 11). Where is the proof that mindfulness meditation works?. Retrieved from www.scientificamerican.com/article/wheres-the-proof-that-mindfulness-meditation-works1/

Stillman, C. M., Feldman, H., Wambach, C. G., Howard, J. H., & Howard, D. V. (2014). Dispositional mindfulness is associated with reduced implicit learning. *Consciousness and Cognition*, 28, 141–150. doi:10.1016/j.concog.2014. 07. 002

Sun, J. (2014). Mindfulness in context: a historical discourse analysis. *Contemporary Buddhism*, 15(2), 394–415. doi:10.1080/14639947.2014.978088

Teasdale, J. D., Segal, Z. V., Williams, J. M. G., Ridgeway, V. A., Soulsby, J. M., & Lau, M. A. (2000). Prevention of relapse/recurrence in major depression by Mindfulness-Based Cognitive Therapy. *Journal of Consulting and Clinical Psychology*, 68(4), 615–623. doi:10.1037/0022-006X.68. 4. 61doi:5

Tomlinson, E. R., Yousaf, O., Vittersø, A. D., & Jones, L. (2018). Dispositional mindfulness and psychological health: a systematic review. *Mindfulness*, 9(1), 23–43. doi:10.1007/s12671-017-0762-6

Van Dam, N. T., van Vugt, M. K., Vago, D. R., Schmalzl, L., Saron, C. D., Olendzki, A., …, & Meyer, D. E. (2018). Mind the hype: a critical evaluation and prescriptive agenda for research on mindfulness and meditation. *Perspectives on Psychological Science*, 13(1), 36–61. doi:10.1177/1745691617709589

Van Gordon, W., Shonin, E., & Griffiths, M. D. (2015). Towards a second generation of mindfulness-based interventions. *Australian & New Zealand Journal of Psychiatry*, 49(7), 591–592. doi:10.1177/0004867415577437

Van Gordon, W., Shonin, E., & Griffiths, M. D. (2016). Are contemporary mindfulness-based interventions unethical?. *British Journal of General Practice*, 66(643), 94. doi:10.3399/bjgp16X683677

Zajonc, A. (2016). Contemplation in education. In K. A. Schonert-Reichl & R. W. Roeser (Eds.), *Handbook of mindfulness in education: emerging theory, research, and programs* (pp. 17–28). doi:10.1007/978-1-4939-3506-2_2

Wallace, R. K. (1970). Physiological effects transcendental meditation. *Science*, 167(3926), 1751–1754. doi:10.1126/science.167.3926.1751

Whitmarsh, S., Uddén, J., Barendregt, H., & Petersson, K. M. (2013). Mindfulness reduces habitual responding based on implicit knowledge: evidence from artificial grammar learning. *Consciousness and Cognition*, 22(3), 833–845. doi:10.1016/j.concog.2013.05.0doi:07

Williams, J. M. G., & Kabat-Zinn, J. (2011). Mindfulness: diverse perspectives on its meaning, origins, and multiple applications at the intersection of science and dharma. *Contemporary Buddhism*, 12(1), 1–18. doi:10.1080/14639947.2011.564811

Witkiewitz, K., Marlatt, G. A., & Walker, D. (2005). Mindfulness-Based Relapse Prevention for alcohol and substance use disorders. *Journal of Cognitive Psychotherapy*, 19(3), 211–228. doi:10.1891/jcop.2005.19.doi:3.211

Wong, V., Chen, J., & Chan, L.-C. (2018). Mindfulness practice in medical education. In M. A. Henning, C. U. Krägeloh, R. Dryer, F. Moir, D. R. Billington, & A. G. Hill (Eds.). *Wellbeing higher education: cultivating a healthy lifestyle among faculty and students* (pp. 94–106). Oxon, United Kingdom: Routledge.

Yapko, M. D. (2014). The spirit of hypnosis: doing hypnosis versus being hypnotic. *American Journal of Clinical Hypnosis*, 56(3), 234–248. doi:10.1080/00029157.2013.815605

2

META-THEORIES AND QUALITATIVE METHODS IN MINDFULNESS RESEARCH

Since the subject matter of mindfulness research involves subjective states and reports of experiences and mental phenomena, one might expect that the majority of research studies about mindfulness-based interventions (MBIs) use a qualitative methodology. It may thus appear as counter-intuitive to discover after a critical review of the mindfulness literature that qualitative research studies on mindfulness are considerably fewer than quantitative studies. The reason for this is open for speculation. One may claim that this discrepancy is reflective of the field of psychology in general, which traditionally has a heavier emphasis on quantitative methodology (Kidd, 2002), although there has been an increasing trend recently towards the use of qualitative approaches (Carrera-Fernández, Guàrdia-Olmos, & Peró-Cebollero, 2014). Additionally, the rapid growth of mindfulness research within health settings – through the development of MBIs such as Mindfulness-Based Stress Reduction (MBSR; Kabat-Zinn, 1990) – likely fuelled the need to demonstrate the effectiveness of such programmes using designs such as randomised controlled trials and the associated quantitative analyses. However, as a result of the widely recognised effectiveness of MBIs (Khoury et al., 2013), research has increasingly focused on the description of the lived experience around mindfulness practice, and more qualitative studies on mindfulness have started to appear.

The present chapter arranges its discussion of the use of a range of different qualitative methods in MBI research by purpose of application. Any discussion of qualitative research would be incomplete without an analysis of the role of ontology and epistemology in such methods of inquiry (Guba & Lincoln, 1994; Ponterotto, 2005). While this inevitably links the topic to some concepts from Buddhist philosophy that informed the development of MBIs, the broader implications of cross-cultural exchanges will be discussed in another chapter. After an outline of the recognition of ontological and epistemological assumptions in MBIs, the focus of the present chapter will then shift to how qualitative or mixed-methods approaches have been used to investigate specific topics related to all aspects around the application of MBIs. While some discussion has also repeatedly outlined the utility of mindfulness in the *process* of conducting qualitative research (Depraz, Varela, & Vermersch, 2003; Stanley, 2012; Woodgate, Tennent, & Zurba, 2017), and there have even been empirical investigations on that subject (Stanley, Barker, Edwards, & McEwen, 2015), this is beyond the scope of the present book. General critical discussion such as commentaries about the sociological role of MBIs within political climates and workplace contexts (e.g. Arthington, 2016; Reveley, 2016) will also not be included in this chapter as it has already been covered in the previous chapter.

Meta-theory in research on mindfulness-based interventions

Philosophy of science recognises the importance of promoting an understanding of meta-theory or the different beliefs and assumptions underlying the process of scientific inquiry (Ponterotto, 2005). This includes ontology (nature of reality), epistemology (study of how knowledge is acquired), axiology (role and place of values in research), rhetorical structure (language used to disseminate research), and methodology (procedures used in research). While qualitative research generally verbalises its assumptions thoroughly and carefully (Guba & Lincoln, 1994; Ponterotto, 2005), quantitative researchers are often silent about ontology and epistemology. As a result, classification of research approaches and associated assumptions is typically offered by qualitative researchers, which leaves them vulnerable to the temptation to portray quantitative research in naïve and stereotypic ways. For example, it is not uncommon to see quantitative research to be linked almost exclusively with so-called positivist ideas, according to which science is perceived as being in pursuit of an absolute truth, using provable hypotheses and promoting bias- and value-free description (Giddings & Grant, 2007).

Of the quantitative approaches that have been used to investigate the therapeutic application of mindfulness, those concerning Acceptance and Commitment Therapy (ACT; Hayes, Strosahl, Wilson, 2011) tend to be most explicit about their philosophical assumptions. ACT is closely embedded within the theory of contextual behavioural science (Hayes, Barnes-Holmes, & Wilson, 2012). Also known as functional contextualism, this philosophy

> views science as an endeavour whose aim is not to give an ontological description of how the world really is but rather to develop ways of speaking that help accomplish scientific goals. From a functional contextual viewpoint, the world is real but is differentiated into units of analysis based on the actions of those doing the analysis. The value of such division is determined by its consequences, both within the lifetime of an individual and across lifetimes throughout human history. Thus, it is not the "ontological truth" of a description that our science is interested in but whether it meets its stated goals.
>
> *Fletcher, Schoendorff, & Hayes, 2010, p.47*

This tradition finds its origins in behavioural psychology, and has thus been heavily influenced by a-ontological ideas of behavioural pragmatism (Krägeloh, 2006) and the radical empiricism of William James (Kerr & Key, 2011). Such thought re-appears within contextual behavioural science under the term ontological agnosticism (Long, 2013).

In contrast to ACT, which is not included within the definitions of MBIs used in the present book, quantitative MBI research in the tradition of MBSR and Mindfulness-Based Cognitive Therapy (MBCT; Segal, Williams, & Teasdale, 2013) provides very scarce references to ontology and epistemology. This can easily be confirmed by conducting a search of common literature databases (e.g. "+MBSR +ontology"). Many of the search hits regarding mindfulness are not directly related to MBIs, such as the argument that the process of learning mindfulness will be beneficial for teaching ontology in an accessible way (Bearance & Holmes, 2015). However, the general absence of explicit discussion of the philosophical underpinnings of MBI research does not mean that a default worldview such as positivism can automatically be assigned. For example, the philosophy underlying ACT may still be applied to research about mindfulness-based approaches more broadly.

Despite the overall more thorough engagement of qualitative research with relevant research paradigms (Guba & Lincoln, 1994; Ponterotto, 2005), qualitative studies about MBIs are generally not very different from quantitative studies in their description of philosophical assumptions. For example, of the five qualitative studies included in a systematic review of qualitative evidence of attitudes about mindfulness by MBSR and MBCT course participants with cancer (Tate, Newbury-Birch, & McGeechan, 2018), none of the studies explicitly discussed philosophical assumptions and instead relied on general references about qualitative methods or did not elaborate much at all. Two of these studies (Chambers, Foley, Galt, Ferguson, & Clutton, 2012; Eyles et al., 2015) reported on the use of a mixed-methods approach, Dobkin (2008) analysed quantitative and qualitative data without referring to her study as mixed methods, and one study reported on a thematic analysis of qualitative data collected within a randomised controlled trial (Hoffman, Ersser, & Hopkinson, 2012). The last study, Mackenzie, Carlson, Munoz, and Speca (2007), used grounded theory to analyse data from semi-structured interviews and a focus group about self-perceived effects of MBSR.

An example of a qualitative study where the authors made their background and philosophical perspective clear was a grounded-theory study by Langdon, Jones, Hutton, and Holttum (2011). Here, the authors described their experience with mindfulness and qualitative research and also stated that their research was informed by a critical realist position. A formal system to evaluate the quality of qualitative studies was used in a review by Morgan, Simpson, and Smith (2015). Using a critical appraisal tool, the researchers categorised 14 studies about health care workers' experience of mindfulness training as either "key paper" ($n=10$), "satisfactory" ($n=3$), or "fatally flawed" ($n=1$). The most common issue noted about the papers were failing to report the methods of data analysis or lack of reflection on the potential impact by the researcher.

Relating mindfulness to Buddhist psychology

Discussion of philosophical assumptions underlying MBI research remains largely confined to work that draws comparisons between Western MBI research and Buddhist philosophy. One example would be a study by Crowder (2016) about Mindfulness-Based Feminist Therapy, where the author discussed how feminist and Buddhist ontologies are able to inform each other. Other conceptual discussion drew attention to the fact that MBI research represents a confluence of traditions with different epistemologies, namely contemplative teaching and practice as well as Western scientific and empiricist traditions (Crane, 2017). Such meeting of diverse traditions not only brings with it the need to communicate with clarity (Crane, 2017), but might even lead to further refinement of relevant concepts as contemplative research may consider equanimity as a more appropriate outcome than mindfulness (Desbordes et al., 2015).

Stanley (2012) discussed mindfulness in the context of Buddhist as well as discursive psychology. While MBIs may be understood by discursive perspectives as promoting a cognitivist view, Stanley (2012) presents a discussion of Buddhist psychology as radically embodied and experiential. Such a shift on experience inevitably draws the paradox that defining it as a subject matter would fail to capture and locate it in the public sphere (Sharf, 2000). Similar arguments have also been presented about the nonconceptual aspects of mindfulness, which methodological techniques such as phenomenology can only approach indirectly (Krägeloh, 2018). Buddhist understandings of experience have been discussed extensively through the Mahāyāna philosophy of emptiness, although Krägeloh (2018) also provided links to the more recently emerging philosophical thought of the Kyoto School, which communicated Buddhist philosophy using Western vocabulary. Within such philosophy, experience can be described as having "an ontological role that defies any reified description and discourse" (Krägeloh, 2018).

The cross-cultural platform of mindfulness research through its historical links to Eastern philosophy might also challenge some of the conventional classifications of schools of thought. The tendency to add the prefix *post* to a term such as in postmodern, posthumanist, and postqualitative (Brinkmann, 2017) is a useful short-hand expression to signal the historical relatedness of sets of theoretical frameworks such as one developing out of the context of another (Giddings & Grant, 2007). However, it must not be misunderstood as accepting the notion of a logical progression of thought. Previous philosophical thought that might have come out of favour over time might be interpreted through new perspectives, such as Confucianism through the lens of postmodernism (Hahm, 2001). Comparisons with East Asian thought also need to be made with the understanding that the relatively early separation between religious and general philosophical vocabulary was primarily a Western phenomenon. It was not until the Meiji period in Japan (1868–1912) that a large number of neologisms using Chinese characters were created within a short period of time (Godart, 2008). This includes the term for philosophy (哲学; Japanese pronunciation: *tetsugaku*), which was used exclusively to refer to Western philosophy during that period, while Eastern ideas were described in the context of religion (Uehara, 2009).

The comparative work necessary for the creation of neologisms as well as particular Western trends and motivations for studying Eastern ideas at particular time periods may have led to the occasional overemphasis of similarities and parallels between Western and Eastern ideas. Sharf (1995), for example, discussed how the popular contemporary image of what characterises Zen is to a large extent derived from specific attempts by Zen partisans in the Meiji period to adapt Buddhism to be fit for the modern age. Another Buddhist tradition that influenced MBIs but cannot be seen as representative of traditional Buddhist thought is that of the Burmese reform movement, also known as the *Vipassana* or insight meditation movement (Sharf, 2015). Coupled with a tendency for Western intellectuals to seek in Buddhism a rational philosophy (Baumann, 1997), one needs to expect that particular kinds of interpretations of Buddhism may have been popularised in the West more than others. Against this backdrop one also finds perceptions in Western philosophy that Eastern thought lacks comparable sophistication in epistemological thinking (Hahm, 2001). Others, in contrast, argued that some of the thought that influenced Eastern Buddhist philosophy does not fit the typical categorisations found in Western philosophy as it does not consider ontology as a theory of being but may instead be promoting meontology, or the theory of nothingness (Schultz, 2012; Chai, 2014).

Given the unclear position of Buddhist ideas in relation to Western philosophy, it is not surprising that Buddhist philosophy and psychology have been interpreted, adapted, and integrated with Western mindfulness research in diverse ways. This includes attempts to contrast the Buddhist soteriological context from Western therapeutic applications in the marketplace or as postmodern activity (Nilsson, 2013). By referring to its axiological characteristics, Beshara (2017) described Buddhism as transmodern because of the fact that its rigour and reflexivity matches that of postmodernism but without the morally reprehensible practices brought about by moral relativism. Beshara (2017) also explained the soteriological aspect of Buddhism through the collapsing (or nondualistic merging) of the absolute truth of the lack of independent existence of phenomena (ontology of transformation) and the epistemology of social change, namely the relative truth about phenomena through psychosocial construction. McWilliams (2014) used the term *process ontology* to explain the notion that reality is seen as events arising within continuous change and the term *pragmatic epistemology* to describe the understanding that one cannot make assertions about an ultimate reality but can only know reality as a socially constructed truth.

The social constructivism of Buddhism results in the logical extension of its process ontology to the question of the self and thus views the self as constructed (McWilliams, 2010). Similar conclusions can be reached through the Buddhist notion of nonconceptualisation (Sharf, 2014), which is more directly linked to current understandings and discourse of mindfulness within the MBI literature (Krägeloh, 2016). Related to nonconceptualisation is the view of lack of a permanent self, or the doctrine of non-self (Sharf, 2014). While deconstruction of the conventional self has also been part of Western therapies such as Gestalt therapy, Buddhist philosophy may be more explicit in this regard, thus triggering discussions about the extent to which such philosophy may be indirectly implied in Western MBIs as well (Murray, 2015). Other attempts to interpret such Buddhist ideas from the perspectives of Western philosophy have been made through embodiment and the phenomenology of being where persons are understood as processes instead of entities (Virtbauer, 2016). Drawing on the phenomenological concept of bracketing, according to which one's judgments are suspended, Buddhism may then be viewed as a "radically experiential phenomenological psychology" (Virtbauer, 2016, p.77).

Meta-theory in first-person perspectives

Buddhism is regularly described as a first-person discourse and contrasted with third-person scientific traditions (e.g. Huxter, 2012). When attempting to explore the process of engaging in meditation and mindfulness techniques from a Western perspective, it is therefore not surprising to find regular references to relevant qualitative research approaches and their associated philosophical frameworks. One of these perspectives is phenomenology. While the English title of Martin Heidegger's (1938/1997) book *Mindfulness* might be seen as an affirmation of such a link, the original German title *Besinnung* connotes aspects of reflection more than mindfulness, for which German typically uses the term *Achtsamkeit*. Nevertheless, parallels between phenomenology and mindfulness have been outlined in detail, which includes interpreting classical philosophical writings of key phenomenologists such as Edmund Husserl and Martin Heidegger through perspectives gained from contemporary understandings of mindfulness and its associated vocabulary (e.g. Depraz et al., 2003). With more recently emerging neuroscientific research on meditation, phenomenology has also been applied to explore links between brain function and the experiences of conscious states (Modestino, 2016) – through an approach known as neurophenomenology (Varela, 1999).

Even though it could be argued that neurophenomenology dismisses ontology as mere speculation (Froese, 2011), other researchers have argued that a recovery of subjective experience as a mode of knowledge is in "need [of] a proper ontology, at least a minimally acceptable ontology, that is not contrary to our scientific corpus of knowledge, yet allows for an access of consciousness to reality beyond the senses, through its own inner experiences" (Walach, 2014, p.13). Within the corresponding epistemology, so-called inner experience can provide potential access to reality through knowledge gained from subjective first-person perspectives. Of course, the expression *inner experience* is misleading in this context, as it implies a distinction between an inner and an outer dimension, which can be criticised as third-person views based on artificial dualism. For that reason, Walach (2014) uses quotation marks when referring to inner experiences. When referring to consciousness more broadly rather than mindfulness, Walach and Römer (2011) introduced the idea of phenomenological dualism together with ontological monism.

First-person methods and meditation have also been promoted under the methodological approach of contemplative inquiry (Zajonc, 2009), although in the context of MBIs no particular philosophical approach appears to be dominant. Here, because of the application of mindfulness as a therapeutic intervention in a variety of contexts with health professionals of diverse backgrounds and educated in a range of treatments paradigms, MBIs have been described as trans-epistemological (Didonna, 2009). As such, MBI practice may be embedded quite comfortably within standard dualist worldviews, such as when seen as a method of self-improvement with

> the self controlling the self, that is, the exercise of one's own 'will-power' to change oneself. The idea that the will has power is based on nineteenth century ideas of energy, including psychic energy. This is another model of the self or the mind that reifies what should more accurately be treated as processes.
>
> *Payne, 2016, p.131*

Another way in which philosophical discussions have been linked to mindfulness is through concepts such as pure awareness, nonconceptual awareness, or nondual awareness. Chiesa and Malinowski (2011), for example, referred to pure awareness as another term for bare attention or direct perception of pure experience that is practised in Zen, Vipassana, and MBSR in contrast to the behaviourally oriented ACT. Krägeloh (2018) outlined how nondual awareness, or the pre-conceptual awareness that precedes the distinction between subject and object, is part of deeper mindfulness practice intended to bring about transformative growth. However, nondual awareness has also been described in diverse ways. Within the context of the Mahāyāna Buddhist philosophy of emptiness, nondual awareness may be considered either as an ontological principle or a linguistic device to refer to nonreifiable or nonobjectifiable experience and is thus unsuitable for phenomenological analysis (Krägeloh, 2018). As shown by a qualitative study of mindfulness teachers providing psychotherapy, nonduality and the corresponding distinction between ultimate and reality truth are difficult to communicate (Gill, Waltz, Suhrbier, & Robert, 2015). This may certainly be the reason that MBIs typically do not cover nondual awareness as it is considered to require more advanced understanding and practice (Mills et al., 2018). On the other hand, nondual awareness has also been conceptualised and investigated empirically as a state associated with meditation practices. In that context, neurophenomenological approaches have led to a revival of introspective methods that utilise similar methods to those of phenomenological research (Bitbol & Petitmengin, 2013). In other cases, introspection has been investigated in terms of introspective accuracy where expert meditators have been shown to have increased tactile sensitivity than novice meditators in a laboratory-based body-scan meditation task (Fox et al., 2016).

Types of qualitative methods used in mindfulness research

There are many sources one can consult to obtain an overview of the range of different qualitative research methods and how they can be classified. For example,

Fossey, Harvey, McDermott, and Davidson (2002) distinguished between the interpretive and critical paradigms of qualitative methods. The former includes hermeneutics and phenomenology and focuses primarily on understanding the meaning of human experiences and actions. The critical paradigm, on the other hand, promotes analysis and awareness of how collective thought is socially and historically constructed. The particular perspectives one can adopt here include Marxism and feminism. Within these paradigms, data are generally collected using interviews, focus groups, or observation (Fossey et al., 2002). In meaning-focused approaches such as phenomenology, data are analysed to reveal the subjective meaning of experiences for the participant without involving the researcher's conceptions. Data are coded for recurrent themes within participants and are then compared across participants to identify common themes. In so-called discovery-focused techniques, in contrast, the primary aim is that of theory building, which is conducted either thematically or using grounded theory (Fossey et al., 2002). This is typically an iterative process involving continuous refinement and reformulation of the theory being developed.

A variety of typologies have been proposed for the various qualitative approaches (Hammersley, 2018), and a way to provide a structure and overview of qualitative research is in terms of the characteristics of the specific methods and what they aim to achieve. This includes ethnography, narrative inquiry, phenomenology, and grounded theory. Mixed methods, or the combination of qualitative and quantitative methods, will also be briefly outlined here.

Within the interpretive paradigm is ethnography (Fossey et al., 2002), although it may also be described as inductive (Vogt, 2014). Ethnography has its origins in cultural anthropology and focuses on observation where the researcher may become a *participant observer*. In the case of MBI research, a mindfulness group or programme is likely to have developed particular beliefs, values, norms, and even set of specialised or idiosyncratic language, and the researcher could observe this culture in action. When searching the MBI literature, very little ethnographic research in the above-mentioned sense can be located, and most search hits would refer to meta-ethnography. This approach, as used by Malpass et al. (2012), for example, is a method for synthesising findings from qualitative research – thus similar to a meta-synthesis (Wyatt, Harper, & Weatherhead, 2014) or the equivalent of systematic literature reviews for quantitative studies. Another variant is auto-ethnography, which involves reports from self-observation. Although this method has been used for quite some time, it is still fairly loosely defined and may even include auto-biographical accounts (Vogt, 2014). With that definition, a reflective piece by Shobbrook-Fisher (2016) about the experience of providing person-centred therapy as a teacher of MBSR might count as auto-ethnography. When searching for auto-ethnographic studies in the context of MBIs, most search hits relate to postgraduate theses, but not many to peer-reviewed publications. An example of a refereed article in this area is an auto-ethnographic study by Laurie and Blandford (2016), who used this method to inform subsequent semi-structured qualitative interviews about the use of a commercially available mindfulness smartphone app.

Very much related to the method of ethnography is that of narrative inquiry, or the insights gained from considering detailed life histories (Tierney, 1998). The process of recollecting life experiences through narration is understood to reveal the truth and meaning of these events and associated emotions. In the context of MBIs, each course participant will have their own story to share, which is generally explored using open-ended interviews. In a study on the experiences of participation in an MBI (Stelter, 2009), the researcher acted as a nonparticipant observer who collected field notes to contextualise the subsequently collected qualitative information from the participants and to establish ecological validity. Course participants posted diaries back to the researcher on a weekly basis, and further information was gathered through semi-structured interviews at three time points throughout the course. Data collection in narrative inquiry can thus be ongoing and iterative, with analysis occurring alongside verification. In the study by Stelter (2009), data were coded and then thematically bundled. The three cases presented in this study illustrated the unique and embodied changes that had occurred as a result of participation in the MBI and how these appeared to be linked to experiences of healing and life changes.

A qualitative method that has become increasingly common in MBI research is interpretative phenomenological analysis (IPA; Malpass et al., 2012; Wyatt et al., 2014; Tate et al., 2018). The aim of IPA is to explore how people create meaning from their experiences (Smith, Flowers, & Larkin, 2009). To gain access to what is present or given in the experience of the awareness of the participant, the researcher gathers descriptions from their participants about the experience and then starts to unpack the common elements that make the experience what it is. During the collaborative process between researcher and participant, intuitive evidence is co-generated that is thought to reveal the essence of the experience (Depraz et al., 2003). In the case of research on MBIs, IPA can provide information about how course participants understand aspects of mindfulness as an intervention. Griffiths, Camic, and Hutton (2009), for example, used IPA to gather experiences of participants in an MBCT programme for cardiac rehabilitation. Between 6 to 12 weeks after the intervention, semi-structured interviews were conducted that lasted between one to two hours. All interviews were tape recorded, transcribed verbatim, and then analysed for themes. A similar study has been conducted by Fitzpatrick, Simpson, and Smith (2010) who explored the experiences of MBCT participation by individuals with Parkinson's disease. In order to gain first-hand experience of what the participants may be experiencing, the first author participated in a separate MBCT course and kept detailed diary notes.

Another commonly found approach with respect to qualitative MBI research (Malpass et al., 2012) is grounded theory. This method differs from IPA in that its aim is to derive a theoretical explanation for the participant's engagement in the activity under investigation. Sources of data can vary widely, including interviews, observations, and even government documents, videos, newspaper articles, or books (Corbin & Strauss, 1990). Due to its emphasis on theory building, there is a continuous interrogative nature to the process, in which data collection and analysis are interlinked, and the relationships between the activity and the emerging theory go through stages of verification. The interactive nature of the process involves the constant re-thinking and re-checking of the emerging concepts, which may require repeated interviews, document analysis, and observations. The basic units of analysis in grounded theory are the concepts extracted from the data, not the actual data *per se* (Corbin & Strauss, 1990). In reference to mindfulness research, grounded theory is likely to be a useful research approach to provide a theoretical structure of mindfulness practice. Mason and Hargreaves (2001), for example, argued that grounded theory was particularly useful for their research purpose as it allows capturing individual differences as well as commonalities in participants' experiences of the MBI. The researchers interviewed seven MBCT participants to inquire about the process by which MBCT may bring about its therapeutic benefits. In other cases, the use of a grounded theory approach was only mentioned indirectly. Schussler, Jennings, Sharp, and Frank (2016) collected qualitative data to expand on the results of a randomised controlled trial about a mindfulness-based professional development programme for teachers. Using four focus groups of three to eight participants, the researchers explored the role of the mindfulness programme in influencing teacher awareness and the role of various aspects of the programme in affecting teachers' health. The authors mentioned the fact that they had used axial coding to reveal contextual information about aspects of mindfulness practice and referred to a seminal reference source for grounded theory (Strauss & Corbin, 1990).

A number of studies in the MBI research literature reported on the use of a mixed-methods approach. Considered as a third paradigm alongside quantitative and qualitative research, mixed-methods research actively integrates and triangulates quantitative and qualitative research either sequentially or simultaneously (Johnson, Onwuegbuzie, & Turner, 2007). This approach is distinguished from multi-method research that generally does not have the same level of integration between quantitative and qualitative analyses (Morse, 2003). For that reason, mixed-methods investigations are generally considered suitable for the purpose of answering complex research questions or for providing breadth that one would not be able to gain with a single methodological approach (Johnson et al., 2007). In the context of MBI research, mixed-methods studies typically collect quantitative data about commonly used intervention outcomes as well as qualitative data to provide more detail. For example, Bernay, Graham, Devcich, Rix, and Rubie-Davies (2016) investigated the effects of an MBI conducted with three primary schools and reported on quantitative data from 124 participants. In order to triangulate these results, teacher observation journals and interview data from six students were also analysed. Some researchers also justified the use of a smaller sample size for the analyses of their quantitative MBI results based on the argument that this type of triangulation from mixed-methods designs results in additional robustness (Birtwell, Dubrow-Marshall, Dubrow-Marshall, Duerden, & Dunn, 2017). In a critical methodological review, Huynh, Hatton-Bowers, and Smith (2018) reviewed 35 articles reporting on a mixed-methods design in the context of mindfulness research. Findings revealed the need for more rigour when applying this methodological approach, particularly when outlining the reasons for choosing mixed methods and identifying the relationship between the quantitative and qualitative aspects of the data analysis.

Reasons for collecting qualitative data in research on mindfulness-based interventions

Gaining more detailed understanding about mindfulness-based interventions through qualitative data

A common reason for collecting and analysing qualitative data in MBI research was to confirm the intervention effect or to obtain a more detailed understanding of how mindfulness is related to positive health outcomes. Often, this approach involved mixed-methods studies such as the ones mentioned above that argued that qualitative data in addition to quantitative data would lead to additional robustness (Bernay et al., 2016; Birtwell et al., 2017). Some of the additional qualitative data were published in separate publications, and such studies may therefore not be considered mixed methods. For example, Morone, Greco, and Weiner (2008a) published quantitative results of a feasibility study of an MBSR-modelled mindfulness meditation intervention for older adults with chronic pain. In another publication, Morone, Lynch, Greco, Tindle, and Weiner (2008b) then reported on qualitative data linked to this intervention, which the authors argued would complement the quantitative study and provide more insights about the potential mechanisms underlying the intervention. Using grounded theory, Morone et al. (2008b) examined diary entries from the participants. While the diaries allowed open-ended entries, they were presented in a structured manner inviting comments about each day's meditation experience. The extracted themes were thus generally specific to the experience of pain reduction and other themes that may typically be investigated in quantitative studies using self-reported outcomes measures.

Similar to Morone et al. (2008b), Schussler et al. (2016) also published their qualitative results separately from their quantitative findings. Jennings, Frank, Snowberg, Coccia, and Greenberg (2013) published a randomised controlled trial of a mindfulness-based professional development programme to improve school teachers' awareness and well-being, which was intended to reduce teachers' stress levels and lead to enhanced classroom learning environments. The purpose of the qualitative data reported by Schussler et al. (2016) was to explore the proximal outcomes of the intervention, particularly which aspects of the programme were and were not effective. This was explored using grounded theory with data collected from four focus groups with three to eight teachers each. In another grounded theory study by Hugh-Jones, Rose, Koutsopoulou, and Simms-Ellis (2018), the focus was more directly on the generation of a preliminary model of positive change – in this case for a workplace MBI. Informed by retrospective accounts from semi-structured interviews with 21 employees in a higher education institution, Hugh-Jones et al. (2018) developed a temporal linear model that outlined the process of change in thinking and experience from participation in the MBI. Aspects of change that had been brought about by participation in an MBI were also investigated by Proulx (2008). Here, six adult participants in a mindfulness-based eating disorder programme were interviewed prior and after the intervention. A novel analysis aspect of this study was the comparisons of participant self-portraits prior and after the intervention in order to illustrate experiences of positive transformation. Such an explicit focus on shifts in perception was also the aim of a study on the experiences of an MBSR programme that had been modified slightly for urban youth (Kerrigan et al., 2011). In this case, semi-structured interviews were conducted to explore to what extent participant experiences were consistent with changes in perceptions described by a conceptual model of the mechanism of mindfulness (Shapiro, Carlson, Astin, & Freedman, 2006).

Allen, Bromley, Kuyken, and Sonnenberg (2009) published a qualitative study that explored the processes underlying the therapeutic effectiveness of MBCT for people with recurrent depression. The authors were particularly interested to enquire how participants may explain the way in which MBCT works. Twelve months after MBCT, 20 participants were thus interviewed about their reflections about what they found helpful and difficult about the programme. Interviews were recorded and transcribed, followed by a thematic analysis conducted using widely recognised guidelines (Braun & Clarke, 2006). Many of the commonly reported dynamics of learning mindfulness were captured in the findings by Allen et al. (2009), although a new theme emerged that helps understand the journey that participants experience when participating in this intervention. The theme of *participant struggle* thus described the participants' initial orientation of striving and the subsequent challenges associated with making time for mindfulness practice during one's daily schedule.

Stelter (2009) specifically stated that the purpose of his qualitative study was not to provide further evidence of the effectiveness of MBIs. Instead, the study aimed to offer a further research perspective by "going in-depth with a small number of selected cases ... to clarify *what* happens and *how* it happens when mindfulness meditation training seems to have a positive effect" (Stelter, 2009, p.145). In a similar fashion, Dennick, Fox, and Walter-Brice (2013) intended to address the lack of sufficient qualitative data on the benefits of MBIs for psychosis. Additionally, citing a study by Abba, Chadwick, and Stevenson (2008), Dennick et al. (2013) argued that previous research had attempted to develop a theoretical understanding of the commonalities of experience in people participating in MBIs, and further knowledge was required about the specific idiosyncratic aspects of lived experience.

Even more different in purpose was a study by Marx, Strauss, and Williamson (2015). Here, quantitative and qualitative data were collected to evaluate the experiences of trainees in a year-long MBCT apprenticeship programme. All 18 trainees completed open-ended questions on a form, and five of these participants were also interviewed face-to-face.

When collecting qualitative data of MBIs, research is also able to gather valuable information about any attitudinal factors and beliefs around mindfulness practice, irrespective of whether the exploration of such attitudes was part of the original research objective or whether such findings were incidental. Mason and Hargreaves (2001), for example, investigated the process by which MBCT may bring about its therapeutic benefits and noted that participants' preconceived ideas and expectations about the interventions may be important factors influencing later experiences during the MBI programme. In a case study report, Dellbridge and Lubbe (2009) illustrated how an adolescent who practised mindfulness in an MBI format took a predominantly task-oriented approach to mindfulness. Solhaug et al. (2018) investigated attitude change in MBSR participants more explicitly with a sample of first-year medical and psychology students. Students who had completed a seven-week mindfulness course as part of a randomised controlled trial participated in a focus group or were interviewed separately. Transcripts were analysed using IPA, which was guided by a specific conceptual framework about the process of mindfulness as a cyclic and dynamic process of intention, attention, and attitude (Shapiro et al., 2006). The results revealed that participants generally viewed the MBI as a way to legitimise self-care and self-compassion. While some students expressed a more instrumental and goal-oriented view of mindfulness practice as primarily focused on enhancing attention and relaxation, students with a deeper engagement tended to value mindfulness as a way of self-exploration and also had more complex conceptions of mindfulness. The study thus highlighted how attentional aspects of mindfulness were easier to understand by course participants than some of the subtler attitudinal elements.

Further advantages of using qualitative methods to explore MBI-related changes are that a broad range of experiences can be documented, which may not be included in item content of quantitative self-report measures. For example, in a study of the long-term effects of MBIs, Mitchell and Heads (2015) explored participants' continued use of mindfulness practice since training. Individuals with chronic psychological issues who had been referred to a brief MBSR intervention approximately four years earlier completed an open-ended questionnaire. The results revealed that the intervention appeared to have had long-lasting effects on emotion regulation and psychological well-being. In a similar fashion, a mixed-methods study by Ridderinkhof, de Bruin, Blom, and Bögels (2018) highlighted findings that standardised questionnaires did not. When evaluating the effects of a mindfulness-based programme for children with autism, the researchers collected qualitative data from evaluation forms with open-ended questions that both children parents had answered. Unlike the data obtained from the quantitative questionnaires, the qualitative open-ended feedback by parents illustrated improvements in social interaction and reduction in sleep problems. In some cases, qualitative data has also provided a way to indicate potential utility of an MBI in pilot trials where quantitative results may present a null result for a range of research design reasons. Wongtongkam, Ward, Day, and Winefield (2014) reported on a trial of a MBI for students at a technical college in Thailand to reduce anger expression and violent behaviour. The intervention was based on the MBSR model, with a few modifications such as inclusion of traditional Thai meditation practices delivered by local Buddhist monks. While the quantitative results from the 40 students in the experimental group did not reveal a significant difference in self-reported outcomes after the intervention in comparison to the control group ($n=56$), the data from semi-structured interviews indicated that the participants had improved in terms of self-regulation skills and self-awareness.

Inquiring about adverse effects or barriers to practising mindfulness

In the MBI literature, qualitative research methods have also provided a useful source of information about potential adverse effects of meditation and mindfulness practice or other reasons preventing MBI participants from continuing their practice. As the importance of documenting and quantifying adverse events in MBIs has been increasingly recognised (Wong, Chan, Zhang, Lee, & Tsoi, 2018), qualitative data can offer detailed contextual information about the circumstances of negative reactions to exercises typically practised in MBIs. Kuijpers, van der Heijden, Tuinier, and Verhoeven (2007) reviewed case studies published in the literature that reported on the presence of acute psychotic states that appeared to be linked to meditation practice. Similarly, Lustyk, Chawla, Nolan, and Marlatt (2009) summarised evidence from case studies about negative reactions associated with meditation. Of the 12 studies reviewed, however, none were about MBIs. Given the fairly low rate of adverse effects generally found in MBIs (Wong et al., 2018), reports of adverse reactions to mindfulness practice have generally been mentioned in relation to broader research questions and have thus not been the focus of explicit systematic investigation. Irving et al. (2014), for instance, examined the experiences of healthcare professionals who completed an MBI adapted from MBSR. While the purpose was to develop a working model of how course participants may experience change during the MBI, this qualitative study also aimed to explore any challenges or negative side effects associated with the intervention. Using grounded theory with data from six focus groups, Irving et al. (2014) found that some participants experienced intense emotional distress and feelings of guilt when making some efforts to engage in self-care behaviours.

While a certain degree of frustration is often described as an important experiential aspect of the intervention and thus not necessarily something perceived to be an undesirable feature of an MBI (Irving et al., 2014), participants also appear to prefer clearer communication regarding the goals of the intervention, particularly the focus on emotional rather than physical pain (Ruskin et al., 2017). Although this indicates the presence of differences between prior expectations and actual experiences for some participants, further research is necessary to explore to what extent such expectation–experience mismatch may be a contributing factor to drop-out rates in MBIs. Participant drop-out in MBIs typically occurs early, with no particular pattern related to demographic profiles and outcome measures at baseline (Dobkin, Irving, & Amar, 2012), nor do there appear to be any links to emotional responding during the early part of the intervention (Harel, Hadash, Levi-Belz, & Bernstein, 2018).

In a feasibility study to explore the acceptability of mindfulness for stroke survivors and caregivers, Jani, Simpson, Lawrence, Simpson, and Mercer (2018) conducted focus groups to obtain feedback about a brief taster MBSR programme. Data were analysed using the so-called framework method (Gale, Heath, Cameron, Rashid, & Redwood, 2013), which outlines a number of steps to be followed in a way that even research team members with limited experience in qualitative research can be involved. This method is not aligned with any particular epistemology and may thus be either inductive or deductive (Gale et al., 2013). In this case, Jani et al. (2018) used an inductive approach, which organised the data into four themes related to the participants' experience of the brief MBSR programme. Participants generally found that the intervention provided a positive experience and that the group format was useful. They appeared to have the perception that MBSR is partly about relaxation but also about controlling emotions, and the two-hour sessions were viewed as too long.

Further types of feedback and contextual data have been gathered through qualitative methods. Ruskin et al. (2017) reported that participants in their MBI for adolescents with chronic pain appreciated the variety of examples used to illustrate various aspects of mindfulness practice. Langdon et al. (2011) explored what factors might hinder continued mindfulness practice after completion of an MBCT. The theory that emerged in this grounded-theory study was that MBI participants undergo a *virtuous practice cycle* over the course of the mindfulness journey and that an important aspect of their practice is the integration of mindfulness into their lifestyle. Concrete obstacles to mindful activity have been described as emerging doubts of benefits or practical issues that get in the way of being able to practice. Time constraints for practice were also a theme that emerged in a mixed-methods study that explored the feasibility of MBSR for women with metastatic breast cancer (Eyles et al., 2015). Here, the researchers found difficulty in recruitment due to unspecified reasons, and a focus group revealed that patients' willingness to participate in the intervention may have been improved if mindfulness had been presented as an intervention to teach skills that can be used not only to address symptoms but also in ways to teach how mindfulness can be embedded into busy working schedules. Lastly, Wilde et al. (2018) explored wider organisational factors that might hinder or facilitate the implementation of mindfulness in secondary schools. Using a qualitative case study design, the researchers conducted focus groups with members of staff and found themes related to facilitators such as the need for sufficient resources or the presence of a staff member who champions the implementation of mindfulness teaching at their school.

Using qualitative research to explore novel applications of mindfulness

Some studies employed qualitative methods to explore the experiences of participants in interventions that extended the application of mindfulness techniques from the original MBSR format and content to a wider range of additional contexts, participant groups, or goals. At times, these explorations involved the use of mixed-methods approaches such as by Longshore and Sachs (2015) where semi-structured interviews were conducted in addition to collecting quantitative data about anxiety and mindfulness as outcome variables. The purpose of this study was to explore the effects of a newly developed mindfulness training programme for sports coaches, which focused on the coach's emotional stability. The role of the qualitative interviews was stated here to evaluate the mechanics of the programme and its impact on the coaches. However, even though the study mentioned a mixed-methods design in its title and abstract, there was no further explanation on the process of integration of these two methodologies, which seems to suggest that the approach may be more accurately described as multi-method (Morse, 2003) rather than mixed-method. Mistretta et al. (2017) used a similar multi-methods approach when collecting quantitative and qualitative data from participants in a sport-related mindfulness-based programme, namely the mindfulness sport performance enhancement (MSPE) training programme (Kaufman, Glass, & Arnkoff, 2009). The qualitative data were collected alongside the quantitative data using open-ended questions about the benefits that participants had observed through taking part in this programme. In addition to gathering richer and more holistic data to complete the quantitative outcome measures, Mistretta et al. (2017) also inquired about the expectations that participants had before commencing the programme, which were coded into categories that included *psychological benefits for sport* such as mental toughness or *psychological benefits outside of sport* such as reduced anxiety and improved sport performance.

MacDonald, Oprescu, and Kean (2018) collected qualitative data to add further contextual information to a randomised controlled trial study to enable conclusions about the efficacy of a mindfulness intervention in sports athletes exposed to long-term stress. While previous studies had demonstrated the effects of mindfulness practice in reducing cortisol levels, MacDonald and Minahan (2018) extended these findings to highly trained wheelchair basketball players during a period of competition and increased training load. Over a period of eight weeks, the researchers provided 50 minutes of mindfulness training five times per week to the experimental group, while the control group were placed on a waiting list. The results of the trial indicated that mindfulness training was effective in controlling stress, as measured by salivary cortisol. For eight of the participants in the study by MacDonald and Minahan (2018), qualitative feedback about the mindfulness intervention was available, which was analysed and reported by MacDonald et al. (2018). This feedback was provided in form of a written narrative in response to the question how the mindfulness training had impacted the participants. The researchers expressed a constructivist stance in their interpretation of the coded themes, which were analysed using a case study method that involves separate analyses prior to cross-case comparisons (Yin, 2013). The extracted themes highlighted several benefits of mindfulness training such as improved sleep and stress management, which was interpreted as indication that this type of mindfulness training may be efficacious for athletes during competition periods.

Other studies collected qualitative data to inform the extent to which standard MBIs are acceptable for new target populations, which can be considered fairly minor variations of a typical MBI structure and programme. For example, Chadwick, Kaur, Swelam, Ross, and Ellett (2011) documented the experiences of people with bipolar disorder when participating in an MBCT course in order to explore to what extent the programme may need to be adapted for this target group. Fitzpatrick et al. (2010) analysed diary data from MBCT participants with Parkinson's disease, Griffiths et al. (2009) explored the usefulness of MBCT as an intervention for cardiac rehabilitation patients, and Williams, McManus, Muse, and Williams (2011) conducted an IPA study to explore the experiences of individuals with severe health anxiety when participating in an MBCT course. When exploring the suitability of a six-week MBI for palliative care in a pilot qualitative study, Chadwick, Newell, and Skinner (2008) showed how people's understanding of mindfulness was aided by participation in group discussions. Some of the studies exploring the application of MBIs for new patient populations provided detailed information about their methods. For example, in their pilot grounded-theory study of mindfulness training for incarcerated adolescents with a substance use history, Himelstein, Saul, Garcia-Romeu, and Pinedo (2014) listed the semi-structured questions they had asked their participants. For their study on MBSR with people with insomnia, Hubbling, Reilly-Spong, Kreitzer, and Gross (2014) provided details on the procedures the researchers undertook to ensure that their focus groups were not biased, such as information on question prompts and body language of the focus group facilitators.

Obviously, the application of MBIs to novel contexts and piloting of any modifications that may be necessary includes the literature on cross-cultural adaptations. As cultural factors will be discussed in a subsequent chapter in the present book, only some notes will be presented here about a selection of the qualitative methods that have been used in this literature. The most straight-forward explorations of cultural adaptability of mindfulness programmes are examples where a manualised programme such as MBSR was tested for use in other countries. For example, Majumdar, Grossman, Dietz-Waschkowski, Kersig, and Walach (2002) expected to replicate the findings from North American studies with their sample of MBSR course participants in Germany. In addition to a range of quantitative outcomes measures, Majumdar et al. (2002) also conducted semi-structured interviews after completion of the eight-week programme and at three-month follow up. Data were analysed using content analysis and presented and discussed in terms of their congruence with some of the quantitative ratings by the participants about their improvements in psychological and physical symptoms. Cross-cultural investigations obviously do not need to take place in another country. In a randomised controlled trial involving a mixed-methods design, Neece, Chan, Klein, Roberts, and Fenning (2018) compared the efficacy of MBSR for Latino and non-Latino parents in the United States. The qualitative part of the study was focused on the experiences of Latino families with MBSR. Qualitative data were collected using a participant satisfaction survey that consisted of 11 open-ended questions. Among the themes extracted from these data was the recommendation to deliver the intervention in Spanish in order to improve its efficacy further. Similarly, Watson, Black, and Hunter (2016) recruited 12 African American participants to explore their views about potential barriers of uptake of a brief mindfulness workshop that they had participated in. In semi-structured focus groups, participants shared some of the reservations they had with the workshop due to some perceived incongruence with African American culture.

Lastly, in addition to new types of applications of MBIs, some qualitative studies explored aspects related to the wider implications and effects of MBI participation. For example, Keane (2014) conducted a mixed-methods study to explore the effect that personal mindfulness practice may have on psychotherapists' ability to engage with their clients in therapy. Out of the 40 psychotherapists who responded to a quantitative questionnaire with also open-ended questions, 34 had completed their training in either MBSR or MBCT. During the second phase of the study, Keane (2014) conducted face-to-face interviews with 12 of the participants. The subsequent thematic analysis of the data suggested that personal mindfulness practice is linked to key therapist abilities such as attention and empathy, which has a positive effect on therapist–client interactions. Similar findings were reported in another mixed-methods study of the effects of MBCT on therapy-relevant characteristics of trainee psychologists (Hopkins & Proeve, 2013), as well as a study using semi-structured interviews with nine midwives analysed using IPA that indicated that mindfulness training is beneficial for midwives in dealing with stress and improving patient care (Hunter, Snow, & Warriner, 2018).

Summary and conclusions

In the mindfulness literature, discussion of ontology and epistemology has typically been conducted as theoretical discussion about the concept of mindfulness or when reflecting on MBIs as a general therapeutic approach. In studies that explored specific topics of MBIs such as effectiveness, delivery, or participant experiences, researchers have usually been silent on the particular philosophical assumptions used. This finding generalises only to some extent to qualitative mindfulness research, and one occasionally encounters statements by researchers about the philosophical perspective that informed their work.

As outlined in this chapter, a variety of qualitative methods have been utilised to explore diverse research questions related to MBIs. The aims of such research have also become more wide-ranging, and qualitative methods have thus been used to gain a more detailed understanding of the effects of MBIs as well as their hypothesised mechanisms of action. Often informed by parallel quantitative analyses such as in mixed- or multi-method studies, qualitative data have also been collected to explore barriers to practising mindfulness, which can directly inform further intervention design features to increase participants' engagement and to reduce drop-out rates. In this regard, qualitative research has also been very informative to outline the types of attitudes and preconceptions that participants might bring into an MBI, which may also play a role in the therapeutic journey of the MBI participants. Lastly, various qualitative methods have been used to explore to what extent MBIs may be modified to expand their original context of application to novel content, aims, and target populations.

Even when researcher biases are acknowledged in the method sections of articles, it is unclear to what extent the reported results and researchers' interpretation of their data need to be qualified or viewed as tentative. Interpretive analyses may be vulnerable to confirmation biases from researchers' preconceptions about mindfulness and mindfulness practice. For example, Dellbridge and Lubbe (2009) interpreted and organised their data according to their understanding of mindfulness gained from a prior review of the literature. The ability of mixed-methods research to triangulate findings therefore presents a substantial methodological advantage (Johnson et al., 2007).

As with the field of psychology in general, the complementary relationship between quantitative and qualitative research continues to be negotiated in conceptual discussions. In such debates, the subtle characteristics of the various research paradigms can often be overlooked (Michell, 2003), resulting in simplified and stereotypic ways in which philosophical approaches are being portrayed. Because of the general lack of clear positioning of quantitative research studies in regard to their ontological and epistemological assumptions, the diversity of philosophical frameworks underlying some of the quantitative research (e.g. Fletcher, 1996; Hayes et al., 2012) may be easily overlooked. It is also important to understand the rhetorical aspects in such methodological debates (Firestone, 1987), and from that point of view discussions about ontological assumptions may be understood as indirectly couched methodological prescriptions (Krägeloh, 2006).

References

Abba, N., Chadwick, P., & Stevenson, C. (2008). Responding mindfully to distressing psychosis: a grounded theory analysis. *Psychotherapy Research*, 18(1), 77–87. doi:10.1080/10503300701367992

Allen, M., Bromley, A., Kuyken, W., & Sonnenberg, S. J. (2009). Participants' experiences of mindfulness-based cognitive therapy: "It changed me in just about every way possible". *Behavioural and Cognitive Psychotherapy*, 37(4), 413–430. doi:10.1017/S135246580999004X

Arthington, P. (2016). Mindfulness: a critical perspective. *Community Psychology in Global Perspective*, 2(1), 87–104. doi:10.1285/i24212113v2i1p87

Baumann, M. (1997). Culture contact and valuation: early German Buddhists and the creation of a 'Buddhism in protestant shape'. *Numen*, 44(3), 270–295. doi:10.1163/1568527971655904

Bearance, D., & Holmes, K. (2015). Ontology through a mindfulness process. *Interchange*, 46(2), 143–152. doi:10.1007/s10780-015-9238-6

Bernay, R., Graham, E., Devcich, D. A., Rix, G., & Rubie-Davies, C. M. (2016). Pause, breathe, smile: a mixed-methods study of student well-being following participation in an eight-week, locally developed mindfulness program in three New Zealand schools. *Advances in School Mental Health Promotion*, 9(2), 90–106. doi:10.1080/1754730X.2016.1154474

Beshara, R. K. (2017). Cutting through false dualism: transformative social change as a transmodern moral framework for critical psychological research. *International Journal of Qualitative Methods*, 16(1), 1–10. doi:10.1177/1609406917705956

Birtwell, K., Dubrow-Marshall, L., Dubrow-Marshall, R., Duerden, T., & Dunn, A. (2017). A mixed methods evaluation of a Mindfulness-Based Stress Reduction course for people with Parkinson's disease. *Complementary Therapies in Clinical Practice*, 29, 220–228. doi:10.1016/j.ctcp.2017.10doi:009

Bitbol, M., & Petitmengin, C. (2013). A defense of introspection from within. *Constructivist Foundations*, 8(3), 269–279.

Braun, V., & Clarke, V. (2006). Using thematic analysis in psychology. *Qualitative Research in Psychology*, 3(2), 77–101. doi:10.1191/1478088706qp063oa

Brinkmann, S. (2017). Humanism after posthumanism: or qualitative psychology after the "posts". *Qualitative Research in Psychology*, 14(2), 109–130. doi:10.1080/14780887.2017.1282568

Carrera-Fernández, M. J., Guàrdia-Olmos, J., & Peró-Cebollero, M. (2014). Qualitative methods of data analysis in psychology: an analysis of the literature. *Qualitative Research*, 14 (1), 20–36. doi:10.1177/1468794112465633

Chadwick, P., Newell, T., & Skinner, C. (2008). Mindfulness groups in palliative care: a pilot qualitative study. *Spirituality and Health International*, 9(3), 135–144. doi:10.1002/shi.341

Chadwick, P., Kaur, H., Swelam, M., Ross, S., & Ellett, L. (2011). Experience of mindfulness in people with bipolar disorder: a qualitative study. *Psychotherapy Research*, 21(3), 277–285. doi:10.1080/10503307.2011.565487

Chai, D. (2014). Meontological generativity: a Daoist reading of the thing. *Philosophy East and West*, 64(2), 303–318. doi:10.1353/pew.2014.0033

Chambers, S. K., Foley, E., Galt, E., Ferguson, M., & Clutton, S. (2012). Mindfulness groups for men with advanced prostate cancer: a pilot study to assess feasibility and effectiveness and the role of peer support. *Supportive Care in Cancer*, 20(6), 1183–1192. doi:10.1007/s00520-011-1195-8

Chiesa, A., & Malinowski, P. (2011). Mindfulness-based approaches: Are they all the same?. *Journal of Clinical Psychology*, 67(4), 404–424. doi:10.1002/jclp.20776

Corbin, J., & Strauss, A. (1990). Grounded theory research: procedures, canons, and evaluative criteria. *Qualitative Sociology*, 13(1), 3–21. doi:10.1007/BF00988593

Crane, R. S. (2017). Implementing mindfulness in the mainstream: making the path by walking it. *Mindfulness*, 8(3), 585–594. doi:10.1007/s12671-016-0632-7

Crowder, R. (2016). Mindfulness based feminist therapy: the intermingling edges of self-compassion and social justice. *Journal of Religion & Spirituality in Social Work: Social Thought*, 35(1–2), 24–40. doi:10.1080/15426432.2015.1080605

Dellbridge, C.-A., & Lubbe, C. (2009). An adolescent's subjective experiences of mindfulness. *Journal of Child & Adolescent Mental Health*, 21(2), 167–180. doi:10.2989/JCAMH.2009.doi:21.2.8.1016

Dennick, L., Fox, A. P., Walter-Brice, A. (2013). Mindfulness groups for people experiencing distressing psychosis: an interpretative phenomenological analysis. *Mental Health Review Journal*, 18(1), 32–43. doi:10.1108/13619321311310096

Depraz, N., Varela, F. J., & Vermersch, P. (Eds.). (2003). *On becoming aware: a pragmatics of experiencing*. Amsterdam, Netherlands: John Benjamins Publishing Company.

Desbordes, G., Gard, T., Hoge, E. A., Hölzel, B. K., Kerr, C., Lazar, S. W., …, & Vago, D. R. (2015). Moving beyond mindfulness: defining equanimity as an outcome measure in meditation and contemplative research. *Mindfulness*, 6(2), 356–372. doi:10.1007/s12671-013-0269-8

Didonna, F. (2009). Mindfulness-based interventions in an inpatient setting. In F. Didonna (Ed.), *Clinical handbook of mindfulness* (pp. 447–463). New York, USA: Springer Science +Business Media.

Dobkin, P. L. (2008). Mindfulness-based stress reduction: What processes are at work?. *Complementary Therapies in Clinical Practice*, 14(1), 8–16. doi:10.1016/j.ctcp.2007.09.doi:004

Dobkin, P. L., Irving, J. A., & Amar, S. (2012). For whom may participation in a mindfulness-based stress reduction program be contraindicated?. *Mindfulness*, 3(1), 44–50. doi:10.1007/s12671-011-0079-9

Eyles, C., Leydon, G. M., Hoffman, C. J., Copson, E. R., Prescott, P., Chorozoglou, M., & Lewith, G. (2015). Mindfulness for the self-management of fatigue, anxiety, and depression in women with metastatic breast cancer: a mixed methods feasibility study. *Integrative Cancer Therapies*, 14(1), 42–56. doi:10.1177/1534735414546567

Firestone, W. A. (1987). Meaning in method: the rhetoric of quantitative and qualitative research. *Educational Researcher*, 16(7), 16–21. doi:10.3102/0013189X016007016

Fitzpatrick, L., Simpson, J., & Smith, A. (2010). A qualitative analysis of mindfulness-based cognitive therapy (MBCT) in Parkinson's disease. *Psychology and Psychotherapy: Theory, Research and Practice*, 83(2), 179–192. doi:10.1348/147608309X471514

Fletcher, G. J. O. (1996). Realism versus relativism in psychology. *American Journal of Psychology*, 109(3), 409–429. doi:10.2307/1423014

Fletcher, L. B., Schoendorff, B., & Hayes, S. C. (2010). Searching for mindfulness in the brain: a process-oriented approach to examining the neural correlates of mindfulness. *Mindfulness*, 1(1), 41–63. doi:10.1007/s12671-010-0006-5

Fossey, E., Harvey, C., McDermott, F., & Davidson, L. (2002). Understanding and evaluating qualitative research. *Australian and New Zealand Journal of Psychiatry*, 36(6), 717–732. doi:10.1046/j.1440-1614.2002.01100.x

Fox, K. C. R., Zakarauskas, P., Dixon, M., Ellamil, M., Thompson, E., & Christoff, K. (2016). Meditation experience predicts introspective accuracy. *PLoS ONE*, 7(9): e45370. doi:10.1371/journal.pone.0045370

Froese, T. (2011). From second-order cybernetics to enactive cognitive science: Varela's turn from epistemology to phenomenology. *System Research and Behavioral Science*, 28(6), 631–645. doi:10.1002/sres.1116

Gale, N. K., Heath, G., Cameron, E., Rashid, S., & Redwood, S. (2013). Using the framework method for the analysis of qualitative data in multi-disciplinary health research. *BMC Medical Research Methodology*, 13, 117. doi:10.1186/1471-2288-13-117

Giddings, L. S., & Grant, B. M. (2007). A Trojan horse for positivism? A critique of mixed methods research. *Advances in Nursing Science*, 30(1), 52–60. doi:10.1177/1478210316637972

Gill, M., Waltz, J., Suhrbier, P., & Robert, L. (2015). Non-duality and the integration of mindfulness into psychotherapy: qualitative research with meditating therapists. *Mindfulness*, 6(4), 708–722. doi:10.1007/s12671-014-0310-6

Godart, G. C. (2008). "Philosophy" or "religion"? The confrontation with foreign categories in late nineteenth century Japan. *Journal of the History of Ideas*, 69(1), 71–91.

Griffiths, K., Camic, P. M., & Hutton, J. M. (2009). Participants experiences of a Mindfulness-based Cognitive Therapy group for cardiac rehabilitation. *Journal of Health Psychology*, 14(5), 675–681. doi:10.1177/1359105309104911

Guba, E. G., & Lincoln, Y. S. (1994). Competing paradigms in qualitative research. In N. K. Denzin, & Y. S. Lincoln (Eds.), *Handbook of qualitative research* (pp. 105–117). London, United Kingdom: Sage Publications.

HahmC. (2001). Postmodernism in the post-cultural context: epistemological and political considerations. *Human Studies*, 24(1–2), 29–44. doi:10.1023/A:1010721805587

Hammersley, M. (2018). What is ethnography? Can it survive? Should it?. *Ethnography and Education*, 13(1), 1–17. doi:10.1080/17457823.2017.1298458

Harel, O., Hadash, Y., Levi-Belz, Y., & Bernstein, A. (2018). Does early emotional responding to initial mindfulness training impact intervention outcomes?. *Mindfulness*. Online First. doi:10.1007/s12671-018-1018-9

Hayes, S. C., Strosahl, K. D., & Wilson, K. G. (2011). *Acceptance and Commitment Therapy: the process and practice of mindful change*. New York, USA: Guilford Press.

Hayes, S. C., Barnes-Holmes, D., & Wilson, K. G. (2012). Contextual Behavioral Science: creating a science more adequate to the challenge of the human condition. *Journal of Contextual Behavioral Science*, 1(1–2), 1–16. doi:10.1016/j.jcbs.2012.09.0doi:04

Heidegger, M. (1997). Besinnung. In F.-W. von Herrmann (Ed.), *Martin Heidegger Gesamtausgabe 66*. Frankfurt am Main, Germany: Vittorio Klostermann. (Original work published 1938)

Himelstein, S., Saul, S., Garcia-Romeu, A., & Pinedo, D. (2014). Mindfulness training as an intervention for substance user incarcerated adolescents: a pilot grounded theory study. *Substance Use & Misuse*, 49(5), 560–570. doi:10.3109/10826084.2013.852580

Hoffman, C. J., Ersser, S. J., & Hopkinson, J. B. (2012). Mindfulness-based stress reduction in breast cancer: a qualitative study. *Complementary Therapies in Clinical Practice*, 18(4), 221–226. doi:10.1016/j.ctcp.2012.06doi:008

Hopkins, A., & Proeve, M. (2013). Teaching mindfulness-based cognitive therapy to trainee psychologists: qualitative and quantitative effects. *Counselling Psychology Quarterly*, 26(2), 115–130. doi:10.1080/09515070.2013.792998

Hubbling, A., Reilly-Spong, M., Kreitzer, M. J., & Gross, C. R. (2014). How mindfulness changed my sleep: focus groups with chronic insomnia patients. *BMC Complementary and Alternative Medicine*, 14, 50. doi:10.1186/1472-6882-14-50

Hugh-Jones, S., Rose, S., Koutsopoulou, G. Z., & Simms-Ellis, R. (2018). How is stress reduced by a workplace mindfulness intervention? A qualitative study conceptualising experiences of change. *Mindfulness*, 9(2), 474–487. doi:10.1007/s12671-017-0790-2

Hunter, L., Snow, S., & Warriner, S. (2018). Being there and reconnecting: midwives' perceptions of the impact of mindfulness training on their practice. *Journal of Clinical Nursing*, 27(5–6), 1227–1238. doi:10.1111/jocn.14169

Huxter, M. (2012). Buddhist mindfulness practices in contemporary psychology: a paradox of incompatibility and harmony. *Psychotherapy in Australia*, 18(2), 26–31.

Huynh, T., Hatton-Bowers, H., & Smith, M. H. (2018). A critical methodological review of mixed methods designs used in mindfulness research. *Mindfulness*. Online First. doi:10.1007/s12671-018-1038-5

Irving, J. A., Park-Saltzman, J., Fitzpatrick, M., Dobkin, P. L., Chen, A., & Hutchinson, T. (2014). Experiences of health care professional enrolled in mindfulness-based medical practice: a grounded theory model. *Mindfulness*, 5(1), 60–71. doi:10.1007/s12671-012-0147-9

Jani, B. D., Simpson, R., Lawrence, M., Simpson, S., & Mercer, S. W. (2018). Acceptability of mindfulness from the perspective of stroke survivors and caregivers: a qualitative study. *Pilot and Feasibility Studies*, 4, 57. doi:10.1186/s40814-018-0244-1

Jennings, P. A., Frank, J. L., Snowberg, K. E., Coccia, M. A., & Greenberg, M. T. (2013). Improving classroom learning environ- ments by cultivating awareness and resilience in education (CARE): results of a randomized controlled trial. *School Psychology Quarterly*, 28 (4), 374–390. doi:10.1037/spq0000035

Johnson, R. B., Onwuegbuzie, A. J., & Turner, L. A. (2007). Toward a definition of mixed methods research. *Journal of Mixed Methods Research*, 1(2), 112–133.

Kabat-Zinn, J. (1990). *Full catastrophe living: using the wisdom of your body and mind to face stress, pain, and illness*. New York, USA: Delacourt.

Kaufman, K. A., Glass, C. R., & Arnkoff, D. B. (2009). Evaluation of Mindful Sport Performance Enhancement (MSPE): a new approach to promote flow in athletes. *Journal of Clinical Sport Psychology*, 3(4), 334–356. doi:10.1123/jcsp.3.doi:4.334

Keane, A. (2014). The influence of therapist mindfulness practice on psychotherapeutic work: a mixed-methods study. *Mindfulness*, 5(6), 689–703. doi:10.1007/s12671-013-0223-9

Kerr, M., & Key, D. (2011). The Ouroboros (Part 1): towards an ontology of connectedness in ecopsychology research. *European Journal of Ecopsychology*, 2, 48–60.

Kerrigan, D., Johnson, K., Stewart, M., Magyari, T., Hutton, N., Ellen, J. M., & Sibinga, E. M. S. (2011). Perceptions, experiences, and shifts in perspective occurring among urban youth participating in a mindfulness-based stress reduction program. *Complementary Therapies in Clinical Practice*, 17(x), 96–101. doi:10.1016/j.ctcp.2010.0doi:8.003

Khoury, B., Lecomte, T., Fortin, G., Masse, M., Therien, P., Bouchard, V., ..., & Hofmann, S. G. (2013). Mindfulness-based therapy: a comprehensive meta-analysis. *Clinical Psychology Review*, 33(6), 763–771. doi:10.1016/j.cpr.2013doi:05.005

Kidd, S. A. (2002). The role of qualitative research in psychology journals. *Psychological Methods*, 7(1), 126–138. doi:10.1037/1082-989X.7.1.doi:126

Krägeloh, C. U. (2006). Pragmatism and a-ontologicalism in a science of behavior. *The Behavior Analyst Today*, 7(3), 325–334.

Krägeloh, C. U. (2016). Importance of morality in mindfulness practice. *Counseling and Values*, 61(1), 97–110. doi:10.1002/cvj.12028

Krägeloh, C. U. (2018). Phenomenological research fails to capture the experience of nondual awareness. *Mindfulness*. Online First. doi:10.1007/s12671-018-0879-7

Kuijpers, H. J., van der Heijden, F. M., Tuinier, S., & Verhoeven, W. M. (2007). Meditation-induced psychosis. *Psychopathology*, 40(6), 461–464. doi:10.1159/000108125

Langdon, S., Jones, F. W., Hutton, J., & Holttum, S. (2011). A grounded-theory study of mindfulness practice following Mindfulness-Based Cognitive Therapy. *Mindfulness*, 2(4), 270–281. doi:10.1007/s12671-011-0070-5

Laurie, J., & Blandford, A. (2016). Making time for mindfulness. *International Journal of Medical Informatics*, 96, 38–50. doi:10.1016/j.ijmedinf.2016.02.0doi:10

Long, D. M. (2013). Pragmatism, realism, and psychology: understanding theory selection criteria. *Journal of Contextual Behavioral Science*, 2(3–4), 61–67. doi:10.1016/j.jcbs.2013. 09. 003

Longshore, K., & Sachs, M. (2015). Mindfulness training for coaches: a mixed-method exploratory study. *Journal of Clinical Sport Psychology*, 9(2), 116–137. doi:10.1123/jcsp.2014-0038

Lustyk, M. K., Chawla, N., Nolan, R. S., & Marlatt, G. A. (2009). Mindfulness meditation research: issues of participant screening, safety procedures, and researcher training. *Advances*, 24(1), 20–30.

MacDonald, L. A., & Minahan, C. L. (2018). Mindfulness training attenuates the increase in salivary cortisol concentration associated with competition in highly training wheelchair-basketball players. *Journal of Sports Science*, 36(4), 378–383. doi:10.1080/02640414.2017.1308001

MacDonald, L. A., Oprescu, F., & Kean, B. M. (2018). An evaluation of the effects of mindfulness training from the perspectives of wheelchair basketball players. *Psychology of Sport & Exercise*. Online First. doi:10.1016/j.psychsport.2017.doi:11.013

Mackenzie, M. J., Carlson, L. E., Munoz, M., & Speca, M. (2007). A qualitative study of self-perceived effects of Mindfulness-based Stress Reduction (MBSR) in a psychosocial oncology setting. *Stress and Health*, 23(1), 59–69. doi:10.1002/smi.1120

Majumdar, M., Grossman, P., Dietz-Waschkowski, B., Kersig, S., & Walach, H. (2002). Does mindfulness meditation contribute to health? Outcome evaluation of a German sample. *Journal of Alternative and Complementary Medicine*, 8(6), 719–730. doi:10.1089/10755530260511720

Malpass, A., Carel, H., Ridd, M., Shaw, A., Kessler, D., Sharp, D., ..., & Wallond, J. (2012). Transforming the perceptual situation: a meta-ethnography of qualitative work reporting patients' experiences of mindfulness-based approaches. *Mindfulness*, 3(1), 60–75. doi:10.1007/s12671-011-0081-2

Marx, R., Strauss, C., & Williamson, C. (2015). Mindfulness apprenticeship: a new model of NHS-based MBCT teacher training. *Mindfulness*, 6(2), 253–263. doi:10.1007/s12671-013-0254-2

Mason, O., & Hargreaves, I. (2001). A qualitative study of mindfulness-based cognitive therapy for depression. *British Journal of Medical Psychology*, 74(2), 197–212. doi:10.1348/000711201160911

McWilliams, S. A. (2010). Inherent self, invented self, empty self: constructivism, Buddhism, and psychotherapy. *Counseling and Values*, 55(1), 79–100. doi:10.1002/j.2161-007X.2010.tb00023.x

McWilliams, S. A. (2014). Foundations of mindfulness and contemplation: traditional and contemporary perspectives. *International Journal of Mental Health and Addiction*, 12(2), 116–128. doi:10.1007/s11469-014-9486-1

Michell, J. (2003). The quantitative imperative: positivism, naïve realism and the place of qualitative methods in psychology. *Theory & Psychology*, 13(1), 5–31. doi:10.1177/0959354303013001758

Mills, P. J., Peterson, C. T., Pung, M. A., Patel, S., Weiss, L., Wilson, K. L., …, & Chopra, D. (2018). Change in sense of nondual awareness and spiritual awakening in response to a multidimensional well-being program. *Journal of Alternative and Complementary Medicine*, 24(4), 343–351. doi:10.1089/acm.2017.0160

Mitchell, M., & Heads, G. (2015). Staying well: a follow up of a 5-week mindfulness based stress reduction programme for a range of psychological issues. *Community Mental Health Journal*, 51(8), 897–902. doi:10.1080/s10597-014-9825-5

Morone, N. E., Greco, C. M., & Weiner, D. K. (2008a). Mindfulness meditation for the treatment of chronic low back pain in older adults: a randomized controlled pilot study. *Pain*, 134(3), 310–319. doi:10.1016/jpain.2007. 04. 03doi:8

Morone, N. E., Lynch, C. S., Greco, C. M., Tindle, H. A., & Weiner, D. K. (2008b). "I felt like a new person." The effects of mindfulness meditation on older adults with chronic pain: qualitative narrative analysis of diary entries. *Journal of Pain*, 9(9), 841–848. doi:10.1016/j.jpain.2008.04doi:003

Morse, J. M. (2003). Principles of mixed methods and multimethod research designs. In A. Tashakkori, & C. Teddlie (Eds.), *Handbook of mixed methods in social and behavioral research* (pp. 189–208). Thousand Oakes, CA: Sage Publications.

Mistretta, E. G., Glass, C. R., Spears, C. A., Perskaudas, R., Kaufman, K. A., & Hoyer, D. (2017). Collegiate athletes' expectations and experiences with mindful sport performance enhancement. *Journal of Clinical Sport Psychology*, 11(3), 201–221. doi:10.1123/jcsp.2016-0043

Modestino, E. J. (2016). Neurophenomenology of an altered state of consciousness: an fMRI case study. *Explore*, 12(2), 128–135. doi:10.1016/j.explore.2015.doi:12.004

Morgan, P., Simpson, J., & Smith, A. (2015). Health care workers' experiences of mindfulness training: a qualitative review. *Mindfulness*, 6(4), 744–758. doi:10.1007/s12671-014-0313-3

Murray, G. (2015). Do I have a self? (and other useful questions from Buddhist mindfulness). *Australian and New Zealand Journal of Psychiatry*, 49(7), 593–594. doi:10.1177/0004867415590460

Neece, C. L., Chan, N., Klein, K., Roberts, L., & Fenning, R. M. (2018). Mindfulness-Based Stress Reduction for parents of children with developmental delays: understanding the experiences of Latino families. *Mindfulness*. Online First. doi:10.1007/s12671-018-1011-3

Nilsson, H. (2013). How mindfulness becomes mindlessness – a hermeneutical approach. *Asian Journal of Humanities and Social Studies*, 1(4), 187–196.

Payne, R. K. (2016). Mindfulness and the moral imperative for the self to improve the self. In R. E. Purser, D. Forbes, & A. Burke (Eds.), *Handbook of mindfulness – culture, context, and social engagement* (pp. 121–134). Cham, Switzerland: Springer International Publishing. doi:10.1007/978-3-319-44019-4_9

Ponterotto, J. G. (2005). Qualitative research in counselling psychology: a primer on research paradigms and philosophy of science. *Journal of Counseling Psychology*, 52(2), 126–136. doi:10.1037/0022-0167.doi:52.2.126

Proulx, K. (2008). Experiences of women with bulimia nervosa in a mindfulness-based eating disorder treatment group. *Eating Disorders*, 16(1), 52–72. doi:10.1080/10640260701773496

Reveley, J. (2016). Neoliberal meditations: how mindfulness training medicalizes education and responsibilizes young people. *Policy Futures in Education*, 14(4), 497–511. doi:10.1177/1478210316637972

Ridderinkhof, A., de Bruin, E., Blom, R., & Bögels, S. M. (2018). Mindfulness-based program for children with autism spectrum disorder and their parents: direct and long-term improvements. *Mindfulness*, 9(3), 773–791. doi:10.1007/s12671-017-0815-x

Ruskin, D., Harris, L., Stinson, J., Kohut, S. A., Walker, K., & McCarthy, E. (2017). "I learned to let go of my pain". The effects of mindfulness meditation on adolescents with chronic pain: an analysis of participants' treatment experience. *Children*, 4, 110. doi:10.3390/children4120110

Schultz, L. (2012). Nishida Kitarō, G.W.F. Hegel, and the pursuit of the concrete: a dialectic of dialectics. *Philosophy East and West*, 62(3), 319–338. doi:10.1353/pew.2012.0051

Schussler, D. L., Jennings, P. A., Sharp, J. E., & Frank, J. L. (2016). Improving teacher awareness and well-being through CARE: a qualitative analysis of the underlying mechanism. *Mindfulness*, 7(1), 130–142. doi:10.1007/s12671-015-0422-7

Segal, Z. V., Williams, J. M. G., & Teasdale, J. D. (2013). *Mindfulness-based cognitive therapy for depression: a new approach to preventing relapse* (2nd ed.). New York, USA: The Guilford Press.

Shapiro, S. L., Carlson, L. E., Astin, J. A., & Freedman, B. (2006). Mechanisms of mindfulness. *Journal of Clinical Psychology*, 62(3), 373–386. doi:10.1002/jclp.20237

Sharf, R. H. (1995). Whose Zen? Zen nationalism revisited. In J. W. Heisig, & J. Maraldo (Eds.), *Rude awakenings: Zen, the Kyoto School, and the question of nationalism* (pp. 40–51). Honolulu, USA: University of Hawai'i Press.

Sharf, R. H. (2000). The rhetoric of experience and the study of religion. *Journal of Consciousness Studies*, 7, 267–287.

Sharf, R. H. (2014). Is nirvāṇa the same as insentience? Chinese struggles with an Indian Buddhist ideal. In J. Kieschnick, & M. Shahar (Eds.), *India in the Chinese imagination – myth, religion, and thought* (pp. 141–170). Philadelphia, USA: University of Pennsylvania Press.

Sharf, R. H. (2015). Is mindfulness Buddhist? (and why it matters). *Transcultural Psychiatry*, 52 (4), 470–484. doi:10.1177/1363461514557561

Shobbrook-Fisher, Z. (2016). Passionate about presence – a reflection on the experience of being a person-centered therapist who teaches mainstream mindfulness. *Person-Centered & Experiential Psychotherapies*, 15(3), 200–212. doi:10.1080/14779757.2016.1196720

Smith, J. A., Flowers, P., & Larkin, M. (2009). *Interpretative phenomenological analysis: theory, method and research*. London, UK: Sage.

Solhaug, I., Eriksen, T. E., de Vibe, M., Haavind, H., Friborg, O., Sørlie, T., & Rosenvinge, J. H. (2018). Medical and psychology student's experiences in learning mindfulness: benefits, paradoxes, and pitfalls. *Mindfulness*. Online First. doi:10.1007/s12671-016-0521-0

Stanley, S. (2012). From discourse to awareness: rhetoric, mindfulness, and a psychology without foundation. *Theory & Psychology*, 23(1), 60–80. doi:10.1177/0959354312463261

Stanley, S., Barker, M., Edwards, V., & McEwen, E. (2015). Swimming against the stream?: mindfulness as a psychosocial research methodology. *Qualitative Research in Psychology*, 12 (1), 61–76. doi:10.1080/14780887.2014.958394

Stelter, R. (2009). Experiencing mindfulness meditation – a client narrative perspective. *International Journal of Qualitative Studies on Health and Well-being*, 4(3), 145–158. doi:10.1080/17482620903013908

Strauss, A., & Corbin, J. (1990). *Basics of qualitative research: grounded theory procedures and techniques*. Newbury Park, USA: Sage.

Tate, K. J., Newbury-Birch, D., & McGeechan, G. J. (2018). A systematic review of qualitative evidence of cancer patients' attitudes to mindfulness. *European Journal of Cancer Care*, 27(2): e12783. doi:10.1111/ecc.12783

Tierney, W. G. (1998). Life history's history: subjects unfold. *Qualitative Inquiry*, 4(1), 49 70. doi:10.1177/107780049800400104

Uehara, M. (2009). Japanese aspects of Nishida's basho – seeing the "form without form". In W. Lam, & C. Cheung (Eds.), *Frontiers of Japanese Philosophy 4: facing the 21st century* (pp. 152–164). Nagoya, Japan: Nanzan Institute for Religion & Culture.

Varela, F. J. (1999). The specious present: a neurophenomenology of time consciousness. In J. Petitot, F. J. Varela, B. Pachoud, & J.-M. Roy (Eds.), *Naturalizing phenomenology: issues in contemporary phenomenology and cognitive science* (pp. 266–329). Stanford: Stanford University Press.

Virtbauer, G. (2016). Presencing process: embodiment and healing in the Buddhist practice of mindfulness of breathing. *Mental Health, Religion & Culture*, 19(1), 68–81. doi:10.1080/13674676.2015.1115474

Vogt, W. P. (2014). *Selecting the right analysis for your data: quantitative, qualitative, and mixed methods*. New York, USA: Guildford Press.

Walach, H., & Römer, H. (2011). Generalized entanglement – a nonreductive option for a phenomenologically dualist and ontologically monist view of consciousness. In H. Walach, S. Schmidt, & W. B. Jonas (Eds.), *Neuroscience, consciousness and spirituality* (pp. 81–95). New York, USA: Springer.

Walach, H. (2014). Towards an epistemology of inner experience. In S. Schmidt, & H. Walach (Eds.), *Meditation – neuroscientific approaches and philosophical implication* (pp. 7–22). Cham, Switzerland: Springer International Publishing. doi:10.1007/978-3-319-01634-4_2

Watson, N. N., Black, A. R., & Hunter, C. D. (2016). African American women's perceptions of mindfulness meditation training and gendered race-related stress. *Mindfulness*, 7(5), 1034–1043. doi:10.1007/s12671-016-0539-3

Wilde, S., Sonley, A., Crane, C., Ford, T., Raja, A., Robson, J., ..., & Kuyken, W. (2018). Mindfulness training in UK secondary schools: a multiple case study approach to identification of cornerstones of implementation. *Mindfulness*. Online First. doi:10.1007/s12671-018-0982-4

Williams, M. J., McManus, F., Muse, K., & Williams, J. M. G. (2011). Mindfulness-based cognitive therapy for severe health anxiety (hypochondriasis): an interpretative phenomenological analysis of patients' experiences. *British Journal of Clinical Psychology*, 50(4), 379–397. doi:10.1111/j.2044-8260.2010.02000.x

Wong, S. Y. S., Chan, J. Y. C., Zhang, D., Lee, E. K. P., & Tsoi, K. K. F. (2018). The safety of mindfulness-based interventions: a systematic review of randomized controlled trials. *Mindfulness*, 9(5), 1344–1357. doi:10.1007/s12671-018-0897-0

Wongtongkam, N., Ward, P. R., Day, A., & Winefield, A. H. (2014). A trial of mindfulness meditation to reduce anger and violence in Thai youth. *International Journal of Mental Health and Addiction*, 12(2), 169–180. doi:10.1007/s11469-013-9463-0

Woodgate, R. L., Tennent, P., & Zurba, M. (2017). Navigating ethical challenges in qualitative research with children and youth through sustaining mindful presence. *International Journal of Qualitative Methods*, 16(1), 1–16. doi:10.1177/1609406917696743

Wyatt, C., Harper, B., & Weatherhead, S. (2014). The experience of group mindfulness-based interventions for individuals with mental health difficulties: a meta-analysis. *Psychotherapy Research*, 24(2), 214–228. doi:10.1080/10503307.2013.864788

Yin, R. K. (2013). *Case study research: design and methods*. Thousand Oaks, CA: Sage Publications.

Zajonc, A. (2009). *Meditation as contemplative inquiry*. Great Barrington, USA: Lindisfarne Books.

3

MEASURING MINDFULNESS

When the first reports from the effects of mindfulness-based interventions (MBIs) were published in the 1980s, mindfulness questionnaires were not available, and pre-test post-test scores were thus only presented for the various outcome measures of interest. With continued growth of, and interest in, mindfulness research, questionnaires were gradually developed to assess various aspects of the multi-faceted mindfulness construct. While behavioural measures have also been proposed and used, self-report questionnaires remain by far the most widely used tools to assess mindfulness (Sauer et al., 2013).

Mindfulness is typically assessed for a variety of reasons and to serve a variety of purposes. This includes research that aims to investigate the mechanism of action of MBIs through some kind of mediation analysis. Nyklíček and Kuijpers (2008), for instance, measured mindfulness to investigate whether changes in mindfulness skills are indeed mediating the effects of Mindfulness-Based Stress Reduction (MBSR) on psychological well-being and quality of life, and the results indicated that there was partial mediation. Also using a sample of MBSR participants, Carmody and Baer (2008) demonstrated that increases in mindfulness skills mediated the positive relationship between formal meditation practice time with psychological well-being and stress. Josefsson, Larsman, Broberg, and Lundh (2011) extended the investigation of the mediating role of meditation practice to a cross-sectional study with individuals in the community. For participants recruited through Buddhist centres as well as a sample of nonmeditating university students, changes in various facets of mindfulness mediated the relationship between meditation practice and psychological well-being.

When modifying the format of MBIs, mindfulness measures are also typically collected to investigate to what extent the modified MBI continues to deliver an intervention with effects comparable to standard MBIs. Cavanagh et al. (2018) tested a brief online MBI and Krägeloh et al. (2018) tested a mindfulness intervention for nonclinical populations delivered via videoconferencing in a group setting. In both cases, mindfulness measures were collected to compare pre- and post-intervention levels. Krägeloh et al. (2018) compared the effect sizes of changes in mindfulness scores with those reported typically in MBI studies. In a study investigating the effectiveness of a blended online mindfulness programme, Montero-Marín et al. (2018) obtained a sufficiently large sample size to explicitly measure whether changes in awareness scores mediated the effects of their new format on positive affect.

Mindfulness measures also play an important role in experimental studies that explore the role of mindfulness in more research investigations about more fundamental psychological processes. In a study by Geisler, Bechtoldt, Oberländer, and Schacht-Jablonowsky (2018), participants completed an eight-minute mindfulness exercise to investigate the effects of brief mindfulness practice on performance on an achievement test. Here, the researchers distinguished between state mindfulness, which is externally moderated and situationally dependent to that of trait mindfulness, which is seen as intrinsically situated and stable over time. The study then explored to what extent the brief mindfulness exercise modified the participants' state of mindfulness, and whether these effects may have moderated the effect of the intervention.

In addition to experimental settings, mindfulness scales have become essential to investigate the relationship between mindfulness and various indicators of well-being, particularly when the focus is on more enduring aspects of mindfulness such as those related to a trait or skill. Practice of mindfulness may not necessarily be a proxy for mindfulness skills as shown in the study by van den Hurk et al. (2011) who tested the mediating role of mindfulness skills in the relationship between mindfulness meditation practice and personality. A common approach has been to test mediation models based on various hypothetical mechanisms of mindfulness, such as when using large convenience samples comprised of university students (Brown, Bravo, Roos, & Pearson, 2015; Coffey & Hartman, 2008). In other studies, mindfulness has a less central focus and has been explored as a predictor of psychological well-being alongside other psychological variables (Klainin-Yobas et al., 2016).

The present chapter presents the range of techniques available to assess mindfulness as well as the approaches that have been used to test their reliability and validity. Later developments are also outlined, such as the application of modern psychometric techniques to scrutinise item performance as well as work to distinguish between state and trait mindfulness and investigations into response shift. The chapter also contains a brief discussion on how measurement of mindfulness has the potential to guide further conceptual development of the construct.

The range of mindfulness inventories

One of the first widely used mindfulness instruments is the Freiburg Mindfulness Inventory (FMI; Buchheld, Grossman, & Walach, 2001), which was developed to assess mindfulness in participants of insight meditation courses. Very soon after, a range of other mindfulness scales were published, two of the most popular ones being the Mindful Attention Awareness Scale (MAAS; Brown & Ryan, 2003) and the Five Facet Mindfulness Questionnaire (FFMQ; Baer, Smith, Hopkins, Krietemeyer, & Toney, 2006). Since the publication of the widely cited articles by Sauer et al. (2013) and Park et al. (2013) that reviewed the mindfulness scales available at that time, many more instruments have been developed and tested. A detailed description of the scales and their specific purposes and advantages is beyond the scope of the present book, and the reader may instead refer to other sources (e.g. Medvedev, Krägeloh, Siegert, & Singh, in preparation).

Mindfulness inventories vary in terms of dimensionality, ranging from unidimensional scales such as the MAAS (Brown & Ryan, 2003) to eight-factor instruments such as the Comprehensive Inventory of Mindfulness Experiences (CHIME; Bergomi, Tschacher, & Kupper, 2014). Questionnaires with more than one subscale tend to have a higher total number of items than unidimensional scales. The eight-factor CHIME, for example, has 37 items, and the five-factor FFMQ has 39 items. Occasionally, more detailed subsequent testing of psychometric properties resulted in recommendations to discard a small number of items. For instance, due to misfits being identified using Rasch analysis, Medvedev, Siegert, Kersten, and Krägeloh (2017) reported that better performance of the FFMQ may be achieved when two items are discarded.

Scores from multidimensional scales are generally presented and interpreted separately by subscales. Although studies may occasionally report a total score from multidimensional scales on its own (Levinson, Stoll, Kindy, Merry, & Davidson, 2014) or in addition to subscale scores (e.g. Fisak & von Lehe, 2012), such use should ideally be informed by prior psychometric analyses, particularly when the subscales of the instrument are not highly correlated. Some psychometric work (Medvedev, Siegert, Kersten, & Krägeloh, 2016a) has explicitly tested whether the use of the total scores may be warranted, which was not the case for the Kentucky Inventory of Mindfulness Skills (KIMS; Baer, Smith, & Allen, 2004) but acceptable for the FFMQ as long as data are converted from ordinal- to interval-level as informed by Rasch analysis (Medvedev et al., 2017). As items and even subscales differ in their ability to predict the relevant latent trait (in this case mindfulness), such ordinal- to interval-level conversions are necessary to ensure that measurement precision is not compromised by the presence of items that are either very easy or very difficult to shift.

It is often noticeable how the factor structure reflects the definition used during questionnaire development. The MAAS, for example, was based on an operational definition of mindfulness as "*open* or *receptive* attention to and awareness of ongoing events and experience" (Brown & Ryan, 2004, p.245). This definition implies a unidimensional mindfulness construct such as that which informed the development of the MAAS. While Brown and Ryan (2004) acknowledged the characteristics of acceptance, they regarded it as the outcome of present-moment awareness rather than another aspect that defines mindfulness. The KIMS (Baer et al., 2004), in contrast, is based on a conceptualisation of mindfulness as a set of skills, such as those taught in Dialectical Behavioural Therapy (DBT; Linehan, 1993), resulting in a scale consisting of four separate subscales.

Other instruments emerged entirely from empirical work, such as the FFMQ (Baer et al., 2006), which was developed through a series of factor analyses after pooling together items from five mindfulness questionnaires. These were the 30-item FMI, 39-item KIMS, 15-item MAAS, and two questionnaires that were unpublished at the time, namely the 12-item Cognitive and Affective Mindfulness Scale (CAMS; Hayes & Feldman, 2004) and the 16-item Mindfulness Questionnaire (MQ). The most suitable factor solution from a series of psychometric analyses resulted in the five-factor structure of the FFMQ. Even though the FFMQ was thus developed primarily based on psychometric criteria, the definitions underlying the mindfulness questionnaires that contributed to the item pool are still reflected in the final set of items of the FFMQ. Four of the five subscales of the FFMQ were identical to those of the KIMS, and one additional one was added. The FFMQ subscales are called *Acting with Awareness, Describing, Nonjudging of Experience, Nonreactivity to Inner Experience*, and *Observing*.

Assessing a range of mindfulness aspects does not necessarily require the use of separately scored subscales. The 12-item Cognitive and Affective Mindfulness Scale-Revised (CAMS-R) is an example of a unidimensional scale that attempts to maintain a broad range of content (Feldman, Hayes, Kumar, Greeson, & Laurenceau, 2007). The goal of the authors was to develop a brief scale that has practical utility, and they recognised the fact that such a short questionnaire would not be able to contain different subscales. If researchers intend to obtain measures on specific aspects of mindfulness, then the FFMQ would appear to be more useful than the CAMS-R.

Generally, the measures of mindfulness that have been developed for use with adult respondents cannot be used with children or adolescents unless they have been previously validated for those populations. For some questionnaires, specific child or adolescent versions are available. For example, Brown, West, Loverich, and Biegel (2011) demonstrated the suitability of the MAAS for adolescent participants between the ages of 14–18 years. This version, called MAAS-A, required removal of one item ("I drive places on 'automatic pilot' and then wonder why I went there") because it was deemed inappropriate for younger adolescents. Lawlor, Schonert-Reichl, Gadermann, and Zumbo (2014) validated a version to be used with children as young as 11, and called this instrument MAAS-C. Unlike the MAAS-A, this instrument contained items with simpler items wordings and a modified Likert response scale.

A measure that has been specifically developed for use with youth above the age of nine is the Child and Adolescent Mindfulness Measure (CAMM; Greco, Baer, & Smith, 2011). Even though the instrument was based on the multidimensional conceptualisation of mindfulness that informed the KIMS, the resulting 10-item questionnaire assesses mindfulness as one factor. However, similar to the multidimensional KIMS, various aspects of mindfulness such as present-moment awareness, nonjudgmental awareness, and nonreactivity are covered by the items. Apart from the MAAS-A, MAAS-C, and CAMM, several other mindfulness measures are available for youth, although more psychometric work is required to achieve the same level of psychometric robustness as that found for adult measures (Goodman, Madni, & Semple, 2017).

Development and relevance of item content for mindfulness inventories

Operational definitions of mindfulness only emerged gradually with the increased spread and awareness of MBIs (Bishop et al., 2004), and even now there is continued debate about how mindfulness should be defined (Chiesa, 2013). Understanding of mindfulness in the context of MBIs has typically been related directly to the types of practices and skills taught and developed in such programmes (Bishop et al., 2004), which also meant that the first measures of mindfulness typically reflected the putative psychological outcomes of mindfulness practice or the skills thought to be developed there. The generation of item content for mindfulness instruments such as the FMI, KIMS, and MAAS was thus often prompted by the scale authors' own understanding of mindfulness. Subsequent item selection was then generally determined through consultation with experienced meditation and mindfulness teachers as it was understood that experts are required to appreciate the trajectory of mindfulness skills that develop from beginning to advanced practice. This approach places mindfulness measures in contrast to some of the other so-called patient-reported outcome measures that are informed more directly by an end-user perspective. Although certainly not all quality of life measures have been developed that way, the World Health Organisation Quality of Life tools (WHOQOL Group, 1995) would be an example of such a bottom-up approach that commenced with extensive focus group work to inform the breadth and nuances in wording of the concept. When mindfulness instruments were first developed, there was arguably much less awareness of the concept for such focus group work to be able to inform item content. However, with increased familiarity of mindfulness practices and its goals, this approach to questionnaire design and development may now start to be fruitful.

As with factor structure, the operational definitions on which instruments had been based also influenced their item wording. The focus of the MAAS (Brown & Ryan, 2003) on present-moment awareness meant that no items about acceptance and related concepts were included. Additionally, while the initial pool of 184 candidate items for the MAAS contained items relating to mindfulness as well as to *lapses* of mindfulness, the final items selected were all exclusively about mindlessness. Brown and Ryan (2003) argued that such negatively worded items that indirectly assess mindfulness have the advantage that they be more "diagnostic" as episodes of lack of mindfulness are likely to be more common and also more accessible to most individuals. However, this view has attracted the criticism, such as expressed by Grossman (2011), that negatively worded items do not necessarily express a putative opposite concept such that depression is not necessarily the opposite of happiness. Among the responses by Brown, Ryan, Loverich, Biegel, and West (2011) to Grossman's comment is the argument that the MAAS is not simply a measure of attention lapses only as it is correlated with a range of outcomes relevant to mindfulness training.

Feldman et al. (2007) acknowledged the fact that item development and selection must not only be guided by the goal to achieve excellent fit indices. When a concept is very narrowly defined, internal consistency may be artificially increased at the expense of breadth of the concept. In their development of the CAMS-R, Feldman et al. (2007) were therefore guided by the theoretical criterion to ensure that a wide range of mindfulness characteristics are represented in item content such as those covered in the comprehensive definition by Bishop et al. (2004). Other questionnaires that were explicitly guided by this bidimensional definition (Bishop et al., 2004) are the Philadelphia Mindfulness Scale (PMS; Cardaciotto, Herbert, Forman, Moitra, & Farrow, 2008) and the Toronto Mindfulness Scale (TMS; Lau et al., 2006).

Offenbächer et al. (2011) used a content-analysis approach to identify and compare concepts covered in ten mindfulness questionnaires. Using the International Classification of Functioning (ICF) as an external reference, Offenbächer et al. (2011) allocated 341 concepts that they had identified in the questionnaires to the 37 categories of the ICF system. Approximately 50% were related to body function, around 22% to activity and participants, and 28% to personal factors, which are not included in the ICF and referred to contextual factors such as lifestyle, habits, coping styles, and other interpersonal characteristics. There was considerable diversity in the content of mindfulness questionnaires as identified using this classification system, and the authors recommended that future work selecting item content for mindfulness questionnaires may benefit from utilisation of a classification system such as the ICF.

Mindfulness scales with specific focus or purpose

As with many other research areas such as coping (McElfatrick et al., 2000) or quality of life (Heniford et al., 2008), mindfulness researchers are faced with the choice of using generic or context-specific mindfulness measures. The advantage of generic scales is that they permit comparisons across different populations, while the advantage of disease- or context-specific scales is that they tend to be more sensitive to changes that are particularly important to the context of interest. Most of the measures of mindfulness for specific applications have been developed by making some kind of modification to the wording of existing mindfulness measures. For example, Kimmes, Jaurequi, May, Srivastava, and Fincham (2017) developed a relationship mindfulness measure by slight modifications of the wording of a five-item version of the MAAS (Van Dam, Earleywine, & Borders, 2010). Tsafou, De Ridder, van Ee, and Lacroix (2016) also made minor re-wording to the MAAS in order to create a measure specifically designed for their purposes, which they named Mindfulness in Physical Activity. Following a similar approach, Adam, Heeren, Day, and de Sutter (2015) developed a mindfulness scale applicable to female sexual encounters. Two experts in clinical sexology modified and generated items based on the French version of the FFMQ, with the instruction to produce four items for each of the five subscales. One item did not exhibit a sufficiently high factor loading, resulting in a final 19-item version.

Other context-specific mindfulness questionnaires were developed by modifying items from more than one generic mindfulness scale, such as in the case of the Athlete Mindfulness Questionnaire (Zhang, Chung, & Si, 2017), Mindful Eating Questionnaire (Framson et al., 2009), Mindful Eating Scale (Hulbert-Williams, Nicholls, Joy, & Hulbert-Williams, 2014), or Mindfulness in Teaching Scale (Frank, Jenning, & Greenberg, 2016). Similar to the development of generic mindfulness scales, theoretical considerations occasionally also played a role. Framson et al. (2009) developed their questionnaire based on a conceptual clustering of items into a group of items related to "observing, noticing, or attending to sensations, perceptions, thoughts, and feelings; and acting with awareness" (p.1440). Subsequent psychometric testing of all candidate items resulted in a 28-item questionnaire with five factors called *Disinhibition, Awareness, External Cues, Emotional Response*, and *Distraction*. Hulbert-Williams et al. (2014) saw aspects of acceptance and nonjudgmental awareness missing from the Mindful Eating Questionnaire. After pooling together 74 items from three widely used generic mindfulness scales and editing them to capture aspects of mindful eating, Hulbert-Williams et al. (2014) conducted exploratory factor analyses (EFA) that were guided by the criteria to develop subscales that measure aspects of attention and nonjudgment and to be more closely aligned with the conceptual structure of generic mindfulness instruments. The resulting 28-item version contains six subscales labelled *Acceptance, Awareness, Nonreactivity, Routine, Act with Awareness*, and *Unstructured Eating*. An example of a context-specific mindfulness scale that was based on particularly elaborate theoretical foundations is the Interpersonal Mindfulness in Parenting scale (IM-P). Duncan (2007) initially developed a 10-item version but later extended it to a 31-item with five subscales corresponding to five dimensions of a theoretical model of mindful parenting (Duncan, Coatsworth, & Greenberg, 2009).

Techniques used to investigate factor structure and other psychometric properties

With increased maturation of mindfulness research, one can find an increasingly larger variety of approaches to testing the psychometric properties of mindfulness instruments. In the earliest period of mindfulness scale development, the focus of psychometric investigations was on investigating tenable factor structures. Data from the FMI (Buchheld et al., 2001; Walach, Buchheld, Buttenmüller, Kleinknecht, & Schmidt, 2006), for example, was analysed exclusively using EFA. In other cases such as the KIMS (Baer et al., 2004), MAAS (Brown & Ryan, 2003), and PMS (Cardaciotto et al., 2008), psychometric investigations included a series of studies where results from EFA were later tested on a different dataset using confirmatory factor analysis (CFA). The purpose of such replications was also to test the generalisability of the proposed factor structure to a variety of populations such as clinical versus nonclinical (Cardaciotto et al., 2008). Once the questionnaires had been established and increasingly used, questions such as generalisability of factor structure to other populations started to be examined more systematically. An example is the study by Cordon and Finney (2008) who used a measurement invariance approach to investigate the equivalence of the psychometric properties of the MAAS across samples of adults with different attachment styles.

When testing the psychometric properties of the KIMS (Baer et al., 2004) and the FFMQ (Baer et al., 2006), the authors used an approach called parcelling, which uses the sum or average scores of more than one item as indicators in classical test theory (CTT) approaches such as EFA or CFA. In other words, instead of individual items, item parcels become the unit of analysis for factor analysis. The use of parcelling has been described as controversial (Little, Cunningham, Shahar, & Widaman, 2002). The advantages of parcelling are that measures will exhibit increased reliability and decreased probability of deviations from the required normal distribution of the data. Additionally, as models with item parcels are more parsimonious, there is a decreased likelihood of various sources of sampling error or residual correlations. The main disadvantage, however, is that parcelling can obscure any underlying factor structure, especially when items are parcelled together that may instead be best assigned to separate factors. For the KIMS and FFMQ, parcelling was only employed after a suitable factor structure had already emerged, and parcels were thus created with items from the same subscales. Baer et al. (2006) also demonstrated that results were similar when such parcels had been created through random assignment of items or had been based on the factor loadings from preceding EFAs of the FFMQ.

The psychometric properties of the KIMS have been challenged based on the argument that parcelling has been an inappropriate technique (Christopher, Charoensuk, Gilbert, Neary, & Pearce, 2009a), but subsequent empirical work with the FFMQ indicated that there does not appear to be much reason for concern. Christopher, Neuser, Michael, and Baitmangalkar (2012) found evidence for the same FFMQ factor structure when their CFA used items as indicators instead of item parcels. In a further study, Tran, Glück, and Nader (2013) also concluded that it does not appear that parcelling resulted in overly inflated model fit in previous studies. However, the authors argued that parcelling likely obscured item redundancy and weak psychometric properties of some items.

More recently, psychometric investigations have been reported that used approaches such as item response theory (IRT) or Rasch analysis. These approaches offer unique advantages to psychometric investigations such as detailed analysis of item performance and the proportion of information value provided by each item about the underlying mindfulness trait. Van Dam et al. (2010) conducted an IRT analysis of the MAAS and reported that, for most items, the Likert-scale response options failed to differentiate between the different levels of trait of the respondents. This means that higher scores on the scale do not clearly predict whether the respondent has overall a higher level of trait mindfulness. Only 5 of the 15 items provided the majority of information about the trait, and these were all items that asked about mindfulness generally and did not refer to specific situations as some of the other items do, such as driving or eating. These findings were replicated in an IRT study of the Estonian version of the MAAS (Seema et al., 2015), as well as the finding that the MAAS tends to be better able to differentiate between individuals with lower levels of mindfulness than those at the higher end.

Other studies have investigated the psychometric properties of commonly used mindfulness scales using Rasch analysis. As with IRT, Rasch analysis provides detailed information about individual item performance. Recently recommended standards for reporting results from Rasch analysis include tables that enable conversion of original ordinal-level data to interval-level data, which can be calculated if the data fit the Rasch model (Leung, Png, Conaghan, & Tennant, 2017). Such conversion adjusts for the fact that items have differing levels of difficulty, and changes in summary scores may represent different degrees of change in the underlying trait depending on where on the continuum the change is occurring. For example, a change from a summary score of 13 to 14 may be easier to occur than a change from 20 to 21, which can be adjusted by converting ordinal- to interval-level scores. Such conversion tables are now available for the CHIME (Medvedev, Bergomi, Röthlin, & Krägeloh, 2018a), FFMQ (Medvedev et al., 2017), KIMS (Medvedev et al., 2016a), MAAS (Medvedev et al., 2016b), and the Korean version of the IM-P (Kim, Krägeloh, Medvedev, Duncan, & Singh, 2018).

Although traditionally Rasch analysis has been applied to unidimensional scales only, more recently emerging approaches have been developed for multidimensional scales (Lundgren-Nilsson, Jonsdottor, Ahlborg, & Tennant, 2013). This involves close inspection of the residuals correlation matrix during the iterative process of model fitting. If there is evidence of local dependency between items, the next iteration can combine these items into what has been referred to as super-items, subtests, or testlets (Wainer & Kiely, 1987). While this is a useful technique to address local response dependency (such as shared variance due to similar item formatting), super-items can also be used to assess multidimensionality in response scales. If it is hypothesised that items share variance due to local trait dependency, an analysis step may combine the relevant items into super-items to reflect this multidimensional structure. This approach was used by Medvedev et al. (2017) when investigating the psychometric properties of the FFMQ. After combining subscale items into super-items, unidimensionality could thus be interpreted as evidence of a common higher-order factor for the subscales. Unlike Van Dam, Hobkirk, Danoff-Burg, and Earleywine (2012) who concluded from their CFA study that the use of a total FFMQ score is not advisable, Medvedev et al. (2017) found evidence for the validity of a total FFMQ score, at least when total scores have been converted from ordinal to interval level based on Rasch analysis.

The super-item approach to assessing multidimensionality in Rasch analysis can be considered equivalent to bifactor modelling in CTT (Lundgren-Nilsson et al., 2013). In such bifactor models, the assumption is made that an overarching single factor explains common variance of all items. However, at least one additional factor can be tested simultaneously for a subgroup of items that is hypothesised to be affected by an additional source of variance such as method effects from similarity in item wording (Mansolf & Reise, 2017). When testing the Spanish version of FFMQ, Aguado et al. (2015) found evidence that a bifactor model with one general mindfulness factor and five orthogonal factors representing each of the subscales provided a better fit than a model with five correlated factors.

Occasionally, studies that investigated the psychometric properties of mindfulness questionnaires reported the results from both CTT approaches as well as IRT or Rasch analysis. For example, Osman, Lamis, Bagge, Freedenthal, and Barnes (2016) first conducted EFA as well as CFA with a large sample ($n>800$) of undergraduate students, followed by IRT, particularly with the aim to investigate DIF by individuals scoring low versus high in terms of nonattachment. The authors justified the use of IRT in terms of the need of applying modern psychometric techniques, especially the advantages of detailed information about individual item functioning. A similar approach was taken by Seema et al. (2015) for their investigation of the psychometric properties of an Estonian translation of the MAAS. First, the authors validated the questionnaire in a series of CTT analyses including EFA, CFA, and factorial invariance testing that compared the factor structure obtained with a sample of participants completing the Estonian version with an age- and gender-matched sample of US participants completing the English-language version. As a second step, Seema et al. (2015) conducted an IRT analysis to compare the informative value of the items of the Estonian version with those obtained for the English version reported by Van Dam et al. (2010). A different justification for the use of multiple methods was provided by Kim, Krägeloh, Medvedev, Duncan, and Singh (2018) when testing the Korean version of the IM-P. Initially, psychometric investigations used both EFA and CFA. However, because the researchers were required to apply substantial conceptual criteria to arrive at a satisfactory model, they also confirmed the adequacy of their model using Rasch analysis on two different samples.

As a measure of the internal consistency reliability of mindfulness scales, Cronbach's alpha is typically reported (e.g. Baer et al., 2004, 2006; Brown & Ryan, 2003). In the context of Rasch analysis, this may occasionally be assessed in terms of the Person Separation Index (PSI). As stated by Medvedev et al. (2017), PSI expresses the ability of the measure to differentiate between individuals who differ in terms of level of trait (in this case mindfulness). Unlike Cronbach's alpha, the calculation of PSI is based on nonlinear transformation that can be conducted with random missing data. Another common type of reliability reported for mindfulness questionnaires is test-retest reliability, which assesses the stability of scores over time. As argued by Jensen, Niclasen, Vangkilde, Petersen, and Hasselbalch (2016), long-term mediation analyses rely on the assumption that trait mindfulness is stable over time when meditation is not practised, which is important to demonstrate empirically. In their study, the Danish version of the MAAS was administered to participants two weeks and also six months after the first administration, and the questionnaire was found to have adequate test-retest reliability. Other studies of the various versions of the MAAS investigated test-retest reliability over a three-week interval (Catak, 2012; Deng et al., 2012). Further examples involved a timeframe of around two weeks for the KIMS (Baer et al., 2004) or one month for the Chinese version of the FFMQ (Deng, Liu, Rodriguez, & Xia, 2011).

Construct validity and sensitivity to change

The lack of a gold standard or clear external referent for what characterises a mindful person (Grossman, 2011) produces some contradictions for the assessment of construct validity of mindfulness measures. On one hand, various demographic or psychological variables are used as criteria to assess discriminant and convergent validity, but on the other hand, the relationship between mindfulness and such variables is still unclear and continues to be explored (Falkenström, 2010). Some of these differences are related to the specific conceptualisation of mindfulness that informed questionnaire development. For example, since the FMI was developed by conceptualising mindfulness as an attribute developed in practitioners of insight meditation (Buchheld et al., 2001), employing the variable meditation experience as a criterion for discriminant validity can be justified accordingly (Walach et al., 2006). The development of the MAAS, in contrast, was based on an understanding of mindfulness as a naturally occurring trait (Brown & Ryan, 2003). However, also here, the authors argued that individuals with meditation experience are expected to have higher levels of awareness and attentional capacity, which was confirmed in their data. In the validation studies of the KIMS (Baer et al., 2004) and FFMQ (Baer et al., 2006), meditation experience was also used as a criterion variable to differentiate between mindfulness scores.

Although the publications reporting on the development of the KIMS (Baer et al., 2004) and FFMQ (Baer et al., 2006) were very detailed, some follow-up analyses explored their psychometric properties further including investigations of discriminant validity. For example, Baer et al. (2008) reported on more comprehensive analyses that explored the role of meditation experience in predicting scores of the five subscales of the FFMQ using three different cross-sectional samples. Additionally, the authors conducted mediational analyses to test to what extent the subscale scores mediated the relationship between meditation experience and psychological well-being. Such results are important as they are able to shed light on whether mindfulness instruments may be sufficiently sensitive to detect the change in mindfulness that one would expect from an MBI. Baer et al. (2008) did find that FFMQ mindfulness facets were significant mediators. Bergomi, Tschacher, and Kupper (2015) argued that analyses about the effects of meditation practice need to include more detail, such as length of experience, type of practice, and whether participants are still practising. In their cross-sectional study of over 400 participants from the general population and over 200 MBSR course participants, mindfulness scores using the CHIME were associated particularly with continued practice at present as opposed to accumulated practice over years. When controlling for demographic variables, there was no difference for type of meditation. In a study using a large online sample of people with a range of meditation experience, Pang and Ruch (2018) revealed potentially complex dynamics in the effects of meditation experience on facets of mindfulness. While meditation practice was associated with the expected higher scores on FFMQ subscales, stopping practice resulted in slower reductions in scores for some subscales than for others. While *Acting with Awareness, Nonjudging,* and *Nonreactivity* gradually decreased, *Observing* and *Describing* generally remained high even after discontinuation of practice.

As the associations between meditation and mindfulness may be different in clinical situations than in nonclinical ones, Goldberg et al. (2016) investigated the construct validity of the FFMQ in a randomised controlled trial of people who completed either MBSR, participated in an active control group, or were part of a waitlist control group. While FFMQ facet scores increased over the course of the MBSR intervention relative to the waitlist group, no changes were noted relative to the active control condition that received a health enhancement programme specifically designed not to produce an effect on mindfulness. A further study using the Spanish version of the MAAS found that the instrument was not sensitive to change, in this case after DBT (Soler et al., 2012). However, other clinical studies did find evidence of change in mindfulness scores mediating the effects of a MBI on psychological outcomes, such as FFMQ scores mediating the effects of MBSR on difficulties in emotional regulation (Keng, Smoski, Robins, Ekblad, & Brantley, 2012) or KIMS scores mediating the effects of Mindfulness-Based Cognitive Therapy (MBCT) on depression (Kuyken et al., 2010). While the evidence may be mixed, the evidence overall does seem to indicate that the commonly used mindfulness instruments are able to detect change. As illustrated in a systematic review and meta-analysis of 20 studies reporting on a MBI (Gu, Strauss, Bond, & Cavanagh, 2015), changes in mindfulness scores significantly mediated the relationship between the intervention and indicators of mental health. In another review, Goldberg et al. (2018) analysed the results from 69 published randomised controlled trials of a MBI. While the improvements in clinical outcome measures tended to be larger for those of mindfulness measures, the study nevertheless provided partial support for the responsiveness of self-report scales. A need to identify specific items with high sensitivity has been recognised by Soler et al. (2014). Based on a dataset of more than 600 participants with and without meditation experience who completed the FFMQ and the Experiences Questionnaire (EQ) that assessed aspects of decentring and rumination (Fresco et al., 2007), Soler et al. (2014) created a 19-item composite index called MINDSENS that consists of ten FFMQ items and nine EQ items. This index was able to discriminate between daily meditators and nonmeditators in over 80% of cases.

When examining instruments for their ability to discriminate between those with and those without meditation and mindfulness practice experience, it is not sufficient only to compare means between relevant groups or to inspect correlations between mindfulness scores and indicators of experience or familiarity with mindfulness. One assumption of any measure that needs to be explicitly tested is that each item differentiates between individuals low and high on the mindfulness continuum to the same extent irrespective of previous mindfulness experience. When investigating such differential item functioning (DIF) using an IRT approach with an online sample of university students, Van Dam, Earleywine, and Danoff-Burg (2009) found evidence that respondents who had equivalent overall mindfulness levels but differed in terms of prior meditation experience endorsed response options on the FFMQ differently, thus challenging the construct validity of the instrument and its suitability as a tool to investigate pre- and post-intervention changes of meditation programmes. As noted by Van Dam et al. (2009), a limitation of their study was that meditators and non-meditators were not matched in terms of other demographic characteristics. When examining DIF with IRT and using a matched sample, Baer et al. (2011) found only minimal DIF of items by meditation experience. Inspection of DIF by meditation experience alongside other fundamental demographic variables such as gender and age groups is also standard practice of Rasch analysis studies that test the psychometric properties of mindfulness instruments. While Goh, Marais, and Ireland (2017) found DIF by meditation experience for 2 of the 15 MAAS items, another Rasch analysis study of the MAAS did not (Medvedev et al., 2016b), nor did studies on other common mindfulness instruments (Medvedev et al., 2016a, 2017, 2018a). In two of these studies, DIF was reported for student versus general population samples, thus requiring the creation of separate ordinal- to interval-data conversion tables for these two populations for the MAAS (Medvedev et al., 2016a) and FFMQ (Medvedev et al., 2017).

The performance of the FFMQ for sample with or without meditation experience has also been explored using CTT approaches. Using a large sample ($n>2000$) of participants recruited through various online forums and mailing lists, Pang and Ruch (2018) found excellent CFA fits for three sub-samples categorised by extent of meditation experience. However, the researchers noted the presence of ceiling effects for three of the subscales, including a relatively large proportion of respondents without meditation experience reaching the maximum score. Unlike previous studies, the FFMQ Observe facet loaded sufficiently high with a higher-order mindfulness factor. Pang and Ruch (2018) speculated that the recruitment procedure may have attracted individuals with higher levels of curiosity and open-mindedness, thus elevating any associations with the *Describing* and *Observing* subscales of the FFMQ.

Apart from experience with meditation and mindfulness practice, another approach of testing construct validity of mindfulness measures has been to use a psychological construct that is considered related to mindfulness. One such construct is nonattachment, which has been defined as "a flexible, balanced way of relating to one's experiences without clinging to or suppressing them" (Sahdra, Ciarrochi, & Parker, 2016, p.819). Psychometric investigations of the nonattachment scale (NAS; Sahdra, Shaver, & Brown, 2010) demonstrated that it is a related yet distinct construct from mindfulness. While nonattachment exhibited the same moderately high correlation coefficients with the FFMQ subscale scores that are also commonly reported for correlations among the FFMQ subscales, a series of CFAs illustrated that nonattachment is most suitably considered as a separate construct. The use of nonattachment as a variable to assess convergent validity may thus be justified, such as in a study reporting on further psychometric properties of the MAAS (Osman et al., 2016).

Relevant to the present discussion is the fact that mindfulness has itself been used as a criterion variable to assess the convergent validity of measures of other, related, psychological constructs. For example, Pinto-Gouveia, Gregório, Dinis, and Xavier (2012) validated the Portuguese version of a questionnaire on psychological inflexibility in the context of Acceptance and Commitment Therapy (Hayes,

Strosahl, & Wilson, 2011) and used the FFMQ as a variable to assess discriminant validity. When validating a mysticism scale for use with Tibetan Buddhists, Chen, Hood, Yang, and Watson (2011) used the MAAS as a measure to assess discriminant validity. The authors argued that scores on the MAAS should not correlate with mysticism as the latter was conceptualised independently of the mental functions that are assessed through the MAAS. However, instead of lack of correlation, the results revealed some small negative correlations with mysticism, although it was not clear whether the authors had reverse scored the negatively worded MAAS.

Lastly, with increased understanding of the effects of mindfulness on the brain (Falcone & Jerram, 2018), it will be increasingly possible to consider neurological markers to assist in the validation of mindfulness instruments. Way, Creswell, Eisenberger, and Lieberman (2010) found a correlation between MAAS scores and measures of baseline amygdala activity. Another example is a study by Zhuang et al. (2017) who reported that MAAS scores were associated with increased volume of brain grey matter in the right precuneus and also mediated the relationship between structural variation in this brain area and depression vulnerability. Of the FFMQ subscales, *Describing, Nonjudging,* and *Nonreactivity* were also associated with greater surface area and cortical thickness in various areas that have been linked to self-awareness, attention, and emotional regulation. However, associations between neurological markers and mindfulness appear complex. Additionally, biomarkers such as heart rate variability are related to mindfulness differently depending on individuals' general anxiety levels (Mankus, Aldao, Kerns, Mayville, & Mennin, 2013).

Mindfulness as state, trait, and skill

A necessary distinction to be made in psychometric measurement is the distinction between psychological states or traits, in other words, whether one is measuring transient or stable aspects of a psychological construct. Some of the mindfulness inventories available are explicit about whether they are measuring mindfulness states or trait mindfulness, and the majority of mindfulness scales can be described as dispositional or trait measures. For example, the MAAS was specifically described by the authors (Brown & Ryan, 2003) as a dispositional measure that assesses mindfulness as a naturally occurring attribute. Most research tends to employ one mindfulness measure, and when the MAAS is selected, it is generally accurately described as a measure of trait mindfulness. Occasionally, the MAAS has been used as a second mindfulness measure, such as when investigating whether trait mindfulness mediates the relationship between yoga participation and mindful eating (Martin, Prichard, Hutchinson, & Wilson, 2013).

The TMS (Lau et al., 2006) is arguably the most widely used state mindfulness scale. Lau et al. (2006) reported evidence for a two-factor structure, which resulted in one six-item subscale named *Curiosity* and one seven-item subscale called *Decentering*. The TMS was developed to be able to evaluate the mechanism that is assumed to be underlying the efficacy of MBIs (Lau et al., 2006), and thus may not measure state as opposed to trait, but, as the authors described it, as a state in the sense of a process or mode of relating to one's experience. TMS scores were found to be correlated with meditation experience and to be increased after completion of the eight-week MBSR course (Lau et al., 2006). Nevertheless, the TMS is also able to detect very short-term effects of mindfulness practice such as demonstrated by Mahmood, Hopthrow, and de Moura (2016) who reported on a study where participants completed a five-minute mindfulness exercise via the internet. The TMS is also available as a trait version, which was developed by changing the instructions and re-wording the TMS items from past to present tense (Davis, Lau, & Cairns, 2009).

Another state scale, the 21-item State Mindfulness Scale (SMS; Tanay & Bernstein, 2013), was developed by considering more traditional conceptualisations of mindfulness as well as the two-component definition of mindfulness by Bishop et al. (2004). The resulting two subscales were named State Mindfulness of Body and State Mindfulness of Mind. Lynch and Wilson (2017) argued that existing state mindfulness measures did not sufficiently capture the same range of diverse characteristics of trait mindfulness scales and thus developed the Mindful State Questionnaire (MSQ). These were developed by re-wording existing trait mindfulness questionnaire items into the present tense – interestingly the same way in which the TMS state version had been modified into a trait version. Re-wording of items was also the approach taken by Brown and Ryan (2003) to produce a state version of the MAAS – in this case, five items were slightly re-worded to produce the five-item state MAAS.

More systematic psychometric research about the distinction between state and trait mindfulness is needed. The number of trait scales clearly surpasses the number of state scales, and there may be the perception that the existing state scales are still inadequate. This is indicated by occasional isolated efforts to modify existing trait scales such as the KIMS through minor re-wording of items (Geisler et al., 2018). However, such practice is risky as the psychometric properties of the new modified scale are uncertain, and validity is thus jeopardised. As Blanke and Brose (2017) found when developing their Multidimensional State Mindfulness Questionnaire (MSMQ), item re-wording to transform a trait measure to a state measure is not always straightforward. Items referring to nonreactivity imply occurrence of a specific event, thus requiring a decoupling of nonreactivity from negative experiences to generate a state measure. However, as found by Blanke and Brose (2017), such re-wording may have changed the meaning of the items to the extent they no longer fit a CFA model alongside other facets of mindfulness.

Some inconsistent findings have been reported about the TMS that highlight the need for further conceptual and empirical work about the function of this instrument. While Lau et al. (2006) justified the development of the TMS based on the need to have a scale that can track progress in MBIs, some clinical evidence appears to suggest that the TMS may not be sensitive enough to detect change in mindfulness as a result of an MBI and that assessment of mindfulness in everyday-life situation may be more suitable for that purpose (Eyles et al., 2015). Klein et al. (2015) also reported that TMS scores did not change after completion of a ten-week mindfulness meditation course, although scores on a measure of trait measure of mindfulness, the PMS (Cardaciotto et al., 2008), did increase. A study by Carmody, Reed, Kristeller, and Merriam (2008), in contrast, did report that both MAAS and TMS increased as a result of an MBSR intervention. However, baseline scores of MAAS and TMS were unrelated, and there was no significant correlation between the change scores of the two measures. Further inconsistent findings between the TMS and the dispositional MAAS and FFMQ scales have also been reported by Thompson and Waltz (2008) who concluded that the TMS may not be a sufficiently sensitive instrument. Additionally, using the FFMQ and SMS in an experimental study that induced mindful states through a brief mindfulness exercise, Bravo, Pearson, Wilson, and Witkiewitz (2018) reported limited association between state and trait mindfulness, and several unexpected interactions with meditation experience were found.

While the above evidence appears to suggest that the relationship between state and trait measures of mindfulness may be complex, attempts have been made to study the distinction between state and trait mindfulness measurements through psychometric investigations. Here, a longitudinal study suggests that the TMS may indeed be more adequately described as a measure that can track how repeated mindful states may gradually develop into a more enduring trait during a MBI (Kiken, Garland, Bluth, Palsson, & Gaylord, 2015), although this might not necessarily apply to all items. As demonstrated by a study across three time points that used Generalisability theory (Medvedev, Krägeloh, Narayanan, & Siegert, 2017), two items of the TMS had no signs of differentiating between trait levels of individuals, although all remaining items can also be accurately described as measuring state rather than trait. Overall, more studies with more sophisticated psychometric techniques are necessary, such as Generalisability theory (e.g. Medvedev et al., 2017) or multilevel confirmatory factor analysis (e.g. Blanke & Brose, 2017) that analyse levels of mindfulness both within a person (state) as well as between persons (trait).

While the distinction between mindfulness as a trait and mindfulness as a state is made regularly in the literature, the distinction between trait mindfulness and mindfulness as a skill is less clear. The KIMS (Baer et al., 2004) is the only questionnaire that explicitly refers to mindfulness as involving a set of skills, particularly those related to the context of DBT. The FFMQ (Baer et al., 2006) does not have this explicit focus, but contains a substantial number of KIMS items and has a similar multidimensional structure. Conceptualising mindfulness as a skill might then place the construct somewhere in the middle of the state-trait continuum, as it is then considered to be something that can be developed with continued training, ideally within the approximately eight-week period typically found in MBIs. Mindfulness as measured by the FFMQ has thus sometimes been "conceptualized as a relatively stable dispositional characteristic that is not expected to change greatly unless an individual engages in mindfulness training" (Eisenlohr-Moul, Walsh, Charnigo, Lynam, & Baer, 2012, p.277). However, within-person variations in FFMQ scores may not merely be random error variance, as weekly fluctuations of scores may predict concomitant changes in psychological outcome variables such as the expression of borderline personality features (Eisenlohr-Moul, Peters, Chamberlain, & Rodriguez, 2016).

Shortened versions of questionnaires

Many studies tend to administer a mindfulness scale alongside other psychological instruments. This includes cross-sectional studies that explore the relationship between several variables of interest, such as when testing proposed mechanisms by which mindfulness brings about health benefits (Short, Mazmanian, Oinonen, & Mushquash, 2016). Other times, a large amount of data is collected from participants in mindfulness interventions to provide detailed information about the effects of the intervention (Neece, 2014), to explore the trajectory of change in mindfulness scores (Ietsugu et al., 2015), or track weekly fluctuations of mindfulness (Eisenlohr-Moul et al., 2016). When collecting data from vulnerable respondents with compromised health, it is also burdensome for participants to complete long self-report questionnaires (Zimmermann, Burrell, & Jordan, 2018). Occasionally, researchers selected a small number of items from existing scales to arrive at an abbreviated mindfulness measure, such as Snippe, Nyklíček, Schroevers, and Bos (2015) who tracked daily mindfulness scores and only presented two items from each of the FFMQ subscales (identified for having had the highest factor loadings). However, to allow comparative studies and in order to have confidence in the validity and reliability of the measure, systematic psychometric investigations are required.

Specific guidelines for the development of short scales are available that recommend that both psychometric criteria as well as content-related considerations are applied (Ziegler, Kemper, & Kruyen, 2014). One such recommendation relates to the fact that shorter scales tend to yield lower values of internal consistency reliability, and by selecting items with the goal to minimise a reduction in reliability one may risk reducing the heterogeneity of item content to the extent that core characteristics are lost. For the MAAS, reliance on primarily psychometric criteria such as information value has resulted in five-item versions where items have been removed that referred to specific situations as opposed to general wording (Seema et al., 2015; Van Dam et al., 2010). Another short version of the MAAS emerged out of an investigation of method effects due to negative item wording. Höfling, Moosbrugger, Schermelleh-Engel, and Heidenreich (2011a) re-worded 13 of the 15 items of the German MAAS into positively worded items and investigated the factor structure of the resulting 28-item questionnaire using a series of CFAs. Satisfactory model fit could only be achieved after selecting ten items based on factor loadings: five original negatively worded items and their corresponding positively worded ones.

Occasionally, researchers specifically sought out to develop a shorter version of one of the main instruments, such as when a briefer 20-item German version of the KIMS was developed (Höfling, Ströhle, Michalak, & Heidenreich, 2011b). In many other cases, however, the development of shortened versions of mindfulness can be described as incidental or as the outcome of further psychometric refinement. The 14-item version of the FMI was developed largely as a result of using the full version of the scale with a sample that included individuals without meditation experience, which resulted in an unstable psychometric structure of the full 30-item version (Walach et al., 2006). Other times, shortened versions emerged when translating instruments into other languages, as illustrated by the translation the full 31-item version of the IM-P scale from the original English (Duncan, 2007; Duncan et al., 2009). For the Dutch (de Bruin et al., 2014) and the Portuguese (Moreira & Canavarro, 2017) versions, the same two items were discarded when testing its psychometric properties. For the Hong Kong Chinese version (Lo et al., 2018), eight items were discarded, and Kim et al. (2018) were only able to obtain an adequate fit for an 18-item version of the Korean version. Particularly when translating into very different languages and cultural contexts, variations are to be expected, and such discrepancies therefore do not necessarily indicate inadequacy of the original scale. In other cases, the validation work after translation of an instrument into a new version was used as an opportunity to create a shorter version to reduce response burden in a specific study, such as the use of a Chinese version of the MAAS in a longitudinal study with adolescents (Black, Sussman, Johnson, & Milam, 2012).

The gradual availability of several short versions for some questionnaires prompted work to explicitly compare the psychometric performance of the different versions. Using IRT, Chiesi, Donati, Panno, Giacomantonio, and Primi (2017) compared the performance of the original 15-item MAAS with that of an 11-item version informed by their IRT results as well as a 5-item version informed by previous IRT work (Van Dam et al., 2010; Osman et al., 2016) and a version comprising of 10 items found to work well psychometrically in a Rasch analysis (Goh et al., 2017). Chiesi et al. (2017) concluded that the MAAS may be shortened but that the 5-item version had inadequate psychometric properties. Similar to Chiesi et al. (2017), Medvedev, Titkova, Siegert, Hwang, and Krägeloh (2018b) tested the suitability of various short versions of the FFMQ (a 24-item Dutch version, 20-item German version, 20-item Chinese version, and 15-item English version) using a mixed sample of university students and members of the general population. Using Rasch analysis, Medvedev et al. (2018b) found that an 18-item version was slightly superior psychometrically to some of the other versions.

Exploring contradictory and counterintuitive findings

Occasional findings that are at odds with expectations may be dismissed as being the result of error variance or as indicating the presence of an unknown confounding variable. In contrast, repeated reports for certain counterintuitive results eventually raise questions about the validity of the measures concerned, thus triggering further investigations. In mindfulness measurements, such patterns of findings have been documented for some of the subscales of multidimensional mindfulness inventories, particularly the *Observing* subscales of the KIMS (Baer et al., 2004) and FFMQ (Baer et al., 2006). A frequently cited study in this context is that by Christopher, Christopher, and Charoensuk (2009b) who administered the MAAS (Brown & Ryan, 2003) and KIMS to 24 Thai monks, 77 Thai university students, and 96 US university students. For the participants in Thailand, the questionnaires had been translated into Thai. As expected, the Thai monks scored highest on the

MAAS. However, the US students had the highest scores on the *Observing* and *Accepting without Judgment* subscales of the KIMS. On the *Describing* subscale, both the Thai and the US students scored significantly higher than the monks.

The results by Christopher et al. (2009b) may perhaps be considered an anomaly related to cultural differences or the small sample size of the study. However, unexpected relationships have frequently been reported about certain subscales. In a longitudinal study by Barnes and Lynn (2010) with undergraduate university students, the *Acting with Awareness, Nonreactivity,* and *Nonjudging* subscales of the FFMQ inversely predicted depressive symptoms over the course of the semester, while *Describing* was unrelated, and *Observing* even positively predicted depressive symptoms. In a study using the Dutch version of the FFMQ in adults with depression, *Observing* and *Describing* also showed only a small or no association with symptoms of depression and anxiety (Bohlmeijer, ten Klooster, Fledderus, Veehof, & Baer, 2011). The authors interpreted these results as indication that these subscales are less sensitive to change than the other FFMQ facets. In another clinical sample of participants with various kinds of mood disorders, Curtiss and Klemanski (2014) also found that the FFMQ Observe subscale predicted anxiety when controlling for the other subscales. The authors concluded that this may indicate that individuals with mood disorders may employ attentional resources in a maladaptive manner, in contrast to the equanimous observation style encouraged and developed in MBIs.

Baer et al. (2006) argued that the FFMQ Observe facet might function differently in people with meditation experience. This hypothesis was later confirmed by Baer et al. (2008) who found that *Observing* was strongly positively correlated with psychological well-being in experienced meditators but either not associated or negatively associated with psychological well-being in nonmeditating samples of educated adults and university students. In meditators, therefore, observing may thus apply to a wide range of external and internal stimuli rather than primarily on unpleasant ones. When testing the psychometric properties of the Dutch version of the FFMQ, de Bruin, Topper, Muskens, Bögels, and Kamphuis (2012) reported a similar result. For a sample of university students, *Observing* was positively associated with variables such as worry and thought suppression (although not significantly), while in a sample of meditators, *Observing* was significantly negatively associated with worry. Observing may thus only serve a beneficial function for meditators. Further support for this explanation comes from a study by Campos et al. (2016) who found that, of the FFMQ subscales, only *Observing* mediated the relationship between meditation frequency and happiness. Lastly, using a person-oriented analysis approach, Lilja, Lundh, Josefsson, and Falkenström (2013) demonstrated that meditators were over-represented in clusters of respondents with high scores and under-represented in clusters with low observing scores, confirming the relevance of the subscale in differentiating between individuals with different mindfulness levels.

Rather than being a matter of whether the FFMQ Observe subscale is relevant in a clinical situation or not (Curtiss & Klemanski, 2014), it appears that extent of meditation experience in the sample is a determining factor of the performance of this subscale. Lack of relationships between the *Observing* subscale and psychological well-being in cross-sectional studies may thus be due to a lack of under-representation of meditators (Baroni, Nerini, Matera, & Stefanile, 2018). This effect may also be related to the fact that the items in the FFMQ Observe subscale tend to be about external perception rather than emotional awareness. When pooling together observing items from various different mindfulness instruments into one survey, Rudkin, Medvedev, and Siegert (2018) found that items of the FFMQ Observe subscale formed a factor that shared the meaning of external perception in contrast to body observation or emotional awareness. This might perhaps also explain why this subscale predicts creativity (Baas, Nevicka, & Ten Velden, 2014) and shows positive correlations with aesthetic experiences evoked by art (Harrison & Clark, 2016).

Content complexity and response shift

The subtleties of the attitudinal aspects of mindfulness can sometimes be difficult to understand for participants who are new to it – irrespective of background and context, whether older adults in nursing homes (McBee, 2009) or young medical students (Solhaug et al., 2018). Compared to some of the other mindfulness instruments available, the MAAS is considered to be more comprehensible by people without mindfulness experience. When translating the instrument from English into Estonian, Seema et al. (2015) noted that items relating to moments of absentmindedness are more easily understood by Estonians, whose language does not have a word for mindfulness.

An instrument that has clearly been recognised as requiring prior familiarisation with mindfulness and related practices is the FMI (Buchheld et al., 2001). The FMI was validated with data from participants in insight meditation retreats, and the authors recommended that the questionnaire be used only with respondents who had some exposure with mindfulness meditation. A cognitive interviewing study by Belzer et al. (2013) presented two groups of participants, namely mindfulness practitioners and those without experience, with the FMI and asked them to think out loud as they were answering the questionnaire. Additional retrospective information was also collected using interviews. The results indicated that individuals without mindfulness experience struggled to understand many of the items, sometimes even referring to them as esoteric.

The phenomenon that items are understood differently by individuals that differ on some characteristic is commonly referred to as response shift. When applied to assessment of mindfulness, the frame of reference for rating self-report items may depend on prior experience with meditation and mindfulness, which also determines how items are understood. When discussing mindfulness measurement, Im (2017) referred to the so-called Dunning-Kruger effect according to which individuals low on an ability or trait fail to recognise their inadequacy and overestimate their ability. In the context of mindfulness, this has often been described as individuals starting to practise mindfulness realising increasingly how absentminded they have been, which thus means that individuals' self-rated mindfulness levels might initially decrease before increasing again (Erisman & Roemer, 2012). Such lack of linearity is of concern for self-rating scales, where it is assumed that any change in score is due to a change in the trait and not due to changes in standards of reference applied when rating items.

Only a few studies have reported empirical data that could provide some information about how common or strong response shift effects may be in mindfulness scales. The above-mentioned studies by Baer et al. (2008) and Curtiss and Klemanski (2014) found that the *Observing* subscale of the FFMQ appears to be understood differently by those with and those without experience with meditation, and the subscale is more predictive of psychological adjustment in meditators. However, a number of statistical techniques are available to investigate response shift specifically. Within the CTT literature, this includes invariance testing that tests to what extent factor structure and loadings are constant over time. Using this approach, Gu et al. (2016) noted that the factor structure of the FFMQ was not equivalent when comparing data from before and after an MBCT intervention, and that the typical five-factor hierarchical structure only applied to post-intervention data. In contrast, when analysing the CHIME, Krägeloh, Bergomi, Siegert, and Medvedev (2018) reported very little response shift from completion of an MBI, although the limited sample size meant that invariance tests could only be conducted separately for each of the eight subscales.

Other studies have used an IRT or Rasch analysis approach, which could reveal response shift via DIF by experience. While Van Dam et al. (2009) reported wide-spread DIF when using the FFMQ, Baer, Samuel, and Lykins (2011) only found DIF for four of the FFMQ items when using demographically matched groups of meditators and nonmeditators. Other Rasch analysis studies (Medvedev et al., 2016a, 2016b, 2017, 2018a) reported very minimal DIF by mindfulness experience, although DIF has occasionally been used as a criterion to discard misfitting items, and these studies have therefore not explicitly researched response shift. Apart from psychometric investigations, future research may consider employing other techniques such as the then-test, which asks participants to provide retrospective ratings that are then compared with actual ratings at that time point (Finkelstein, Quaranto, and Schwartz, 2014). A further approach may be offered by so-called end-state mindfulness scales that attempt to differentiate between the process of attentional and attitudinal aspects of practice and its outcomes, or end states (Noguchi, 2017). As with other meditation outcome measures such as the Effects of Meditation Scale (Reavley & Pallant, 2009), response shift will not be an issue, although they allow only limited ability to track change as their use with true beginners of mindfulness practice would be meaningless.

Behavioural or experience-specific measures

Most trait mindfulness questionnaires involve asking participants to provide retrospective information such as when reflecting on their general tendency to behave. In contrast to trait measures, state mindfulness scales are able to inquire about self-reported mindfulness in relation to specific events. However, their format of delivery to respondents has typically been similar to those for trait measures, namely as a series of questions administered in one session. In laboratory situations or clinical environments where the event of interest such as a preceding mindfulness exercise is arranged in the presence of the researcher, such a mode of delivery does not pose an issue. It does, however, when the purpose of the study is to inquire about mindfulness states in various naturalistic settings or as they fluctuate during the day.

Using an experience-sampling approach, Brown and Ryan (2003) sent messages to participants through a pager at quasi-random intervals three times a day. The pager signals prompted participants to record the experiences they had at the time and to complete five questions of the state version of the MAAS as well as questions about their affect state. State mindfulness was associated with higher levels of pleasant affect and lower unpleasant affect when controlling for trait mindfulness, and those with generally higher levels of trait mindfulness were more likely to indicate higher states of mindfulness generally. Gotink et al. (2016) conducted an experience-sampling study where individuals who had previously participated in an MBI course were invited to engage in prolonged mindful walking, which could range from a one- to three-day period. Participants completed self-report questionnaires before and after the walking periods but were also provided with smartphones, which prompted them several times a day to answer 18 Likert-scale items that included questions about their mood as well as some FFMQ questions. These data informed the feasibility of the mindful walking intervention and indicated how positive affect and state mindfulness are related in – as the authors described it – an "upward spiral from one moment to the next" (p.1118). Because of the increased use of technology-based approaches to deliver mindfulness interventions, experience-sampling methods are increasingly used. Another example is a study by Minami et al. (2018) who used a smartphone-assisted MBI for smokers with mood disorders. Here, participants were prompted five times a day by the phone to practise mindfulness by listening to an audio recording and also to report their affect, behaviours, and state mindfulness. Some evidence suggests that experience-sampling methods appear more sensitive to be able to detect change in MBIs than when the same CAMS-R and psychological distress items were delivered through traditional paper-and-pencil formats (Moore, Depp, Wetherell, & Lenze, 2016).

The terms *process-oriented* or *process-related* have been used in different ways to mark a contrast with other types of measurement approaches. Erisman and Roemer (2012) developed the Mindful Process Questionnaire (MPQ) to assess the process of how mindfulness is applied, such as how often one uses mindfulness intentionally or notices absentmindedness and re-directs attention back to the present moment. This is in contrast to other measures that assess mindfulness as the result of practice and thus successful application of mindfulness techniques. While MPQ scores were correlated with FFMQ and MAAS scores, it predicted variance of depression beyond these so-called outcome-oriented measures of mindfulness. Lacaille, Sadikaj, Nishioka, Flanders, and Knäuper (2015) argued that the content of the MPQ items resembled those of trait measures too closely and re-worded them to create a measure that is more sensitive to changes in mindful responding over time. For that purpose, they also reduced the number of items from eight to four to develop a scale called Daily Mindful Responding Scale (DMRS). The psychometric properties of the DMRS were tested using Generalisability theory, multilevel CFA, as well as latent growth curve modelling, supporting the validity and reliability of the measure both for between- and also within-person comparisons. Another process-related measure, the Applied Mindfulness Process Scale (AMPS), has been proposed by Li, Black, and Garland (2016). Unlike the MPQ that describes how individuals move from mindlessness to mindfulness, the AMPS is more focused on the use of mindfulness to cope with emotional states.

While Erisman and Roemer (2012) used the term *outcome-oriented* mindfulness to refer to measures such as the FFMQ and MAAS and *process-oriented* to refer to MPQ, other researchers used the expression *process-related* to the FFMQ and MAAS (May & Reinhardt, 2018). Here, process-related measures such as self-report ratings are described as focusing on internal processes that are presumed to characterise mindfulness, and *outcome-related* measures focus on the external manifestations of mindfulness. One example of the latter would be the self-other agreement (SOA) method that compares self-ratings on standard mindfulness questionnaires with ratings by a close other participant (May & Reinhardt, 2018). These scores can then be compared using correlation analysis or calculation of difference scores. As predicted, self-rated scores on the FFMQ were generally higher than those rated by others. However, while the results suggest that outside observers are able to detect to what extent mindfulness is manifested in others, the association between self- and other-rated scores was small, with correlation coefficients ranging from .19 to 25.

Hakan, Neal, and Lothes (2017) proposed a further way of assessing the manifestation of mindfulness, namely the overt reflection of the Buddhist concept of right mindfulness as the absence of automatic social judgments. They argued that individuals high in mindfulness will be less likely to engage in automatic negative judgments about people who are not directly known to them. Participants were asked to complete a survey that was disguised as a public opinion survey that presented some pictures of people including some celebrities. When asked to rate the individuals shown in the pictures for intelligence, style, and morality, those ratings were correlated with participants' scores on the FFMQ and MAAS. In contrast to expectations, significant inverse associations were found only for two of the FFMQ subscales and negative social judgment scores. However, involvement in mindfulness activities and yoga predicted less negative social judgment, and the researchers thus concluded that the results indicated some counterintuitive findings when using the FFMQ and MAAS. Even if this conclusion was justified and social judgments are indeed a valid alternative to self-report mindfulness measures, it is difficult to see how the covert nature of administering this social judgment survey could become standard practice of measuring mindfulness.

The last cluster of measures to be mentioned in this section includes those related to meditation performance and experience. Piron's (2001) Meditation Depth Index (MEDI) is a 30-item questionnaire that asks respondents to rate their meditation experience using a Likert-scale format. Based on factor analyses, the items are arranged across five subscales called *Hindrances, Relaxation, Personal self, Transpersonal qualities*, and *Transpersonal self*. Other measures have been described as behavioural or performance measures and have primarily been developed for use in laboratory-type situations. In a study by Burg and Michalak (2011), participants meditated with earphones on and holding a computer mouse. At the end each of 22 phases during the meditation session that lasted for approximately 18 minutes, a signal was played, and participants were instructed to indicate by left or right mouse click whether they had sensed their breath at the moment the signal played or whether they had been absentminded prior to the signal. Additionally, participants could signal any time when they had noticed mind wandering. A score was then calculated that consisted of the total number of phases during which the mind never wandered. When used with a sample of 42 under-graduate university students, these scores were moderately correlated with the *Acting with Awareness* and *Accepting without Judgment* subscales of the KIMS but not with *Observing* and *Describing*.

A slightly different approach to measuring breath awareness during meditation has been taken by Levinson et al. (2014). Here, participants were instructed to press a button each time they were aware of their breath. Every ninth time, they were asked to press another button in order for the accuracy in their counting to be evaluated. Scores of breath counting accuracy (as number of correctly completed nine-breath cycles divided by total number of cycles) were associated with the participants' scores on the MAAS and FFMQ, although the correlations were low ($r=.20$ and $r=.21$, respectively). Lim, Teng, Patanaik, Tandi, and Massar (2018) found that individuals who had a high breath counting score tended to exhibit more task readiness as measured by functional magnetic resonance imaging. Another study (Wong, Massar, Chee, & Lim, 2018) developed more detailed measures out of the breath counting technique that includes miscount and reset rate in addition to accuracy. While Wong et al. (2018) found breath counting to have good test-retest reliability, correlation with MAAS scores did not reach statistical significance.

The Meditation Breath Attention Scores (MBAS) is a further performance measure that has been explored with a fair amount of detail (Frewen, Evans, Maraj, Dozois, & Partridge, 2008). To calculate the MBAS score, experimenters ring a bell at five three-minute intervals when participants engage in a 15-minute meditation. While keeping their eyes closed, participants then provide a hand signal if their attention was focused on their breathing, which thus yields a score ranging from 0 to 5. Frewen, Rogers, Flodrowski, and Lanius (2015) later developed an online version of the MBAS where participants can respond by mouse click or by touching a smartphone or tablet screen.

Frewen et al. (2008) reported that MBAS scores were moderately correlated with MAAS and KIMS scores, except for the *Describing* subscale of the KIMS. In follow-up studies, the pattern of associations with other mindfulness measures was inconsistent. In one study (Frewen, Lundberg, MacKinley, & Wrath, 2011), there was mixed evidence for an association with the FFMQ, and later work also only reported a weak association with the *Acting with Awareness* subscale of the FFMQ (Frewen, Hargraves, DePierro, D'Andrea, & Flodorowski, 2016). The MBAS was also not consistently related to state mindfulness, sometimes not correlating with the TMS (Frewen et al., 2011) or correlating with only one of the TMS subscales (Frewen, Unholzer, Logie-Hagan, & MacKinley, 2014). Given the nonnormal distribution of the MBAS scores (Frewen et al., 2016), scores may need to be interpreted through sub-group comparisons instead. However, the MBAS still demonstrated adequate test-retest reliability and was found to be sensitive to change as a result of repeated meditation experience (Frewen et al., 2014).

In order to explore to what extent MBAS scores may be related to subjective experiences during meditation, Frewen et al. (2011) developed a questionnaire that Frewen et al. (2016) later referred to as the Meditation Experiences Questionnaire (MEQ). For that purpose, Frewen et al. (2011) had collected open-ended feedback from participants after meditation, which they then converted into 13 phrases summarising common phenomenological experiences that could be rated on a Likert scale. Although there was limited support in the initial study for the association between MEQ and MBAS scores (Frewen et al., 2011), other studies reported stronger correlations (Frewen et al., 2014, 2016).

Further conceptual development through mindfulness measurement

Edwin Boring is often remembered for the statement that intelligence is what an intelligence test measures (van der Maas, Kan, & Borsboom, 2014). Similarly, one can generalise the argument and claim that mindfulness is what a mindfulness instrument measures. As shown above, the development of psychometric instruments to assess mindfulness progressed iteratively, with definitions directing the content of mindfulness questionnaire items and empirical data from such self-report instruments such as item performance and questionnaire structure in turn leading to further refinements of definitions of the construct (Hanley, 2016). Part of this development is driven by the need to avoid conceptual redundancy, which can sometimes only be demonstrated through collection of empirical data. As with other subjective self-report instruments such as quality of life, happiness, and psychological well-being (Camfield & Skevington, 2008), the delineations between mindfulness and various related psychological constructs are not always without ambiguity. The Self-Compassion Scale (Neff, 2003), for instance, contains six subscales, one of which is labelled mindfulness. The strength of the association between mindfulness questionnaires and other related constructs is also often found to be moderately high or shows inconsistent patterns (e.g. Brown & Ryan, 2004; Hanley, 2016; Hanley & Garland, 2017; Hollis-Walker & Colismo, 2011; Kong, Wang,

& Zhao, 2014). If correlation coefficients between mindfulness scales and other measures are similarly high as correlations among mindfulness subscales themselves, this can be interpreted as evidence that conceptual clarity has not been achieved (Campbell & Fiske, 1959). Some of this conceptual overlap may be related to the fact that measures may not distinguish clearly enough between mindfulness as an explicit outcome as opposed to an aspect or quality in the expression of another concept (such as in the case of self-compassion). Similar arguments have been made about religiousness and quality of life, where correlations with measures of psychological well-being may be artificially inflated due to items being worded as religious coping (Krägeloh, Billington, Henning, & Chai, 2015).

A fair amount of discussion has taken place about whether mindfulness is best to be conceptualised as a unidimensional construct or multidimensional, and in the latter case, what the different dimensions of a multidimensional construct would be. Adequate psychometric properties are easier to achieve in a unidimensional model such as the MAAS, although there may be the risk that the concept loses its content coverage. The inconsistent and sometimes contradictory findings regarding the *Describing* and *Observing* subscales of the FFMQ (Baer et al., 2006) have sometimes resulted on proposals to drop these facets, such as in the Three-Facet Mindfulness Scale (Truijens, Nyklíček, van Son, & Pop, 2016). Since the comprehensive factor analysis work by Baer et al. (2006), there have also been continued efforts to conduct factor analyses with items from several other instruments (e.g. Siegling & Petrides, 2016). Perhaps further strategies may be needed to avoid applying similar approaches repeatedly and thus potentially reacting to error variation due to sample or methodological detail rather than revealing any stable theoretical structure. Other possible avenues for future research include exploring the extent to which aspects of mindfulness vary with specific types of mindfulness practices (e.g. Hildebrandt, McCall, & Singer, 2017). Other research has also explored different types of mindfulness profiles rather than assuming that an overall high level of mindfulness generalises to all specific facets (Sahdra et al., 2017).

Summary and conclusion

Self-report instruments remain the most common way to assess levels of mindfulness, both as a state as well as a trait. The variety of definitions of mindfulness is matched by the variety of mindfulness self-report instruments that are available. While this could be interpreted as an indication of theoretical confusion, it could also be seen as a sign of maturity of the field. Having a variety of mindfulness questionnaires available enables researchers to concentrate on different aspects and nuances of mindfulness, such as focusing on present-moment awareness or aspects that are taught in some specific MBIs.

Since the early 2000s, we have seen the arrival of a larger variety of approaches to testing psychometric properties. Many of these are able to provide detailed information about item-level performance or the informational value of including specific items. Some early attempts have been made with random forests methods (Sauer, Lemke, Zinn, Buettner, & Kohls, 2015) or facet benchmarking (Siegling,

Furnham, & Petrides, 2018), although it is more common to find the application of techniques such as IRT or Rasch analysis. In Rasch analysis, the trend of reporting tables for conversion of ordinal-level data to interval-level data has also been a very recent development that is yet to be taken on more widely. The challenge here is how to communicate about the use of such scale conversions and how best to assist researchers who are unfamiliar with such approaches.

A major disadvantage of self-report measures of mindfulness remains the issue of subjective standards that may shift (and to some extent are even expected to shift) with mindfulness practice. The issue of response shift has started to be studied in the literature, but remains to be explored in more detail. With the continued development of techniques and approaches to assessing mindfulness, our understanding of the construct will also continue to evolve. Apart from the work on response shift, there is very little mention in the mindfulness measurement literature regarding the presence of other types of response bias, such as when participants may be inclined to want to portray their attitudes or behaviour more positively or more in line with the expectations associated with a mindfulness programme. Baer (2011) argued that this possibility seems unlikely as participants are often found to readily disclose when they may have engaged in less than the recommended home practice time for mindfulness exercises, and published MBI studies generally contain a range of responses including participants who report little or no benefit from such interventions. However, future research may investigate the presence of any response biases more explicitly.

Systematic conceptual work is necessary to advance our understanding of mindfulness and its subtle aspects. The continued development of new questionnaires should not be regarded as a threat to conceptual coherence but as a way to explore contextual factors in mindfulness and generalisability of mindfulness across different contexts and populations. The field has only recently started to explore more formally the distinction between mindfulness as state versus trait (Medvedev et al., 2018). More recently, a number of performance or behavioural measures have been proposed that involve recording the awareness of breath and thus may be less affected by response biases. As with other objective indicators such as neurological measures and other biomarkers, their relationship with self-report measures appear complex, and more work is required to establish the reliability and validity of such approaches.

References

Adam, F., Heeren, A., Day, J., & de Sutter, P. (2015). Development of the sexual Five-Facet Mindfulness Questionnaire (FFMQ-S): validation among a community sample of French-speaking women. *Journal of Sex Research*, 52(6), 617–626. doi:10.1080/00224499.2014.894490

Aguado, J., Luciano, J. V., Cebolla, A., Serrano-Blanco, A., Soler, J., & García-Campayo, J. (2015). Bifactor analysis and construct validity of the five facet mindfulness questionnaire (FFMQ) in non-clinical Spanish samples. *Frontiers in Psychology*, 6, 404. doi:10.3389/fpsyg.2015.00404

Baas, M., Nevicka, B., & Ten Velden, F. S. (2014). Specific mindfulness skills differentially predict creative performance. *Personality and Social Psychology Bulletin*, 40(9), 1092–1106. doi:10.1177/0146167214535813

Baer, R. A., Smith, G. T., & Allen, K. B. (2004). Assessment of mindfulness by self-report – the Kentucky Inventory of Mindfulness Skills. *Assessment*, 11(3), 191–206. doi:10.1177/1073191104268029

Baer, R. A., Smith, G. T., Hopkins, J., Krietemeyer, J., & Toney, L. (2006). Using self-report assessment methods to explore facets of mindfulness. *Assessment*, 13(1), 27–45. doi:10.1177/1073191105283504

Baer, R. A., Smith, G. T., Lykins, E., Button, D., Krietemeyer, J., Sauer, S., …, & Williams, J. M. G. (2008). Construct validity of the Five Facet Mindfulness Questionnaire in meditating and nonmeditating samples. *Assessment*, 15(3), 329–342. doi:10.1177/1073191107313003

Baer, R. A. (2011). Measuring mindfulness. *Contemporary Buddhism*, 12(1), 241–261. doi:10.1080/14639947.2011.564842

Baer, R. A., Samuel, D. B., & Lykins, E. L. B. (2011). Differential item functioning on the Five Facet Mindfulness Questionnaire is minimal in demographically matched meditators and nonmeditators. *Assessment*, 18(1), 3–10. doi:10.1177/1073191110392498

Barnes, S. M., & Lynn, S. J. (2010). Mindfulness skills and depressive symptoms: a longitudinal study. *Imagination, Cognition and Personality*, 30(1), 77–91. doi:10.2190/IC.30.1.e

Baroni, D., Nerini, A., Matera, C., & Stefanile, C. (2018). Mindfulness and emotional distress: the mediating role of psychological well-being. *Current Psychology*. Online First. doi:10.1007/s12144-016-9524-1

Belzer, F., Schmidt, S., Lucius-Hoene, G., Schneider, J. F., Orellana-Rios, C. L., & Sauer, S. (2013). Challenging the construct validity of mindfulness assessment: a cognitive interview study of the Freiburg Mindfulness Inventory. *Mindfulness*, 4(1), 33–44. doi:10.1007/s12671-012-0165-7

Bergomi, C., Tschacher, W., & Kupper, Z. (2014). Konstruktion und erste Validierung eines Fragebogens zur umfassenden Erfassung von Achtsamkeit [Construction and initial validation of a questionnaire for the comprehensive investigation of mindfulness]. *Diagnostica*, 60(3), 111–125. doi:10.1026/0012–1924/a000109

Bergomi, C., Tschacher, W., & Kupper, Z. (2015). Meditation practice and self-reported mindfulness: a cross-sectional investigation of meditators and non-meditators using the Comprehensive Inventory of Mindfulness Experiences (CHIME). *Mindfulness*, 6(6), 1411–1421. doi:10.1007/s12671-015-0415-6

Bishop, S. R., Lau, M., Shapiro, S., Carlson, L., Anderson, N. D., Carmody, J., … Devins, G. (2004). Mindfulness: a proposed operational definition. *Clinical Psychology: Science and Practice*, 11(3), 230–241. doi:10.1093/clipsy/bph077

Black, D. S., Sussman, S., Johnson, C. A., & Milam, J. (2012). Psychometric assessment of the Mindful Attention Awareness Scale (MAAS) among Chinese adolescents. *Assessment*, 19(1), 42–52. doi:10.1177/1073191111415365

Blanke, E. S., & Brose, A. (2017). Mindfulness in daily life: a multidimensional approach. *Mindfulness*, 8(3), 737–750. doi:10.1007/s12671-016-0651-4 [Erratum. Blanke, E. S., & Brose (2017). *Mindfulness*, 8(6), 1727–1731. doi:10.1007/s12671-017-0769-z]

Bohlmeijer, E., ten Klooster, P. M., Fledderus, M., Veehof, M., & Baer, R. (2011). Psychometric properties of the Five Facet Mindfulness Questionnaire in depressed adults and development of a short form. *Assessment*, 18(3), 308–320. doi:10.1177/1073191111408231

Bravo, A. J., Pearson, M. R., Wilson, A. D., & Witkiewitz, K. (2018). When traits match states: examining the associations between self-report trait and state mindfulness following a state mindfulness induction. *Mindfulness*, 9(1), 199–211. doi:10.1007/s12671-017-0763-5

Brown, D. B., Bravo, A. J., Roos, C. R., & Pearson, M. R. (2015). Five facets of mindfulness and psychological health: evaluating a psychological model of the mechanisms of mindfulness. *Mindfulness*, 6(5), 1021–1032. doi:10.1007/s12671-014-0349-4

Brown, K. W., & Ryan, R. M. (2003). The benefits of being present: mindfulness and its role in psychological well-being. *Journal of Personality and Social Psychology*, 84(4), 822–848. doi:10.1037/0022-3514.8doi:4.4.822

Brown, K. W., & Ryan, R. M. (2004). Perils and promise in defining and measuring mindfulness: observations from experience. *Clinical Psychology: Science and Practice*, 11(3), 242–248. doi:10.1093/clipsy/bph078

Brown, K. W., West, A. M., Loverich, T. M., & Biegel, G. M. (2011). Assessing adolescent mindfulness: validation of an adapted Mindful Awareness Scale in adolescent normative and psychiatric populations. *Psychological Assessment*, 23(4), 1023–1033. doi:10.1037/a0021338

Brown, K. W., Ryan, R. M., Loverich, T. M., Biegel, G. M., & West, A. M. (2011). Out of the armchair and into the streets: measuring mindfulness advanced knowledge and improves interventions: reply to Grossman (2011). *Psychological Assessment*, 23(4), 1041–1046. doi:10.1037/a0025781

Buchheld, N., Grossman, P., & Walach, H. (2001). Measuring mindfulness in insight meditation (Vipassana) and meditation-based psychotherapy: The development of the Freiburg Mindfulness Inventory (FMI). *Journal for Meditation and Meditation Research*, 1, 11–34.

Burg, J. M., & Michalak, J. (2011). The healthy quality of mindful breathing: associations with rumination and depression. *Cognitive Therapy and Research*, 35(2), 179–185. doi:10.1007/s10608-010-9343-x

Camfield, L., & Skevington, S. M. (2008). On subjective well-being and quality of life. *Journal of Health Psychology*, 13(6), 764–775. doi:10.1177/1359105308093860

Campbell, D. T., & Fiske, D. W. (1959). Convergent and discriminant validation by the multitrait-multimethod matrix. *Psychological Bulletin*, 56(2), 81–105. doi:10.1037/h0046016

Campos, D., Cebolla, A., Quero, S., Bretón-López, J., Botella, C., Soler, J., …, & Baños, R. M. (2016). Meditation and happiness: mindfulness and self-compassion may mediate the meditation-happiness relationship. *Personality and Individual Differences*, 93, 80–85. doi:10.1016/j.paid.2015. 08. 040

Cardaciotto, L., Herbert, J. D., Forman, E. M., Moitra, E., & Farrow, V. (2008). The assessment of present-moment awareness and acceptance: the Philadelphia Mindfulness Scale. *Assessment*, 15(2), 204–223. doi:10.1177/1073191107311467

Carmody, J., & Baer, R. A. (2008). Relationship between mindfulness practice and levels of mindfulness, medical and psychological symptoms and well-being in a mindfulness-based stress reduction program. *Journal of Behavioral Medicine*, 31(1), 23–33. doi:10.1007/s10865-007-9130-7

Carmody, J., Reed, G., Kristeller, J., & Merriam, P. (2008). Mindfulness, spirituality, and health-related symptoms. *Journal of Psychosomatic Research*, 64(4), 393–403. doi:10.1016/j.jpsychores.2007.06.doi:015

Catak, P. D. (2012). The Turkish version of Mindful Attention Awareness Scale: preliminary findings. *Mindfulness*, 3(1), 1–9. doi:10.1007/s12671-011-0072-3

Cavanagh, K., Churchard, A., O'Hanlon, P., Mundy, T., Votolato, P., Jones, G., …, & Strauss, C. (2018). A randomised controlled trial of a brief online mindfulness-based intervention in a non-clinical population: replication and extension. *Mindfulness*. Online First. doi:10.1007/s12671-017-0856-1

Chen, Z., Hood, R. W., Yang, L., & Watson, P. J. (2011). Mystical experience among Tibetan Buddhists: the common core thesis revisited. *Journal for the Scientific Study of Religion*, 50(2), 328–338. doi:10.1111/j.1468-5906.2011.01570.x

Chiesa, A. (2013). The difficulty of defining mindfulness: current thought and critical issues. *Mindfulness*, 4(3), 255–268. doi:10.1007/s12671-012-0123-4

Chiesi, F., Donati, M. A., Panno, A., Giacomantonio, M., & Primi, C. (2017). What about the different shortened versions of the Mindful Attention Awareness Scale? *Psychological Reports*, 120(5), 966–990. doi:10.1177/0033294117711132

Christopher, M. S., Charoensuk, S., Gilbert, B. D., Neary, T. J., & Pearce, K. L. (2009a). Mindfulness in Thailand and the United States: a case of apples versus oranges? *Journal of Clinical Psychology*, 65(6), 590–612. doi:10.1002/jclp.20580

Christopher, M. S., Christopher, V., & Charoensuk, S. (2009b). Assessing "Western" mindfulness among Thai Theravāda Buddhist monks. *Mental Health, Religion & Culture*, 12(3), 303–314. doi:10.1080/13674670802651487

Christopher, M. S., Neuser, N. J., Michael, P. G., & Baitmangalkar, A. (2012). Exploring the psychometric properties of the Five Facet Mindfulness Questionnaire. *Mindfulness*, 3(2), 124–131. doi:10.1007/s12671-011-0086-x

Coffey, K. A., & Hartman, M. (2008). Mechanisms of action in the inverse relationship between mindfulness and psychological distress. *Complementary Health Practice Review*, 13(2), 79–91. doi:10.1177/1533210108316307

Cordon, S. L., & Finney, S. J. (2008). Measurement invariance of the Mindful Attention Awareness Scale across adult attachment style. *Measurement and Evaluation in Counseling and Development*, 40(4), 228–245. doi:10.1080/07481756.2008.11909817

Curtiss, J., & Klemanski, D. H. (2014). Factor analysis of the Five Facet Mindfulness Questionnaire in a heterogeneous clinical sample. *Journal of Psychopathology and Behavioral Assessment*, 36(4), 683–694. doi:10.1007/s10862-014-9429-y

Davis, K. M., Lau, M. A., & Cairns, D. R. (2009). Development and preliminary validation of a trait version of the Toronto Mindfulness Scale. *Journal of Cognitive Psychotherapy*, 23(3), 185–197. doi:10.1891/0889-839doi:1.23.3.185

de Bruin, E. I., Topper, M., Muskens, J. G. A. M., Bögels, S. M., & Kamphuis, J. H. (2012). Psychometric properties of the Five Facets Mindfulness Questionnaire (FFMQ) in a meditating and a non-meditating sample. *Assessment*, 19(2), 187–197. doi:10.1177/1073191112446654

de Bruin, E. I., Zijlstra, B. J., Geurtzen, N., van Zundert, R. M., van de Weijer-Bergsma, E., Hartman, E. E., …, & Bögels, S. M. (2014). Mindful parenting assessed further: Psychometric properties of the Dutch version of the Interpersonal Mindfulness in Parenting Scale (IM-P). *Mindfulness*, 5(2), 200–212. doi:10.1007/s12671-12012-0168-0164

Deng, Y.-Q., Liu, X.-H., Rodriguez, M. A., & Xia, C.-Y. (2011). The Five Facet Questionnaire: psychometric properties of the Chinese version. *Mindfulness*, 2(2), 123–128. doi:10.1007/s12671-011-0050-9

Deng, Y.-Q., Li, S., Tang, Y.-Y., Zhu, L.-H., Ryan, R., & Brown, K. (2012). Psychometric properties of the Chinese translation of the Mindful Attention Awareness Scale (MAAS). *Mindfulness*, 3(1), 10–14. doi:10.1007/s12671-011-0074-1

Duncan, L. G. (2007). *Assessment of mindful parenting among parents of early adolescents: Development and validation of the Interpersonal Mindfulness in Parenting scale.* Unpublished dissertation. The Pennsylvania State University, USA.

Duncan, L. G., Coatsworth, J. D., & Greenberg, M. T. (2009). A model of mindful parenting: Implications for parent-child relationships and prevention research. *Clinical Child and Family Psychology Review*, 12(3), 255–270. doi:10.1007/s10567-10009-0046-0043

Eisenlohr-Moul, T. A., Walsh, E. C., Charnigo, R. J., Lynam, D. R., & Baer, R. A. (2012). The "what" and the "how" of dispositional mindfulness: using interactions among subscales of the Five-Facet Mindfulness Questionnaire to understand its relation to substance use. *Assessment*, 19(3), 276–286. doi:10.1177/1073191112446658

Eisenlohr-Moul, T. A., Peters, J. R., Chamberlain, K. D., & Rodriguez, M. A. (2016). Weekly fluctuations in nonjudging predict borderline personality disorder feature expression in women. *Journal of Psychopathology and Behavioral Assessment*, 38(1), 149–157. doi:10.1007/s10862-015-9505-y

Erisman, S. M., & Roemer, L. (2012). A preliminary investigation of the process of mindfulness. *Mindfulness*, 3(1), 30–43. doi:10.1007/s12671-011-0078-x

Eyles, C., Leydon, G. M., Hoffman, C. J., Copson, E. R., Prescott, P., Chorozoglou, M., & Lewith, G. (2015). Mindfulness for the self-management of fatigue, anxiety, and depression in women with metastatic breast cancer: a mixed methods feasibility study. *Integrative Cancer Therapies*, 14(1), 42–56. doi:10.1177/1534735414546567

Falcone, G., & Jerram, M. (2018). Brain activity in mindfulness depends on experience: a meta-analysis of fMRI studies. *Mindfulness*. Online First. doi:10.1007/s12671-12018-0884–0885

Falkenström, F. (2010). Studying mindfulness in experiences meditators: a quasi-experimental approach. *Personality and Individual Differences*, 48, 305–310. doi:10.1016/j.paid.2009.10.doi:022

Feldman, G., Hayes, A., Kumar, S., Greeson, J., & Laurenceau, J.-P. (2007). Mindfulness and emotion regulation: the development and initial validation of the Cognitive and Affective Mindfulness Scale-Revised (CAMS-R). *Journal of Psychopathology and Behavioral Assessment*, 29(3), 177–190. doi:10.1007/s10862-006-9035-8

Finkelstein, J. A., Quaranto, B. R., & Schwartz, C. E. (2014). Threats to the internal validity of spinal surgery outcome assessment: recalibration response shift or implicit theories of change? *Applied Research in Quality of Life*, 9(2), 215–232. doi:10.1007/s11482-013-9221-2

Fisak, B., & von Lehe, A. C. (2012). The relation between the five facets of mindfulness and worry in a non-clinical sample. *Mindfulness*, 3(1), 15–21. doi:10.1007/s12671-011-0075-0

Framson, C., Kristal, A. R., Schenk, J. M., Littman, A. J., Zeliadt, S., & Benitez, D. (2009). Development and validation of the Mindfulness or mindlessness? A modified version of the Mindful Eating Questionnaire. *Journal of the American Dietetic Association*, 109(8), 1439–1444. doi:10.1016/j.jada.2009.05.doi:006

Frank, J. L., Jennings, P. A., & Greenberg, M. T. (2016). Validation of the Mindfulness in Teaching Scale. *Mindfulness*, 7(1), 155–163. doi:10.1007/s12671-12015-0461-0

Fresco, D. M., Moore, M. T., van Dulmen, M. H. M., Segal, Z. V., Ma, S. H., Teasdale, J. D., & Williams, J. M. G. (2007). Initial psychometric properties of the Experiences Questionnaire: validation of a self-report measure of decentering. *Behavior Therapy*, 38(3), 234–246. doi:10.1016/j.beth.2006.08.003

Frewen, P. A., Evans, E. M., Maraj, N., Dozois, D. J. A., & Partridge, K. (2008). Letting go: mindfulness and negative automatic thinking. *Cognitive Therapy and Research*, 32(6), 758–774. doi:10.1007/s10608-007-9142-1

Frewen, P., Lundberg, E., MacKinley, J., & Wrath, A. (2011). Assessment of response to mindfulness meditation: Meditation Breath Attention Scores in association with subjective measures of state and trait mindfulness and difficulty letting go of depressive cognition. *Mindfulness*, 2(4), 254–269. doi:10.1007/s12671-011-0069-7

Frewen, P. A., Unholzer, F., Logie-Hagan, K. R.-J., & MacKinley, J. D. (2014). Meditation Breath Attention Scores (MBAS): test-retest reliability and sensitivity to repeated practice. *Mindfulness*, 5(2), 161–169. doi:10.1007/s12671-012-0161-y

Frewen, P., Rogers, N., Flodrowski, L., & Lanius, R. (2015). Mindfulness and Metta-Based Trauma Therapy (MMTT): initial development and proof-of-concept of an internet resource. *Mindfulness*, 6(6), 1322–1334. doi:10.1007/s12671-015-0402-y

Frewen, P. A., Hargraves, H., DePierro, J., D'Andrea, W., & Flodrowski, L. (2016). Meditation Breath Attention Scores (MBAS): development and investigation of an internet-based assessment of focused attention during meditation practice. *Psychological Assessment*, 28(7), 830–840. doi:10.1037/pas0000283

Geisler, F. C. M., Bechtoldt, M. N., Oberländer, N., & Schacht-Jablonowsky, M. (2018). The benefits of a mindfulness exercise in a performance situation. *Psychological Reports*. Online First. doi:10.1177/0033294117740135

Goh, H. E., Marais, I., & Ireland, M. J. (2017). A Rasch model analysis of the Mindful Attention Awareness Scale. *Assessment*, 24(3), 387–398. doi:10.1177/1073191115607043

Goldberg, S. B., Wielgosz, J., Dahl, C., Schuyler, B., MacCoon, D. S., Rosenkranz, M., …, & Davidson, R. J. (2016). Does the Five Facet Mindfulness Questionnaire measure what we think it does? Construct validity evidence from an active controlled randomized clinical trial. *Psychological Assessment*, 28(8), 1009–1014. doi:10.1037/pas0000233

Goldberg, S. B., Tucker, R. P., Greene, P. A., Simpson, T. L., Hoyt, W. T., Kearney, D. J., & Davidson, R. J. (2018). What can we learn from randomized clinical trials about the construct validity of self-report measures of mindfulness? A meta-analysis. *Mindfulness*. Online First. doi:10.1007/s12671-018-1032-7

Goodman, M. S., Madni, L. A., & Semple, R. J. (2017). Measuring mindfulness in youth: review of current assessments, challenges, and future directions. *Mindfulness*. Online First. doi:10.1007/s12671-017-0719-9

Gotink, R. A., Hermans, K. S. F. M., Geschwind, N., De Nooij, R., De Groot, W. T., & Speckens, A. E. M. (2016). Mindfulness and mood stimulate each other in an upward spiral: a mindful walking intervention using experience sampling. *Mindfulness*, 7(5), 1114–1122. doi:10.1007/s12671-12016-0550-0558

Greco, L. A., Baer, R. A., & Smith, G. T. (2011). Assessing mindfulness in children and adolescents: development and validation of the Child and Adolescent Mindfulness Measure (CAMM). *Psychological Assessment*, 23(3), 606–614. doi:10.1037/a0022819

Grossman, P. (2011). Defining mindfulness by how poorly I think I pay attention during everyday awareness and other intractable problems for psychology's (re)invention of mindfulness: comment on Brown et al. (2011). *Psychological Assessment*, 23(4), 1034–1040. doi:10.1037/a0022713

Gu, J., Strauss, C., Bond, R., & Cavanagh, K. (2015). How do mindfulness-based cognitive therapy and mindfulness-based stress reduction improve mental health and wellbeing? A systematic review and meta-analysis of mediation studies. *Clinical Psychological Review*, 37, 1–12. doi:10.1016/j.cpr.2015.01.doi:006

Gu, J., Strauss, C., Bond, R., Crane, C., Barnhofer, T., Karl, A., Cavanagh, K., & Kuyken, W. (2016). Examining the factor structure of the 39-item and 15-item versions of the Five Facet Mindfulness Questionnaire before and after Mindfulness-Based Cognitive Therapy for people with recurrent depression. *Psychological Assessment*, 28(7), 791–802. doi:10.1037/pas0000263

Hakan, R. L., Neal, J. M., & Lothes, J. (2017). Social judgments as a measure of right mindfulness. *Sage Open*. Online First. doi:10.1177/2158244016686811

Hanley, A. W. (2016). The mindful personality: associations between dispositional mindfulness and the Five Factor Model of personality. *Personality and Individual Differences*, 91, 154–158. doi:10.1016/j.paid.201doi:5.11.054

Hanley, A. W., & Garland, E. L. (2017). Clarity of mind: structural equation modeling of associations between dispositional mindfulness, self-concept clarity and psychological well-being. *Personality and Individual Differences*, 106, 334–339. doi:10.1016/j.paid.2016.10.028

Harrison, N. R., & Clark, D. P. A. (2016). The observing facet of trait mindfulness predicts frequency of aesthetic experiences evoked by the arts. *Mindfulness*, 7(4), 971–978. doi:10.1007/s12671-016-0536-6

Hayes, A. M. & Feldman, G. (2004). Clarifying the construct of mindfulness in the context of emotion regulation and the process of change in therapy. *Clinical Psychology: Science and Practice*, 11(3), 255–262. doi:10.1093/clipsy.bph080

Hayes, S. C., Strosahl, K. D., & Wilson, K. G. (2011). *Acceptance and Commitment Therapy: the process and practice of mindful change*. New York, USA: Guilford Press.

Heniford, B. T., Walters, A. L., Lincourt, A. E., Novitsky, Y. W., Hope, W. W., & Ker-
cher, K. W. (2008). Comparison of generic versus specific quality-of-life scales for mesh
hernia repairs. *Journal of the American College of Surgeons*, 206(4), 638–644. doi:10.1016/j.
jamcollsurg.2007.11.doi:025

Hildebrandt, L. K., McCall, C., & Singer, T. (2017). Differential effects of attention-,
compassion-, and socio-cognitively based mental practices on self-reports of mindfulness
and compassion. *Mindfulness*, 8(6), 1488–1512. doi:10.1007/s12671-017-0716-z

Höfling, V., Moosbrugger, H., Schermelleh-Engel, K., & Heidenreich, T. (2011a). Mindfulness
or mindlessness? A modified version of the Mindful Attention and Awareness Scale (MAAS).
European Journal of Psychological Assessment, 27(1), 59–64. doi:10.1027/1015-5759/a000045

Höfling, V., Ströhle, G., Michalak, J., & Heidenreich, T. (2011b). A short version of the
Kentucky Inventory of Mindfulness Skills. *Journal of Clinical Psychology*, 67(6), 639–645.
doi:10.1002/jclp.20778

Hollis-Walker, L., & Colosimo, K. (2011). Mindfulness, self-compassion, and happiness in
non-meditators: a theoretical and empirical examination. *Personality and Individual Differences*, 50(2), 222–227. doi:10.1016/j.paid.2010.09.0doi:33

Hulbert-Williams, L., Nicholls, W., Joy, J., & Hulbert-Williams, N. (2014). Initial validation
of the Mindful Eating Scale. *Mindfulness*, 5(6), 719–729. doi:10.1007/s12671-013-0227-5

Ietsugu, T., Crane, C., Hackmann, A., Brennan, K., Gross, M., Crane, R. S., ..., & Barnhofer, T. (2015). Gradually getting better: trajectories of change in rumination and
anxious worry in Mindfulness-Based Cognitive Therapy for prevention of relapse to
recurrent depression. *Mindfulness*, 6(5), 1088–1094. doi:10.1007/s12671-014-0358-3

Im, S. (2017). What is measured by self-report measures of mindfulness?: conceptual and measurement issues. In A. Masuda & W. T. O'Donohue (Eds.). *Handbook of Zen, mindfulness, and
behavioral health*, pp. 215–235. New York, USA: Springer. doi:10.1007/978-3-319-54595-0_17

Jensen, C. G., Niclasen, J., Vangkilde, S. A., Petersen, A., & Hasselbalch, S. G. (2016).
General inattentiveness is a long-term reliable trait independently predictive of psychological health: Danish validation studies of the Mindful Attention Awareness Scale. *Psychological Assessment*, 28(5), e70–87. doi:10.1037/pas0000196

Josefsson, T., Larsman, P., Broberg, A. G., & Lundh, L.-G. (2011). Self-reported mindfulness mediates the relation between meditation experience and psychological well-
being. *Mindfulness*, 2(1), 49–58. doi:10.1007/s12671-011-0042-9

Keng, S.-L., Smoski, M. J., Robins, C. J., Ekblad, A. G., & Brantley, J. G. (2012).
Mechanisms of change in Mindfulness-Based Stress Reduction: self-compassion and
mindfulness as mediators of intervention outcomes. *Journal of Cognitive Psychotherapy*, 26
(3), 270–280. doi:10.1891/0889-8391.26doi:3.270

Kiken, L. G., Garland, E. L., Bluth, K., Palsson, O. S., & Gaylord, S. A. (2015). From a state to a
trait: trajectories of state mindfulness in meditation during intervention predict changes in trait
mindfulness. *Personality and Individual Differences*, 81, 41–46. doi:10.1016/j.paid.2014.12.0doi:44

Kim, E., Krägeloh, C. U., Medvedev, O. N., Duncan, L. G., & Singh, N. N. (2018).
Interpersonal Mindfulness in Parenting scale: testing the psychometric properties of a
Korean version. *Mindfulness*. Online First. doi:10.1007/s12671-12018-0993-0991

Kimmes, J. G., Jaurequi, M. E., May, R. W., Srivastava, S., & Fincham, F. D. (2017).
Mindfulness in the context of romantic relationships: initial development and validation
of the Relationship Mindfulness Measure. *Journal of Marital and Family Therapy*. Online
First. doi:10.1111/jmft.12296

Klainin-Yobas, P., Ramirez, D., Fernandez, Z., Sarmiento, J., Thanoi, W., Ignacio, J., &
Lau, Y. (2016). Examining the predicting effect of mindfulness on psychological well-
being among undergraduate students: a structural equation modelling approach. *Personality
and Individual Differences*, 91, 63–68. doi:10.1016/j.paid.2015.11.0doi:34

Klein, R., Dubois, S., Gibbons, C., Ozen, L. J., Marshall, S., Cullen, N., & Bédard, M. (2015). The Toronto and Philadelphia Mindfulness Scales: associations with satisfaction with life and health-related symptoms. *International Journal of Psychology & Psychological Therapy*, 15(1), 133–142.

Kong, F., Wang, X., & Zhao, J. (2014). Dispositional mindfulness and life satisfaction: the role of core self-evaluation. *Personality and Individual Differences*, 56, 165–169. doi:10.1016/j.paid.2013.09.0doi:02

Krägeloh, C. U., Billington, D. R., Henning, M. A., & Chai, P. P. M. (2015). Spiritual quality of life and spiritual coping: Evidence for a two-factor structure of the WHOQOL Spirituality, Religiousness, and Personal Beliefs module. *Health and Quality of Life Outcomes*, 13:26. doi:10.1186/s12955-015-0212-x

Krägeloh, C. U., Bergomi, C., Siegert, R. J., & Medvedev, O. N. (2018). Response shift after a mindfulness-based intervention: Measurement invariance testing of the Comprehensive Inventory of Mindfulness Experiences. *Mindfulness*, 9(1), 212–220. doi:10.1007/s12671-017-0764-4

Kuyken, W., Watkins, E., Holden, E., White, K., Taylor, R. S., Byford, S., ..., & Dalgleish, T. (2010). How does mindfulness-based cognitive therapy work? *Behaviour Research and Therapy*, 48(11), 1105–1112. doi:10.1016/j.brat.2010.08.0doi:03

Lacaille, J., Sadikaj, G., Nishioka, M., Flanders, J., & Knäuper, B. (2015). Measuring mindful responding in daily life: validation of the Daily Mindful Responding Scale (DMRS). *Mindfulness*, 6(6), 1422–1436. doi:10.1007/s12671-015-0416-5

Lau, M. A., Bishop, S. R., Segal, Z. V., Buis, T., Anderson, N. D., Carlson, L., ..., & Carmody, J. (2006). The Toronto Mindfulness Scale: development and validation. *Journal of Clinical Psychology*, 62(12), 1445–1467. doi:10.1002/jclp.20326

Lawlor, M. S., Schonert-Reichl, Gadermann, A. M., & Zumbo, B. D. (2014). A validation study of the Mindful Attention Awareness Scale adapted for children. *Mindfulness*, 5(6), 730–741. doi:10.1007/s12671-12013-0228-0224

Levinson, D. B., Stoll, E., L., Kindy, S. D., Merry, H. L., & Davidson, R. J. (2014). A mind you can count on: validating breath counting as a behavioral measure of mindfulness. *Frontiers in Psychology*, 5, 1202. doi:10.3389/fpsyg.2014.01202

Leung, Y. Y., Png, M. E., Conaghan, P., & Tennant, A. (2017). A systematic literature review on the application of Rasch analysis in musculoskeletal disease: A special interest group report of OMERACT 11. *Journal of Rheumatology*, 41(1), 159–164. doi:10.3899/jrheum.130814

Li, M. J., Black, D. S., & Garland, E. L. (2016). The Applied Mindfulness Process Scale (AMPS): a process measure for evaluating mindfulness-based interventions. *Personality and Individual Differences*, 93, 6–15. doi:10.1016/j.paid.2015doi:10.027

Lilja, J. L., Lundh, L.-G., Josefsson, T., & Falkenström, F. (2013). Observing as an essential facet of mindfulness: a comparison of FFMQ patterns in meditating and non-meditating individuals. *Mindfulness*, 4(3), 203–212. doi:10.1007/s12671-012-0111-8

Lim, J., Teng, J., Patanaik, A., Tandi, J., & Massar, S. A. A. (2018). Dynamic functional connectivity markers of objective trait mindfulness. *NeuroImage*, 176, 193–202. doi:10.1016/j.neuroimage.2018.doi:04.056

Linehan, M. M. (1993a). *Cognitive-behavioural treatment of borderline personality disorder*. New York, USA: Guilford Press.

Little, T. D., Cunningham, W. A., & Shahar, G. (2002). To parcel or not to parcel: exploring the question, weighing the merits. *Structural Equation Modeling*, 9(2), 151–173. doi:10.1207/S15328007SEM0902_1

Lo, H. H. M., Yeung, J. W. K., Duncan, L. G., Ma, Y., Siu, A. F. Y. S., Chan, S. K. C., ..., & Ng, S. M. (2018). Validation of the Interpersonal Mindfulness in Parenting scale in Hong Kong Chinese. *Mindfulness*. Online First. doi:10.1007/s12671-12017-0879-0877

Lundgren-Nilsson, Å., Jonsdottir, I. H., Ahlborg, G., & Tennant, A. (2013). Construct validity of the psychological general well being index (PGWBI) in a sample of patients undergoing treatment for stress-related exhaustion: a Rasch analysis. *Health and Quality of Life Outcomes*, 11, 2. doi:10.1186/1477-7525-11-2

Lynch, J., & Wilson, C. E. (2017). Exploring the impact of choral singing on mindfulness. *Psychology of Music*. Online First. doi:10.1177/0305735617729452

Mahmood, L., Hopthrow, T., & de Moura, G. R. (2016). A moment of mindfulness: computer-mediated mindfulness practice increases state mindfulness. *PLoS ONE*, 11(4), e0153923. doi:10.1371/journal.pone.0153923

Mankus, A. M., Aldao, A., Kerns, C., Mayville, E. W., & Mennin, D. S. (2013). Mindfulness and heart rate variability in individuals with high and low generalized anxiety symptoms. *Behaviour Research and Therapy*, 51(7), 386–391. doi:10.1016/j.brat.2013.doi:03.005

Mansolf, M., & Reise, S. P. (2017). When and why the second-order and bifactor models are distinguishable. *Intelligence*, 61, 120–129.

Martin, R., Prichard, I., Hutchinson, A. D., & Wilson, C. (2013). The role of body awareness and mindfulness in the relationship between exercise and eating behavior. *Journal of Sport & Exercise Psychology*, 35(6), 655–660. doi:10.1123/jsep.35.6.6doi:55

McBee, L. (2009). Mindfulness-based elder care: communicating mindfulness to frail elders and their caregivers. In F. Didonna (Ed.). *Clinical handbook of mindfulness*, pp. 431–445. New York, USA: Springer.

McElfatrick, S., Carson, J., Annett, J., Cooper, C., Holloway, F., & Kuipers, E. (2000). Assessing coping skills in mental health nurses: is an occupation specific measure better than a generic coping skills scale? *Personality and Individual Differences*, 28, 965–976. doi:10.1016/S0191-8869(99)00152-X

Medvedev, O. N., Siegert, R. J., Kersten, P., & Krägeloh, C. U. (2016a). Rasch analysis of the Kentucky Inventory of Mindfulness Skills. *Mindfulness*, 7(2), 466–478. doi:10.1007/s12671-015-0475-7

Medvedev, O. N., Siegert, R. J., Feng, X. J., Billington, D. R., Jang, J. Y., & Krägeloh, C. U. (2016b). Measuring trait mindfulness: how to improve the precision of the Mindful Attention Awareness Scale using a Rasch model. *Mindfulness*, 7(2), 384–395. doi:10.1007/s12671-015-0454-z

Medvedev, O. N., Siegert, R. J., Kersten, P., & Krägeloh, C. U. (2017). Improving the precision of the Five Facet Mindfulness Questionnaire using a Rasch approach. *Mindfulness*, 8(4), 995–1008. doi:10.1007/s12671-016-0676-8

Medvedev, O. N., Krägeloh, C. U., Narayanan, A., & Siegert, R. J. (2017). Measuring mindfulness: applying generalizability theory to distinguish between state and trait. *Mindfulness*, 8(4), 1036–1046. doi:10.1007/s12671-017-0679-0

Medvedev, O. N., Bergomi, C., Röthlin, P., & Krägeloh, C. U. (2018a). Assessing the psychometric properties of the Comprehensive Inventory of Mindfulness Experiences (CHIME) using Rasch analysis. *European Journal of Psychological Assessment*. Online First. doi:10.1027/1015-5759/a000453

Medvedev, O. N., Titkova, E. A., Siegert, R. J., Hwang, Y.-S., & Krägeloh, C. U. (2018b). Evaluating short versions of the Five Facet Mindfulness Questionnaire using Rasch analysis. *Mindfulness*. Online First. doi:10.1007/s12671-017-0881-0

Medvedev, O. N., Krägeloh, C. U., Siegert, R. J., & Singh, N. N. (Eds.) (in preparation). *Handbook of Assessment in Mindfulness*. New York, USA: Springer.

Minami, H., Brinkman, H. R., Nahvi, S., Arnsten, J. H., Rivera-Mindt, M., Wetter, D. W.,…, & Brown, R. A. (2018). Rationale, design and pilot feasibility results of a smartphone-assisted, mindfulness-based intervention for smokers with mood disorders: Project mSMART MIND. *Contemporary Clinical Trials*, 66, 36–44. doi:10.1016/j.cct.2017.12.doi:014

Montero-Marin, J., Gaete, J., Araya, R., Demarzo, M., Manzanera, R., Álvarez de Mon, M., & García-Campayo, J. (2018). Impact of a blended web-based mindfulness programme for general practitioners: a pilot study. *Mindfulness*, 9(1), 129–139. doi:10.1007/s12671-017-0752-8

Moore, R. C., Depp, C. A., Wetherell, J. L., & Lenze, E. J. (2016). Ecological momentary assessment versus standard assessment instruments for measuring mindfulness, depressed mood, and anxiety among older adults. *Journal of Psychiatric Research*, 75, 116–123. doi:10.1016/j.jpsychires.2016.doi:01.011

Moreira, H., & Canavaro, M. C. (2017). Psychometric properties of the Interpersonal Mindfulness in Parenting Scale in a sample of Portuguese mothers. *Mindfulness*, 8(3), 69–706. doi:10.1007/s12671-12016-0647-0

Neece, C. L. (2014). Mindfulness-Based Stress Reduction for parents of young children with developmental delays: implications for parental mental health and child behavior problems. *Journal of Applied Research in Intellectual Disabilities*, 27(2), 174–186. doi:10.1111/jar.12064

Neff, K. D. (2003). The development and validation of a scale to measure self-compassion. *Self and Identity*, 2(3), 223–250. doi:10.1080/15298860390209035

Noguchi, K. (2017). Mindfulness as an end-state: construction of a trait measure of mindfulness. *Personality and Individual Differences*, 106, 298–307. doi:10.1016/j.paid.2016.10.doi:047

Nyklíček, I., & Kuijpers, K. F. K. (2008). Effects of mindfulness-based stress reduction intervention on psychological well-being and quality of life: Is increased mindfulness indeed the mechanism? *Annals of Behavioral Medicine*, 35(3), 331–340. doi:10.1007/s12160-008-9030-2

Offenbächer, M., Sauer, S., Hieblinger, R., Hufford, D. J., Walach, H., & Kohls, N. (2011). Spirituality and the International Classification of Functioning, Disability and Health: content comparison of questionnaires measuring mindfulness based on the International Classification of Functioning. *Disability and Rehabilitation*, 33(25–26), 2434–2445. doi:10.3109/09638288.2011.573902

Osman, A., Lamis, D. A., Bagge, C. L., Freedenthal, S., & Barnes, S. M. (2016). The Mindful Attention Awareness Scale: further examination of dimensionality, reliability, and concurrent validity estimates. *Journal of Personality Assessment*, 98(2), 189–199. doi:10.1080/00223891.2015.1095761

Pang, D., & Ruch, W. (2018). Scrutinizing the components of mindfulness: insights from current, past, and non-meditators. *Mindfulness*. Online First. doi:10.1007/s12671-018-0990-4

Park, T., Reilly-Sprong, M., & Gross, C. R. (2013). Mindfulness: a systematic review of instruments to measure an emergent patient-reported outcome (PRO). *Quality of Life Research*, 22(10), 2639–2659. doi:10.1007/s11136-013-0395-8

Pinto-Gouveia, J., Gregório, S., Dinis, A., & Xavier, A. (2012). Experiential avoidance in clinical and non-clinical samples: AAQ-II Portuguese version. *International Journal of Psychology & Psychological Therapy*, 12(2), 139–156.

Piron, H. (2001). The Meditation Depth Index (MEDI) and the Meditation Depth Questionnaire (MEDEQ). *Journal for Meditation and Meditation Research*, 1, 50–67.

Reavley, N., & Pallant, J. F. (2009). Development of a scale to assess the meditation experience. *Personality and Individual Differences*, 47(6), 547–552. doi:10.1016/j.paid.2009.05doi:007

Rudkin, E., Medvedev, O. N., & Siegert, R. J. (2018). The Five-Facet Mindfulness Questionnaire: why the observing subscale does not predict psychological symptoms. *Mindfulness*, 9(1), 230–242. doi:10.1007/s12671-12017-766-762

Sahdra, B. K., Shaver, P. R., & Brown, K. W. (2010). A scale to measure nonattchment: a Buddhist complement to Western research on attachment and adaptive functioning. *Journal of Personality Assessment*, 92(2), 116–127. doi:10.1080/00223890903425960

Sahdra, B., Ciarrochi, J., & Parker, P. (2016). Nonattachment and mindfulness: related but distinct constructs. *Psychological Assessment*, 28(7), 819–829. doi:10.1037/pas0000264

Sahdra, B. K., Ciarrochi, J., Parker, P. D., Basarkod, G., Bradshaw, E. L., & Baer, R. (2017). Are people mindful in different ways? Disentangling the quantity and quality of mindfulness in latent profiles and exploring their links to mental health and life effectiveness. *European Journal of Personality*, 31(4), 347–365. doi:10.1002/per.2108

Sauer, S., Walach, H., Schmidt, S., Hinterberger, T., Lynch, S., Büssing, A., & Kohls, N. (2013). Assessment of mindfulness: review on state of the art. *Mindfulness*, 4(1), 3–17. doi:10.1007/s12671-012-0122-5

Sauer, S., Lemke, J., Zinn, W., Buettner, R., & Kohls, N. (2015). Mindful in a random forest: assessing the validity of mindfulness items using random forests methods. *Personality and Individual Differences*, 81, 117–123. doi:10.1016/j.paid.2014.09.011

Seema, R., Quaglia, J. T., Brown, K. W., Sircova, A., Konstabel, K., & Baltin, A. (2015). The Estonian Mindful Attention Awareness Scale: assessing mindfulness without a distinct linguistic present tense. *Mindfulness*, 6(4), 759–766. doi:10.1007/s12671-014-0314-2

Short, M. M., Mazmanian, D., Oinonen, K., & Mushquash, C. J. (2016). Executive function and self-regulation mediate dispositional mindfulness and well-being. *Personality and Individual Differences*, 93, 97–103. doi:10.1016/j.paid.2015.08.doi:007

Siegling, A. B., & Petrides, K. V. (2016). Zeroing in on mindfulness facets: similarities, validity, and dimensionality across three independent measures. *PLoS ONE*, 11(4), e0153073. doi:10.1371/journal.pone.0153073

Siegling, A. B., Furnham, A., & Petrides, K. V. (2018). Facet benchmarking: advanced application of a new instrument refinement method. *Personality and Individual Differences*, 120, 288–298. doi:10.1016/j.paid.2016.doi:12.014

Snippe, E., Nyklíček, I., Schroevers, M. J., & Bos, E. H. (2015). The temporal order of change in daily mindfulness and affect during mindfulness-based stress reduction. *Journal of Counseling Psychology*, 62(2), 106–114. doi:10.1037/cou0000057

Soler, J., Tejedor, R., Feliu-Soler, A., Pascual, J. C., Cebolla, A., Soriano, J., …, & Perez, V. (2012). Psychometric proprieties of Spanish version of Mindful Attention Awareness Scale (MAAS). *Actas Españolas De Psiquiatría*, 40(1), 19–26.

Soler, J., Cebolla, A., Feliu-Soler, A., Demarzo, M. M. P., Pascual, J. C., Baños, R., & García-Campayo, J. (2014). Relationship between meditative practice and self-reported mindfulness: the MINDSENS composite index. *PLoS ONE*, 9(1), e86622. doi:10.1371/journal.pone.0086622

Solhaug, I., Eriksen, T. E., de Vibe, M., Haavind, H., Friborg, O., Sørlie, T., & Rosenvinge, J. H. (2018). Medical and psychology student's experiences in learning mindfulness: benefits, paradoxes, and pitfalls. *Mindfulness*. Online First. doi:10.1007/s12671-016-0521-0

Tanay, G., & Bernstein, A. (2013). State Mindfulness Scale (SMS): development and initial validation. *Psychological Assessment*, 25(4), 1286–1299. doi:10.1037/a0034044

Thompson, B. L., & Waltz, J. (2007). Everyday mindfulness and mindfulness meditation: overlapping constructs or not? *Personality and Individual Differences*, 43(7), 1875–1885. doi:10.1016/j.paid.2007.06.doi:017

Tran, U. S., Glück, T. M., & Nader, I. W. (2013). Investigating the Five Facet Mindfulness Questionnaire (FFMQ): construction of a short form and evidence of a two-factor higher order structure of mindfulness. *Journal of Clinical Psychology*, 69(9), 951–965. doi:10.1002/jclp.21996

Truijens, S. E. M., Nyklíček, I., van Son, J., & Pop, V. J. M. (2016). Validation of a short form Three Facet Mindfulness Questionnaire (TFMQ-SF) in pregnant women. *Personality and Individual Differences*, 93, 118–124. doi:10.1016/j.paid.2015.06.doi:037

Tsafou, K.-E., De Ridder, D. T. D., van Ee, R., & Lacroix, J. P. W. (2016). Mindfulness and satisfaction in physical activity: a cross-sectional study in the Dutch population. *Journal of Health Psychology*, 21(9), 1817–1827. doi:10.1177/1359105314567207

Van Dam, N. T., Earleywine, M., & Danoff-Burg, S. (2009). Differential item function across meditators and non-meditators on the Five Facet Mindfulness Questionnaire. *Personality and Individual Differences*, 47, 516–521. doi:10.1016/j.paid.2009.05.doi:005

Van Dam, N. T., Earleywine, M., & Borders, A. (2010). Measuring mindfulness? An Item Response Theory analysis of the Mindful Attention Awareness Scale. *Personality and Individual Differences*, 49, 805–810. doi:10.1016/j.paid.2010.0doi:7.020

Van Dam, N. T., Hobkirk, A. L., Danoff-Burg, S., Earleywine, M. (2012). Mind your words: positive and negative items create method effects on the Five Facet Mindfulness Questionnaire. *Assessment*, 19(2), 198–204. doi:10.1177/1073191112438743

van den Hurk, P. A. M., Wingens, T., Giommi, F., Barendregt, H. P., Speckens, A. E. M., & van Schie, H. T. (2011). On the relationship between the practice of mindfulness meditation and personality: an exploratory analysis of the mediating role of mindfulness skills. *Mindfulness*, 2(3), 194–200. doi:10.1007/s12671-011-0060-7

van der Maas, H. L. J., Kan, K.-J., & Borsboom, D. (2014). Intelligence is what the intelligence test measures. Seriously. *Journal of Intelligence*, 2, 12–15. doi:10.3390/jintelligence2010012

Wainer, H., & Kiely, G. L. (1987). Item clusters and computerized adaptive testing: a case for testlets. *Journal of Educational Measurement*, 24(3), 185–201. doi:10.1111/j.1745-3984.1987.tb00274.x

Walach, H., Buchheld, N., Buttenmüller, V., Kleinknecht, N., & Schmidt, S. (2006). Measuring mindfulness: the Freiburg Mindfulness Inventory (FMI). *Personality and Individual Differences*, 40, 1543–1555. doi:10.1016/j.paid.2005.doi:11.025

Way, B. M., Creswell, J. D., Eisenberger, N. I., & Lieberman, M. D. (2010). Dispositional mindfulness and depressive symptomatology: correlations with limbic and self-referential neural activity during rest. *Emotion*, 10(1), 12–24. doi:10.1037/a0018312

WHOQOL Group (1995). The World Health Organization Quality of Life assessment (WHOQOL): position paper from the World Health Organization. *Social Science and Medicine*, 41(10), 1403–1409. doi:10.1016/0277-9536(95)00112-K

Wong, K. F., Massar, S. A. A., Chee, M. W. L., & Lim, J. (2018). Towards an objective measure of mindfulness: replicating and extending the features of the breath-counting task. *Mindfulness*. Online First. doi:10.1007/s12671-12017-0880-0881

Zhang, C.-Q., Chung, P.-K., & Si, G. (2017). Assessing acceptance in mindfulness with direct-worded items: the development and initial validation of the Athlete Mindfulness Questionnaire. *Journal of Sport and Health Science*, 6(3), 311–320. doi:10.1016/j.jshs.2015.09doi:010

Zhuang, K., Bi, M., Li, Y., Xia, Y., Guo, X., Chen, Q., ..., & Qiu, J. (2017). A distinction between two instruments measuring dispositional mindfulness and the correlations between those measurements and the neuroanatomical structure. *Scientific Reports*, 7, 6252. doi:10.1038/s41598-017-06599-w

Ziegler, M., Kemper, C. J., & Kruyen, P. (2014). Short scales: five misunderstandings and ways to overcome them. *Journal of Individual Differences*, 35(4), 185–189. doi:10.1027/1614-0001/a000148

Zimmermann, F. F., Burrell, B., & Jordan, J. (2018). The acceptability and potential benefits of mindfulness-based interventions in improving psychological well-being for adults with advanced cancer: a systematic review. *Complementary Therapies in Clinical Practice*, 30, 68–78. doi:10.1016/j.ctcp.2017.doi:12.014

4

QUANTITATIVE RESEARCH ON THE EFFECTIVENESS OF MINDFULNESS-BASED INTERVENTIONS

With mindfulness-based interventions (MBIs) steadily emerging as a mainstream health intervention (Harrington & Dunne, 2015), a large volume of quantitative research has been produced with the aim to investigate the effectiveness of a wide range of mindfulness applications (Dimidjian & Segal, 2015). Since the development of Mindfulness-Based Stress Reduction (MBSR) in the 1970s (Kabat-Zinn, 1982), a variety of other MBIs have been tested, each focusing on a different health issue or participant population. Some of the first well-known variants of MBSR include Mindfulness-Based Cognitive Therapy (MBCT) to decrease the likelihood of relapse after depression (Segal, Williams, & Teasdale, 2002), Mindfulness-Based Relapse Prevention (MBRP) for alcohol and drug problems (Witkiewitz, Marlatt, & Walker, 2005), Mindfulness-Based Eating Awareness Therapy (MB-EAT) for eating disorders (Kristeller, Baer, & Quillian-Wolever, 2006), and Mindfulness-Based Relationship Enhancement (MBRE) to enrich the relationships of nondistressed couples (Carson, Carson, Gill, & Baucom, 2004). Since 2010, the number of articles reporting on very context- or population-specific MBI adaptations has increased dramatically. These diverse applications range from Mindfulness-Based Resilience Training to address stress experienced by police officers (Christopher et al., 2016) and Mindfulness-Based Self-Leadership Training to teach achievement-oriented self-regulation and self-leadership (Sampl, Maran, & Furtner, 2017), to Mindfulness-Based Childbirth Education that combine MBSR with skills-based antenatal education (Fisher, Hauck, Bayes, & Byrne, 2012) and Mindfulness-Based Program for Infertility to target emotional distress in people dealing with fertility problems (Galhardo, Moura-Ramos, Cunha, & Pinto-Gouveia, 2018). In some cases, modifying an MBI resulted in an extension of the MBSR label. An example would be the MBSR-tics programme, which is an MBSR programme that had been modified slightly in terms of content for the treatment of Tourette Syndrome and Chronic Tic Disorder (Reese et al., 2015).

The present chapter focuses on the quantitative research conducted on standardised MBIs, where mindfulness is used as a central part of a time-limited and often manualised intervention, typically with the objective of improving a clearly defined health outcome. An intervention can be defined as an act or process that is undertaken to prevent or treat a condition, and MBIs that have a focus on improving health can be categorised in this manner. Such mindfulness programmes, which generally have a secular approach, have been described as first-generation MBIs (Van Gordon, Shonin, & Griffiths, 2015). This mode of categorisation would classify second-generation MBIs as those that have an overtly spiritual presentation. Second-generation MBIs are more likely to have a broader objective, such as exposing participants to a larger range of meditation practices, undergoing a process of ongoing spiritual development, achieving personal transformation, and application of mindfulness in everyday life. The present authors acknowledge that this may not be a distinction that is routinely accepted, nor can a clear separation of MBIs be made. There is, of course, some overlap, as well as some MBIs that do not fit clearly into either category, such as some eHealth interventions.

Gradually emerging evidence base for mindfulness-based interventions

The structured MBSR programme was initially presented under the name *Stress Reduction and Relaxation Program* as a 10-week intervention where participants met in groups for two hours each week (Kabat-Zinn, 1982). Eventually, MBSR came to be offered as a standard eight-week intervention, although total contact time increased as classes were lengthened to 2.5 hours, and participants also met for a further 6-hour class during a weekend day of the sixth week (Carmody & Baer, 2009). The initial focus of MBSR was to address symptoms of chronic pain, which included patients with any kind of condition accompanied by chronic pain who were referred to the programme by a physician (Kabat-Zinn, 1982). These were typically patients who did not respond well to traditional medical and psychological treatments (Kabat-Zinn, 2003) and were thus given an opportunity to apply mindfulness as a different kind of approach to change their psychological stance towards their condition.

In the context of MBIs, Kabat-Zinn (1994) defined mindfulness as "paying attention in a particular way: on purpose, in the present moment, and non-judgmentally" (p. 4). The techniques taught in the programme reflect this definition and consist of a range of meditative practices such as insight meditation, breathing exercises, body scan, hatha yoga, mindful walking, and mindful eating. Through this variety of techniques as well as group discussion, participants gradually learn to focus their attention to the present moment and to accept thoughts as they appear nonjudgmentally without getting caught up in their literal content as this can sometimes lead to rumination and anxiety. Mindfulness practitioners in MBSR, and MBIs in general, learn to be comfortable with unpleasant experiences and emotions, as well as gain insight into the distinction between actual physical pain and the unnecessary psychological suffering produced by maladaptive corollary cognitions (Kabat-Zinn, 1990; Ruskin et al., 2016). MBI participants are also taught how to apply these skills to their everyday life, reinforced through diary writing and daily home-based meditation practice.

Given the initial focus of MBSR on alleviation of symptoms from chronic pain conditions, early research compared pre- and post-intervention measures of pain ratings by participants (Kabat-Zinn, 1982). Subsequent studies soon started to include a comparison group of individuals who received pain treatment typically provided to patients with chronic pain conditions, and the results indicated that relevant outcome measures only improved for the experimental group that participated in the MBI (Kabat-Zinn, Lipworth, & Burney, 1985). The effects were also found to be enduring with most measures of symptoms of pain and related psychological distress remaining relatively unchanged at follow-up points that ranged from 2½ to 48 months (Kabat-Zinn, Lipworth, Burney, & Sellers, 1986). Fuelled by the success of these early applications of mindfulness interventions, further studies then tested the effects of MBIs for contexts other than chronic pain. Such studies were typically in the form of proof-of-principle studies about specific hypothesised outcomes, such as the effects of mindfulness in increased melatonin levels and thus lowering risks of cancer (Massion, Teas, Hebert, Wertheimer, & Kabat-Zinn, 1995) or responsiveness to phototherapy and photochemotherapy as defined by rate of skin clearing in patients with the skin condition psoriasis (Kabat-Zinn et al., 1998). Evidence of the positive effects of MBSR on antibody reaction in response to an influenza vaccine could also be interpreted as the intervention being linked to improved immune functioning (Davidson et al., 2003).

Evidence reported in literature reviews and meta-analyses

Given the steadily growing number of studies on MBIs, systematic and meta-analytic reviews have been published regularly to provide comprehensive overviews of the evidence base documented in the academic literature (Gotink et al., 2015). Some of the earlier work often reported that MBIs are associated with the expected positive health outcomes but that more robust studies are needed to provide conclusive evidence. Grossman, Niemann, Schmidt, and Walach (2004), for example, found 20 MBSR studies that met the criteria for inclusion into their meta-analysis, of which only six were controlled trials. While the studies fairly consistently revealed a moderate effect size of MBSR for various health outcomes, the authors listed the following common methodological shortcomings of the studies: potential confounding from participants receiving concurrent interventions in addition to mindfulness, inadequate statistical power, and lack of information about therapist-related factors such as treatment adherence and trainer competence. In a conceptual review, Baer (2003) also noted that studies reported up until then often did not include a control group or only a waitlist control group and thus did not adequately control for demand characteristics or placebo effects. In principle, treatment-as-usual (TAU) control groups are preferable, but those studies that did so often had medical treatment or unspecified mental health approaches as comparative TAU.

A more recent meta-analysis by Bohlmeijer, Prenger, Taal, and Cuijpers (2010) specifically aimed to provide information about further research developments about MBSR and chronic pain since the reviews by Baer (2003) and Grossman et al. (2004). Analysing eight randomised controlled trials (RCTs), Bohlmeijer et al. (2010) found that the overall effect size of MBSR on depression was small (d=0.26). For anxiety, the effect size was small to moderate (d=0.47), although it decreased to 0.24 when studies of lower quality had been excluded. Due to the lack of follow-up data in most studies, the meta-analysis could not explore to what extent these effects were long-term. Bohlmeijer et al. (2010) discussed how these results were comparable to those reported for psychotherapy and pharmacotherapy, and the authors concluded that MBSR may best be used in conjunction with cognitive behavioural therapy.

Hofmann, Sawyer, Witt, and Oh (2010) conducted a meta-analysis of the effects of MBSR as well as MBCT on anxiety and depression. The selection criteria included a wide range of clinical samples, and their meta-analysis was conducted on 39 studies with more than 1,000 participants in total. Effect sizes were moderate and significantly larger than placebo effect sizes. Additionally, effects were found to be unrelated to year of publication of the study, number of treatment sessions, and were maintained at follow-up. Hofmann et al. (2010) explicitly addressed the issue of expectancy effects according to which researchers conducting a meta-analysis may be affected by their own expectations regarding the outcomes. The authors stated that they had been rather critical regarding the effects of MBIs and referred to a prior article that they had published as evidence for their initial stance. Given their prior expectations to obtain a null result, the authors concluded that it was unlikely that their findings had been affected by such expectancy biases.

More recent systematic literature reviews and meta-analyses generally confirm the findings of the earlier work and continue to comment on the need for higher quality studies. Fjorback, Arendt, Ørnbøl, Fink, and Walach (2011), for example, systematically reviewed 21 RCTs using MBSR or MBCT with at least 33 participants. Medium effect sizes were found, but the authors also commented on the need for more studies with active control groups and more data on follow-up effects. In perhaps one of the most comprehensive meta-analyses of the effects of MBIs, Khoury et al. (2013) analysed 209 studies (>12,000 participants) reporting on an MBI that addressed a clinical outcome of either physical or psychological nature. Overall, effect sizes were moderate, and MBI can be considered similarly effective as cognitive behavioural therapy. MBIs were more effective in addressing psychological issues, such as anxiety, for which large effect sizes were reported. One of the moderators explored was the meditation experience of the therapist, which was found to be associated with positive outcomes at the end of treatment. Khoury et al. (2013) stated that their liberal inclusion criteria served to address their own expectancy biases, and their recommendations for the future included more methodologically robust studies, particularly those that are able to test various relevant moderators and meditators.

With an emerging evidence base for MBIs, particularly for general psychological distress, literature reviews subsequently focused increasingly on the application of mindfulness in particular contexts or for particular target populations. Given the fact that such a focus decreases the sample pool of studies, it is not surprising to continue to see recommendations for more robust studies. For example, in a systematic literature review about the effectiveness of MBIs for substance use, Chiesa and Serretti (2014) concluded that MBIs reduced substance use issues more than waitlist controls and concluded that the findings had limited generalisability due to methodological issues such as small sample size or lack of information about methods used. For a variety of other specific applications, literature reviews have presented similar tentative conclusions that MBIs are safe and potentially useful interventions but that the evidence base is still small and that more methodologically rigorous studies are needed. This, for example, includes MBIs for fibromyalgia (Lauche, Cramer, Dobos, Langhorst, & Schmidt, 2013), Parkinson's disease (McLean, Lawrence, Simpson, & Mercer, 2017), psychosis (Aust & Bradshaw, 2017), cancer care (Shennan, Payne, & Fenlon, 2011), or sleep disturbance (Winbush, Gross, & Kreitzer, 2007).

The effectiveness of MBIs in nonclinical settings has also been documented extensively for a variety of applications. This includes MBSR for family caregivers to deal with stress, depression, and anxiety (Li, Yuan, & Zhang, 2016), MBSR in generally healthy individuals for stress reduction (Chiesa & Serretti, 2009), or MBSR for other diverse health and well-being outcomes (Khoury, Sharma, Rush, & Fournier, 2015). Other studies outlined the evidence for MBIs and mental health during pregnancy (Dhillon, Sparkes, & Duarte, 2017; Shi & MacBeth, 2017), MBIs to address psychological distress in organisational settings (Virgili, 2015), and MBIs in schools to address cognitive performance and stress resilience (Zenner, Herrnleben-Kurz, & Walach, 2014). Similar to the application of MBIs to specific patient populations, the more specific the focus of nonclinical MBIs became, the fewer studies could be identified by such reviews. A common conclusion also mentioned general methodological limitations such as the need for more RCTs with larger sample sizes, appropriate comparison groups, and follow-up data.

Other reviews and meta-analyses did not distinguish between clinical and non-clinical applications. For MBIs with specific age groups, the literature is now comprehensive enough to permit stronger conclusions about the effectiveness of the intervention as well as potential moderators. Klingbeil et al. (2017) reviewed 76 group-design studies with more than 6,000 youth participants in an MBI. The range of study designs allowed comparisons of effect sizes by quality, which confirmed previous findings that effect sizes were generally smaller in more robust designs. While effect sizes in controlled studies were generally small, larger effects were noted in follow-up studies, indicating that ongoing mindfulness practice was beneficial. Some of the remaining methodological issues raised by Klingbeil et al. (2017) were the fact that studies still tended to provide insufficient information about treatment integrity, implementation fidelity, or the amount of personal practice that participants engaged in.

Whether the focus of the above-mentioned reviews and meta-analyses was on a specific application or population group or whether inclusion criteria were broad, analyses of the outcomes did not impose any specific restrictions or focus on particular measures. Some reviews, in contrast, have taken another approach and conducted a review that maps the effects of MBIs on one specific outcome. This includes a study on pain intensity that analysed results from studies with chronic pain patients, fibromyalgia, mixed diagnoses, nursing home residents, and healthy pregnant women (Reiner, Tibi, & Lipsitz, 2013). Here, findings revealed that the effects of MBIs were more consistently positive for samples with clinical pain. Another example is the systematic review by O'Leary, O'Neill, and Dockray (2016) who reviewed the effects of MBIs on cortisol as a biomarker for stress. Again, a wide range of studies was included, and results revealed that significant changes of MBIs on cortisol levels were only observed in within-participant studies and not in RCTs.

As noted by Dimidjian and Segal (2015), it is noticeable that there is generally fairly little discussion about the distinction between efficacy and effectiveness of MBIs. While efficacy research typically focuses on how the intervention effect can be maximised, effectiveness studies also tend to investigate any moderating variables that affect the relationship between the intervention and the outcome, such as external patient-, provider-, or system-level factors (Singal, Higgins, & Waljee, 2014). Certainly, such research is best placed along a continuum, but the mindfulness literature often does not distinguish between the terms clearly enough and could thus give the impression that these terms are synonymous (e.g. Mak, Whittingham, Cunnington, & Boyd, 2018; Khoury et al., 2015). A quasi-experimental study by Juul, Pallesen, Piet, Parsons, and Fjorback (2018) compared the effects of MBSR when conducted with a community sample with the effects reported in selected reference trials. These were efficacy RCTs that the authors had selected based on inclusion of a similar participant population. While the community MBSR yielded smaller effect sizes than these efficacy trials, Juul et al. (2018) argued that lower effect sizes are not uncommon in effectiveness studies that tend to include a more heterogeneous participants pool. Additionally, the authors illustrated how baseline stress levels in their study tended to be less than those reported in the comparison efficacy trials, and within-sample comparisons revealed that those participants with higher initial stress levels tended to experience larger health improvements from participating in the MBSR intervention.

Research on clinical effectiveness can also involve analyses of cost effectiveness (Dimidjian & Segal, 2015), and here only a few sporadic examples can be found in the mindfulness literature. This includes a study by Prioli et al. (2017) that compared the cost effectiveness of Mindfulness-Based Art Therapy with that of a standard breast cancer support group, a cost analysis of a mindfulness-based professional development programme for teachers (Doyle, Brown, Rasheed, Jones, & Jennings, 2018), an investigation of the effectiveness and cost-effectiveness of MBCT (Kuyken et al., 2015), and a benefit-cost analysis of teaching a mindfulness-based procedure to adult offenders with intellectual disabilities (Singh et al., 2008a).

Investigating mechanisms of action in mindfulness-based interventions

Demonstration of the effectiveness of MBIs naturally raised the question of the mechanism of action underlying such interventions. Such investigations tended to include a larger number of outcome measures than the early demonstrations of the overall utility of MBIs that typically addressed only the direct goal of the intervention such as improvement of pain symptoms in chronic pain patients. Studies exploring or testing mechanisms of action, in contrast, included a range of psychological variables that could assist in highlighting a cascade of changes in the variables that are hypothesised to bring about positive health effects for the mindfulness practitioner.

Carmody, Baer, Lykins, and Olendzki (2009) reported an empirical test of a model that described a hypothesised mechanism of action proposed by Shapiro, Carlson, Astin, and Freedman (2006). According to this model, mindfulness involved the three interwoven aspects of intention, attention, and attitude. As Shapiro et al. (2006) did not recommend any specific measures to operationalise the concepts in their model, Carmody et al. (2009) selected several psychological self-report instruments that they considered as suitable. Using a sample of more than 300 participants in MBSR classes, Carmody et al. (2009) tested the extent of the association between mindfulness and psychological distress and how this was mediated by changes in self-regulation, values clarification (or the recognition what one truly values), behavioural and cognitive flexibility, as well as willingness to remain in contact with unpleasant thoughts and feelings. These variables were not found to be significant mediators between mindfulness and psychological distress. However, partial evidence of the model was obtained when the mindfulness score was calculated as a combination of the Five Facet Mindfulness Questionnaire (Baer, Smith, Hopkins, Krietemeyer, & Toney, 2006) and the Experiences Questionnaire (Fresco, Segal, Buis, & Kennedy, 2007) as a measure of so-called reperceiving, or the fundamental shift in which experience is perceived as a result of mindfulness practice, such as decentring, defusion, or distancing.

The role of mindfulness in the process of bringing about health benefits has since been studied using an increasingly wider range of variables that are hypothesised to be relevant in such relationships. In such models, mindfulness has sometimes been included as a mediator, and other times relevant psychological variables were tested to explain how the effects of mindfulness practice are mediated by psychological processes. Kuyken et al. (2010), for example, found that self-compassion and mindfulness scores mediated the effects of MBCT on depressive symptoms, and Keng, Smoski, Robins, Ekblad, and Brantley (2012) demonstrated that self-compassion and mindfulness mediated the effects of participation in MBSR on worry and emotional regulation. In other mediation studies about MBSR, Nyklíček and Kuijpers (2008) reported that changes in mindfulness skills were partially mediating the effects of the mindfulness intervention on psychological well-being and quality of life, and Nila, Holt, Ditzen, and Aguilar-Raab (2016) found that different aspects of mindfulness such as acceptance and decentring were mediating the association between the intervention effect and distress tolerance as well as resilience. Gu, Strauss, Bond, and Cavanagh (2015) conducted a systematic literature review and meta-analysis of studies that had explored the mechanism of therapeutic effects of mindfulness from MBSR and MBCT. In the 20 studies that were analysed, a range of variables were investigated using mediation analysis: mindfulness, repetitive negative thinking such as rumination and worry, self-compassion, psychological flexibility, emotional and cognitive reactivity, and ability to retrieve autobiographical memories. Using narrative synthesis to structure the results, the review revealed consistent and strong evidence for cognitive and emotional reactivity in mediating the effects of MBIs on mental health outcomes. Moderate but consistent evidence was found for mindfulness and repetitive negative thinking as mediators, with only preliminary evidence for self-compassion and psychological flexibility. Another systematic review by van der Velden et al. (2015) focused specifically on MBCT. This analysis of 23 studies confirmed the tenability of theoretical models of action for MBCT, although the authors also concluded that more rigorously designed studies are required.

Overall, increasingly more empirical data are becoming available about the specific role of mindfulness, and a larger variety of models are proposed as the mechanisms of action, which prompted the need to summarise and structure this literature. Chiesa, Anselmi, and Serretti (2014) provided a comprehensive review of the literature on the psychological mechanisms of MBIs and outlined future areas of improvement such as clearer conceptualisation of mindfulness and its overlap with related concepts such as self-compassion. The use of different methods to investigate mechanisms of mindfulness also provided valuable converging evidence. One such method includes time series analyses of day-to-day changes during MBIs. When within-subject variations in outcome measures were followed daily since starting MBSR, changes in mindfulness levels tended to precede those of affect and ruminative thinking rather than the other way around (Snippe et al., 2015a; Snippe, Nyklíček, Schroevers, & Bos, 2015b).

Attempts to isolate separate components of the effects of mindfulness-based interventions

Related to the question about relevant mediating variables in the relationship between MBIs and intended health outcomes is whether the effects of MBIs can be dismantled and whether it is possible to isolate the beneficial effects of specific practices and psychological processes from those that may be functionally redundant. This is particularly relevant to MBIs as these interventions typically teach a variety of techniques, some of which aimed at changing the way cognitions and emotions are reacted to, and these typically require the participants to also facilitate a state of physical relaxation as a pre-requisite for mindfulness exercises. Even though MBSR was originally called *Stress Reduction and Relaxation Program* (Kabat-Zinn, 1982), Kabat-Zinn (2003) emphasised that the similarities between relaxation and mindfulness are only superficial and that the true aim of the latter is to bring about transformative experience. This assertion was subsequently investigated explicitly by a number of empirical studies. In an RCT reported by Jain et al. (2007), full-time university students were either part of a no-treatment waitlist control group, a somatic relaxation group, or participated in mindfulness meditation modelled on MBSR but delivered in a shortened one-month format. Both somatic relaxation and meditation resulted in large reductions in psychological distress, but the meditation group had large improvements in positive states of mind and also significant reductions in rumination and distraction compared to the control group. With between 24 to 30 participants in three groups, the study by Jain et al. (2007) possessed a sufficiently large sample size to be able to detect effects of moderate to large size (Hertzog, 2008), and larger sample sizes would be required when investigating variables that may be expected to yield smaller effect sizes. In an even slightly less powered RCT with a community sample, Agee, Danoff-Burg, and Grant (2009) compared the effects of a five-week mindfulness meditation course adapted from MBSR with a five-week course teaching progressive muscle relaxation. Although participants in the mindfulness group tended to engage with the home practice tasks more than the participants in the relaxation group, both interventions resulted in post-treatment reductions in psychological distress. The authors speculated that the lack of a group difference in the treatment effect may have been due to the shortened duration of the mindfulness intervention as well as the small sample size overall.

A laboratory study with brief mindfulness and relaxation exercises for university students confirmed the difference between the effects of mindfulness meditation and somatic relaxation (Lancaster, Klein, & Knightly, 2016). While participants in the former condition reported significant reductions in both negative and positive affect, participants in the progressive muscle relaxation condition experienced significantly less cognitive anxiety, and women in the progressive muscle relaxation group experienced less somatic anxiety. This study thus revealed potentially complex interactions, and the results need to be followed up by further studies with larger sample sizes and longer interventions.

Instead of comparing mindfulness with other techniques and practices such as relaxation, other studies aimed to identify the beneficial effects of specific aspects of mindfulness practice with each other. One such example is a study by Lindsay, Young, Smyth, Brown, and Creswell (2018) that explored to what extent acceptance is the critical element in the emotion-regulation mechanism underlying the effects of mindfulness. In a three-arm RCT of a smartphone-delivered intervention, Lindsay et al. (2018) allocated stressed adults sampled from the community to a) one group receiving training in both monitoring of present-moment experiences as well as acceptance, b) another group to only monitoring of physical and psychological experiences without acceptance training, and c) a third group functioned as an active control group receiving training in coping. Only the group practising monitoring combined with acceptance exhibited reduced cortisol and systolic blood pressure after the intervention, indicating that acceptance training appears to be an essential aspect in the stress-reducing role of mindfulness training. Similar to the variable acceptance, studies have also attempted to isolate the specific role of empathy and compassion in mindfulness training. This has been investigated through arranging mindfulness interventions that separated out concentration-focused mindfulness practice from those focused on ethics and compassion (Bayot, Vermeulen, Kever, & Mikolajczak, 2018). However, more research is required as the study by Bayot et al. (2018) revealed some contradictory findings such as no effect of either the mindfulness intervention or the ethics-oriented training on empathy.

Further approaches to isolating the effects of MBIs involved comparing the effects of specific practices when delivered on their own as opposed to when integrated into a therapeutic package. For that purpose, Blanck et al. (2018) conducted a systematic literature review and meta-analysis to explore the effects of stand-alone mindfulness exercises on symptoms of anxiety and depression when such exercises were not integrated into a larger therapeutic framework. The dynamics in MBIs are generally complex, involving elements in addition to mindfulness practice such as psychoeducation, social support from other group members, and teacher-related factors. To separate the effects of the practice of mindfulness exercises from such contextual factors, Blanck et al. (2018) searched for peer-reviewed articles that reported data on interventions where mindfulness exercises were conducted repeatedly and as the primary focus, either face to face or through an online format. Compassion-focused programmes and manualised interventions such as MBSR that included group discussion and psychoeducation were thus not included. When compared with inactive controls, stand-alone mindfulness exercises were associated with reductions of anxiety and depression in the order of small to medium effect sizes. When compared with active controls, the effect size decreased for anxiety, and the effect was no longer significant for depression. As the effect sizes were less than those reported in meta-analyses of MBIs, Blanck et al. (2018) concluded that MBIs outperformed stand-alone mindfulness exercises and that MBIs provided benefits additional to mere performance of formal mindfulness exercises. However, this conclusion was limited by the fact that studies investigating the effects of stand-alone mindfulness exercises tended to involve nonclinical samples.

Another area of research that has been receiving increasingly more attention is the role of movement and the body in mindfulness. While yoga has traditionally and historically been linked to spirituality and mindfulness (Büssing, Hedtstück, Khalsa, Ostermann, & Heusser, 2012; Jarry, Chang, & La Civita, 2018), it can also be practised as largely a physical activity, and is often seen that way in the West (Sistig, Lambrecht, & Friedmann, 2015). For that reason, the term *mindful yoga* is occasionally used as a way of differentiation from the purely physical interpretation of yoga (Sistig et al., 2015). In mindful yoga, the main goal is not the perfection of postures but the training of awareness of the breath as well as noticing external and internal stimuli. The inclusion of yoga exercises within MBSR provided a stimulus for recent research on the effects of yoga, either as a separate intervention or embedded within an MBI (Pascoe, Thompson, & Ski, 2017). Additionally, specifically yoga-based stress management programmes have been proposed and tested

(Stück, Meyer, Rigotti, Bauer, & Sack, 2003), and standardised psychometric instruments are available for yoga research (MacDonald & Friedman, 2009). Yoga-based interventions have been shown empirically to involve similar mechanisms of health benefits as MBIs, such as through developing mindfulness and self-compassion (Gard et al., 2012). Hunt, Al-Braiki, Dailey, Russell, and Simon (2018) conducted an RCT to investigate the role of the yoga-based and mindfulness-based elements within MBIs. Participants were assigned to a) a mindfulness training group that did not engage in any movement exercises, b) a yoga-only group without explicit mindfulness training, c) a combined yoga and mindfulness group, d) an active placebo group consisting of party games, access to a therapy dog, and healthy snacks, and lastly e) a no-treatment control group. All four active treatments were associated with positive effects on anxiety and dysphoric affect. The combined yoga and mindfulness group resulted in slightly better outcomes. The authors concluded that the inclusion of yoga exercises appears to be beneficial to the effectiveness of MBIs, although more research is needed to explore to what extent the benefits of yoga are more attributable to physical activity or some other component that is embedded within this practice.

Laboratory-based studies on the effects of mindfulness practice

A number of studies explored the effects of mindfulness practice in laboratory situations and could thus be considered as investigations into more fundamental psychological processes relevant to mindfulness. The purpose of such work was often to confirm the findings from MBIs in more controlled environments and to test various hypotheses about what drives the beneficial effects that have been observed in clinical settings. Given the time restrictions typically found in laboratory settings, studies tended to focus on investigating the role of specific short-term exercises that are commonly taught in MBIs.

Some of the laboratory-based studies explored which particular type of cognitive performance may be enhanced by meditation-related exercises. Eisenbeck, Luciano, and Valdivia-Salas (2018), for instance, assigned 46 university students to a group listening to an audio recording that guided a focused breathing exercise or a control exercise recording, both of which 13 minutes in length. In subsequent attention and memory tasks, the experimental group performed significantly better in a memory task, but there were no differences in the attention or mood evaluations tasks. The results regarding the effects of mindfulness training are inconsistent and may depend on the emotional valence of the stimuli to be remembered. Alberts and Thewissen (2011) administered a 20-minute mindfulness intervention to university students followed immediately by a memory task of emotional stimuli. Compared to control participants who completed the memory task right away, participants in the experimental group remembered a significantly lower proportion of negative words, possibly indicating a diminished negativity bias induced by mindfulness. This finding is slightly in contrast with the results from a study that investigated recall bias after a 12-week laboratory-based meditation course (Roberts-Wolfe, Sacchet, Hastings, Roth, & Britton, 2012). Here, participants in the meditation group were found to have greater improvements in efficiency to process positively valenced stimuli than participants in an active control group who engaged in practice-based learning of music.

Other studies explored the effects of mindfulness on creativity and critical thinking. Ostafin and Kassman (2012) reported on the results of two studies that explored the link between mindfulness and performance on tasks that are considered to involve different amounts of creative and insightful problem solving. First, a cross-sectional study conducted with university students discovered a link between trait mindfulness and insight problem solving, while mindfulness was unrelated to problem solving in tasks not requiring insight. The authors subsequently confirmed these findings in an experimental study with a smaller sample of students who had been randomly assigned to listening either to a 10-minute audio recording presenting a guided meditation exercise or an audio recording of the same length that presented a text on natural history. In another laboratory-based study on mindfulness meditation, Noone and Hogan (2018) assigned university students with no meditation experience to a group listening to 10-minute meditation audio recording or to a mind-wandering control task that had been used in a previous research study (Arch & Craske, 2006) and was considered to have high ecological validity as a relevant active control condition. Noone and Hogan (2018) found no direct effect of mindfulness meditation on measures of critical thinking, although a significant increase was reported for participants who already possessed a relatively lower tendency towards applying effort to thinking or those who were generally less likely to think in a flexible and open manner.

The purpose of other mindfulness studies was to focus on the short-term effects of mindfulness exercises on psychological processes that are considered to be more directly related to how MBIs address psychological distress. In a study comparing the immediate short-term effects of different stress–management techniques, Feldman, Greeson, and Senville (2010) randomly assigned female university students to engaging in 15-minute exercises of mindful breathing, progressive muscle relaxation, or loving-kindness meditation. All of these were presented in an audio recording. As predicted, participants in the mindful breathing group reported significantly increased decentring, or the tendency to view their thoughts with more objectivity. The other two conditions, in contrast, resulted in significantly more reductions in repetitive thinking and negative reactions to thoughts, and the overall results confirmed the role of decentering as a mechanism that distinguished mindfulness practice from other stress–management techniques. In conjunction with converging evidence from cross-sectional studies that reported associations between dysfunctional breathing patterns and anxiety (e.g. Crockett, Cashwell, Tangen, Hall, & Young, 2016), a more detailed understanding of the role of breathing practice in MBIs is starting to emerge.

Some of the laboratory-based mindfulness studies attempted to manipulate the mood of their participants in various ways to explore the role of mindfulness in emotional regulation. In a study by Arch and Craske (2006), mood manipulation was only applied to one of the comparison groups and served to amplify any contrasts between emotional processing from mindfulness practice as opposed to how it might occur naturally in stressful everyday life situations. For that purpose, the researchers assigned university students to either a group who engaged in a 15-minute focused breathing exercise, a group who were instructed to let their minds wander freely, or a group who were explicitly instructed to catastrophise about their principal worry. When shown neutral, positive, or negative slides sourced from a manual for affective ratings, the participants in the focused breathing group maintained moderately positive responses to neutral slides, while the participants in the other groups responded more negatively to them. Additionally, the focused breathing group exhibited a higher willingness to view additional optional negative slides after the exercise. While there were no differences for other measures and other types of slides, the study provided some evidence for the immediate effects of focused breathing in individuals who were specifically required not to have any experience with meditation or mindfulness.

Other studies provided an experimental manipulation of mood states for all of their participants. In a study on mindful acceptance and dysfunctional attitudes, Keng, Seah, Tong, and Smoski (2016) exposed 79 university students with elevated depressive symptoms to an autobiographical mood induction procedure that fostered a sad mood by combining negative autobiographical recall with mood-suggestive classical music. Participants were then randomly allocated to listening to a 15-minute audio recording giving a brief mindful acceptance exercise adapted from MBCT or to listening to a 15-minute clip that instructed them to let their thoughts wander freely without any particular focus. The effects of the experimental condition were moderated by participants' trait mindfulness levels such that those with high trait mindfulness had reduced implicit dysfunctional attitude scores after the intervention and scores increased for those participants with lower trait mindfulness. Of note is that, before finishing the experiment, the researchers attempted to alleviate the negative mood of the participants by playing a funny videoclip followed by debriefing with one of the experimenters.

Among the research on fundamental processes of mindfulness, a particularly important role has been played by studies that investigated the effects of mindfulness and meditation practice on the brain. Generally, such neuroscience research has been perceived as providing objective and scientific converging evidence of the benefits of clinical applications such as MBIs (Holmes, Craske, & Graybiel, 2014). Typically, neuropsychological studies include those that explored the state change effects of short-term meditation on the brain as well as longer-term changes from prolonged meditation and mindfulness practice such as enduring functional and structural changes that can thus be noticed outside meditative situations. Some of the early studies explored the associations between meditation practice and brain structure using cross-sectional designs (e.g. Hölzel et al., 2008), but controlled studies were subsequently more commonly reported. This includes a controlled longitudinal study published by Hölzel et al. (2011), where 33 participants without meditation experience were allocated to an MBSR intervention or a waitlist control condition. As a result of the programme, grey matter in the experimental group increased in density for brain regions involved in emotion regulation, learning, memory, perspective taking, and self-related cognitions. These areas include the hippocampus, posterior cingulate cortex, cerebellum, and temporo-parietal junction. In another controlled study on neuroanatomical changes from MBSR training (Santarnecchi et al., 2014), the mindfulness intervention was associated with increased cortical thickness of the right insular lobe and somatosensory cortex – areas associated with interoception, awareness of body movements, and emotional awareness.

With increased interest in brain imaging studies on the effects of MBIs, several systematic literature reviews and meta-analyses have been published. Fox et al. (2014) analysed the effects of MBSR together with those of other meditation techniques, making it difficult to isolate the effects of MBIs. Gotink, Meijboom, Vernooij, Smits, and Hunink (2016), in contrast, specifically compared the effects of MBSR and MBCT with those of other meditation practices. While many of the functional and structural changes were similar, such as in the prefrontal cortex, cingulate cortex, insula, and hippocampus, MBSR was also associated with changes in the amygdala and thus consistent with improved emotion regulation. Similarly, Young et al. (2018) systematically reviewed the evidence for changes in brain functioning as a result of participation in a manualised eight-week MBI. In contrast to other previous reviews, there was insufficient evidence to link MBIs to increased activity in specific regions of the prefrontal cortex, and evidence was clearer for changes in the insula. The latter brain region has been linked to higher-order cognitive functioning such as awareness of interoceptive experiences. Some of the inconsistent findings may be related to the level of meditation experience of the participants. As found in a meta-analysis of functional magnetic resonance imaging studies exploring brain activity during mindfulness meditation (Falcone & Jerram, 2018), increased activity in the insula was found more consistently for novice meditators, while experienced meditators presented with foci in the medial frontal gyrus and globus pallidus regions.

Because of the original development of MBSR specifically to address symptoms of chronic pain, a number of fundamental research studies also focused specifically on the effects of mindfulness practice and the perception of pain. This could be considered as research following up the findings reported from therapeutic interventions and giving them a scientific basis by demonstrating their effect at the physiological level. While evidence from cross-sectional work (Lee et al., 2017a) seems to suggest that self-reported mindfulness levels do not predict perception of pain but only positively moderate the effect of pain perception on stress, an experimental study reported by Zeidan, Gordon, Merchant, and Goolkasian (2009) found that participants rated pain from electrical stimulation less severely after a mindfulness meditation intervention involving three days of 20-minute mindfulness practice. There are other examples of studies that provided laboratory-based evidence to confirm the utility of specific clinical applications of MBIs. These include an RCT about the effects of MBSR on telomerase length and activity as psychobiomarkers for the relationship between stress and disease in women with breast cancer (Lengacher et al., 2014) and a quasi-experimental nonrandomised study of the relationship between MBSR with endocrine and immune function in individuals infected with the human immunodeficiency virus (Robinson, Mathews, & Witek-Janusek, 2003).

Research on modifications of format and content of mindfulness-based interventions

In response to the emergence of the large number of new MBIs that have been proposed since MBSR and MBCT, increased discussion has taken place about how much modification can be made without losing the core intention and integrity of the original programme. In that context, Dobkin, Hickman, and Monshat (2014) advised that adaptations need to involve consultation with instructors of established MBIs such as MBSR and also need to maintain the link between practice and science. Crane et al. (2017) proposed some guidelines to assist programme developers to communicate the distinction between the adapted population- or context-specific elements of their MBI and core invariant elements common to all MBIs. According to these guidelines, some of the essential elements of MBIs are that they are "informed by theories and practices that draw from the confluence of contemplative traditions, science, and the major disciplines of medicine, psychology and education" (p.4). Additionally, MBIs involve sustained intensive training that supports the development of increased attentional and emotional self-regulation but also positive qualities such as compassion, wisdom, and equanimity. In contrast, elements that can be adapted without losing the commonality with other MBIs are contextualisation of curriculum to specific contexts and populations as well as necessary variations in the structure, length, and delivery format of the programme.

Some of the adaptations of MBIs for different participant populations may appear relatively minor if there are strong similarities in the main objectives of the programme, such as when addressing psychological distress and teaching resilience to stress. There is currently no clear direction or consensus a) at what point studies should be encouraged simply to describe in their method section the extent to which they have made minor modifications to an established programme such as MBSR (e.g. Langer, Cangas, Salcedo, & Fuentes, 2012; Petersen & la Cour, 2016), b) whether to use an addition to the acronym to signal a noteworthy modification in order to contextualise the programme (e.g. MBSR-tics for Tourette Syndrome; Reese et al., 2015), or c) whether to introduce a whole new name altogether, such as Cognitive Behavioural Therapy and Mindfulness Training (CBT/MT) for youth involved in the criminal justice system (Leonard et al., 2013).

In some cases, the separate name and acronym of what is perceived as novel and unique about the new mindfulness interventions can be justified by a sufficient theoretical basis and empirical evidence. For example, the MB-EAT programme (Kristeller et al., 2006) is presented as a modification of MBSR to address eating issues and is grouped as a first-generation MBI like MBSR and MBCT (Van Gordon et al., 2015). While the focus of mindfulness practice has shifted towards eating situations in MB-EAT, this intervention still considers the fundamental psychological processes of mindfulness to be related to those of other MBIs. Furthermore, participants are still encouraged to develop increased awareness of their emotions and cognitions, although exercises that are covered in more detail in MB-EAT tend to be those related to signals of hunger and satiety as well as triggers for eating (Kristeller et al., 2006). The hypothesised mechanism of action for MB-EAT has also been tested empirically. For example, a cross-sectional study, Beshara, Hutchinson, and Wilson (2013), identified mindful eating as a mediator of the relationship between mindfulness and serving size, thus confirming the potential utility of mindful eating interventions in addressing healthy eating.

A commonly reported modification of MBIs relates to variations of the length of the programme or total number of contact hours with course participants. Such work has often been prompted by participant feedback, particularly from patients suffering from conditions such as stroke or cancer (Jani, Simpson, Lawrence, Simpson, & Mercer, 2018; Zimmermann, Burrell, & Jordan, 2018). As a result, a number of studies investigated to what extent MBI session length or programme duration could be reduced without negatively impacting on its effectiveness. While work has been published showing that even single-session mindfulness interventions can have measurable effects, the results from such studies have limited generalisability to standard MBIs of eight-week duration. Given the brevity, such interventions struggle to deliver the transformative aspects of mindfulness practice, not only in terms of time to deliver the content but also opportunities for participants for reflection and deepening their learning. Brief mindfulness interventions such as the single-session mindfulness training by Lim and Qu (2017) therefore typically focus on attentional or cognitive aspects of mindfulness rather than those based on emotions and attitudes. Additionally, single-trial mindfulness interventions can only be considered to induce state changes in outcomes and have also been appropriately assessed that way (e.g. Hussein, Egan, & Mantzios, 2017; Mahmood, Hopthrow, & Randsley de Moura, 2016), while the trajectory of change in outcome variables in MBIs such as MBSR and MBCT has been shown to be gradual (Ietsugu et al., 2015; Snippe, Dziak, Lanza, Nyklíček, & Wichers, 2017).

When conducting a shortened five-week (10-hour) MBSR intervention with university students, Bergen-Cico, Possemato, and Cheon (2013) found that scores of mindfulness and self-compassion increased significantly but that depression and anxiety did not, and the authors recommended that longer interventions may be required. This finding is in contrast with the overall conclusion from a review by Carmody and Baer (2009). When analysing data from 30 MBI studies with in-class hours varying from 6 to 26, Carmody and Baer (2009) found no significant correlation between MBI length and mean effect size. However, before being able to conclude that intervention length within the above range is irrelevant, the authors recommended that future work investigate the effects of total in-class hours using experimental designs. Some progress has been made since, such as by a quasi-experimental study by Demarzo et al. (2017) that found that both the standard eight-week MBSR course as well as an abbreviated four-week MBSR generated significant improvements in a number of outcome variables compared to a no-intervention control group. There was only slight evidence to indicate that the standard MBSR programme led to larger improvements than the abbreviated one. The issue of optimal length or dosage has also been raised in conceptual and critical discussions of the mindfulness literature. Van Dam et al. (2018a), for example, argued that not enough is known about the issue and that optimal length and intensity of MBIs is likely to depend heavily on the intended outcome of the MBI. In this regard, shortened mindfulness interventions have not always been intended as direct alternatives to standardised MBIs. For example, Moore (2008) reported on a brief mindfulness course for clinical psychologists aimed to assist them in future personal and professional applications of mindfulness.

Another major area where substantial modifications to MBIs have taken place is the application of mindfulness using eHealth technology such as with online formats or delivered through a smartphone. The latter application is particularly interesting or even counterintuitive as research has linked mobile phones to being a significant source of distraction: In an experimental study, participants who had access to their cell phones during a 20-minute lecture had worse test performance than participants without access (Lee, Kim, McDonough, Mendoza, & Kim, 2017b). Interestingly, the effect was not moderated by the level of mindfulness of the participants, when categorised as low versus high level. However, despite the potential to provide additional challenges to present-moment awareness of participants, the ubiquity of mobile technology has also been increasingly identified as a chance to explore methods to deliver MBIs. The very source of distraction, therefore, may potentially be used to teach participants to learn how to regulate their attention.

Much of the eHealth research on mindfulness has investigated the effects of mindfulness apps for use on smartphones, such as the popular audio-guided mindfulness meditation app Headspace. A study by Wylde, Mahrer, Meyer, and Gold (2017) explored the effects of using this app with novice nurses as an intervention for coping with stress as compared to traditional mindfulness training. Nurses recruited during the first year of the study were allocated to the smartphone-delivered mindfulness programme, and nurses recruited in the following year participated in a traditional four-week face-to-face mindfulness programme adapted from MBSR. While both interventions resulted in increased scores on acting with awareness and nonreactivity, which were positively related to compassion satisfaction and negatively to compassion fatigue, the smartphone intervention resulted in more highly increased compassion satisfaction and decreased burnout. However, a moderation effect was noted in that nurses with existing symptoms of posttraumatic stress benefited less from the intervention than those without. The authors hypothesised that the reduced effects of the traditional face-to-face intervention may have been due to the difficulty in generalising mindfulness skills to everyday-life situations without the availability of a phone or support of a therapist.

When delivered through a web-based format, eHealth applications of MBIs tend to follow the original format more closely. An example is the study by Dimidjian et al. (2014) who tested the effects of a web-based training programme based on MBCT to reduce residual depressive symptoms. Using a quasi-experimental design, participants were allocated to a web-based MBCT intervention or TAU for depression by matching pairs of participants based on their depression propensity scores. Compared to previously reported effects of in-person MBCT programmes, the web-based programme resulted in similarly sized effects on reduced rumination and increased mindfulness. Systematic literature reviews and meta-analyses have generally confirmed such findings although such work often included a wide range of different eHealth delivery formats (O'Connor, Munnelly, Whelan, & McHugh, 2018; Spijkerman, Pots, & Bohlmeijer, 2016). Additionally, in contrast to the definition of MBIs by Crane et al. (2017) that was used in the present book, the reviews by Spijkerman et al. (2016) also classified Acceptance and Commitment Therapy (Hayes, Strosahl, Wilson, 2011) as an MBI and thus included it in their review, while O'Connor et al. (2018) included an even wider range under the term *third-wave treatments*. Overall, these reviews indicated that such treatments, when delivered in an eHealth format, provide comparable effects as standard face-to-face delivery methods, although there may be a tendency for effects to be slightly smaller.

Another procedural variation of MBIs that has been investigated is to what extent MBIs may be delivered to individual participants as opposed to delivered in a group format. As this increases the time commitment required from researchers, such interventions often relied on the use of audio-recordings. Wahbeh, Lane, Goodrich, Miller, and Oken (2014), for example, reported on the development of a one-on-one mindfulness meditation intervention adapted from MBCT that delivered six weekly 90-minute training sessions and home practice. For that purpose, sessions were held in a small room with a reclining chair and a computer that was used to play audio-recordings, although a facilitator was present who could assist when needed. While the intervention resulted in the expected outcomes, the use of audio-recordings in the one-on-one group still meant that this difference in delivery format was another aspect in which the experimental manipulation differed from the traditional face-to-face group format. A further study that investigated the effects of single meditation training as opposed to a group format was an RCT published by Matiz, Fabbro, and Crescentini (2017). Here, the researchers compared the effects of an eight-week mindfulness course inspired by MBSR with those from a group who met as a group only during the first session but then commenced autonomous practice using guided audio-recordings. No group differences were noted in the extent to which outcome measures improved. In another example of an adapted MBI, procedural deviations were not the purpose of the investigation, but nevertheless inherent in the intervention and adequately described in the Method section. In this case, a different combination of individual and group-based content delivery was provided: Morrison, Goolsarran, Rogers, and Jha (2014) reported on the use of an MBI focused on cognitive training in order to reduce mind wandering in university students. Based on the structure of MBSR, the seven-week programme included a weekly 20-minute instructor-led mindfulness session as well as two separate 20-minute individual practice sessions with a supervisor where participants listened to audio-recordings providing attention-focused exercises. Compared to a waitlist control, participants in the mindfulness group showed evidence of reduced mind wandering, although working memory performance was not different between the two groups.

Given the fact that eHealth interventions often involve the introduction of several new elements such as timing of practice, single delivery as opposed to group format, or reliance on audio-recordings, some research has attempted to limit modifications to some specific procedural aspects only. Krägeloh et al. (2018), for example, trialled a format with participants recruited in a university setting where the main facilitator was present only during the first session and then delivered the group MBI using videoconferencing. While the intervention resulted in medium to large effects for a number of outcome measures, results could only be compared against a waitlist control group, and further work is required to compare the effects of specific procedural variations more explicitly. Another technology-assisted MBI was employed in a nonexperimental pre-test post-test study by Bazarko, Cate, Azocar, and Kreitzer (2013), this time for nurses employed in a corporate setting. In a modified MBSR programme, nurses participated in six of the eight sessions via telephone conferencing. The study concluded that this format has the potential to offer a cost-effective and convenient alternative for participants who may find it difficult to attend traditional face-to-face group sessions.

Because of the heavy reliance of eHealth studies on audio-visual material to deliver aspects of their interventions, research has now also started to investigate to what extent various aspects of such delivery may be differently effective. Campillo, Ricarte, Ros, Nieto, and Latorre (2018) randomly assigned participants to engage in a 30-minute mindfulness exercise that primarily used visual stimuli to instigate concentration and attention-based activities, while another group received the material in an auditory format. For both groups, scores for attention increased and scores for positive emotions decreased, while negative emotions decreased more for the auditory group. While this may indicate that mindfulness practice is more immediately effective if emotional material is delivered in an auditory format, more research is required about these effects in more prolonged standardised MBIs.

Pilot studies, feasibility studies, and study protocols

Ideally, modifications to the format and content of MBIs would involve the use of pilot work (Dobkin et al., 2014), which has often occurred. Given the large volume of pilot and feasibility studies that have been published about mindfulness interventions, a separate section in this chapter can be justified.

There is no commonly agreed definition of the terms pilot study and feasibility study. The literature has often been using these term interchangeably, although there may be a tendency for feasibility studies to have a more flexible methodology as opposed to pilot studies, which may focus more on sample size estimation or control group selection procedures (Arain, Campbell, Cooper, & Lancaster, 2010). Occasionally, authors may be tempted to use the term pilot study in the hope that reviewers might regard their manuscript more favourably. In that case, however, the term pilot *work* may then be a more appropriate term to distinguish it from pilot *studies* that have specific hypotheses or pilot *trials* that also include other pre-planned design features (Arain et al., 2010). Pilot studies are generally conducted for the following reasons: assess the feasibility of specific steps in the research such as recruitment or retention rates, assess time and budget implications, gauge the impact of the study on personnel and other management issues, assess the safety of the intervention, or estimate the potential treatment effect size (Thabane et al., 2010).

Pilot and feasibility studies have often been conducted for mindfulness interventions designed for target populations deemed to be sufficiently unique or requiring adaptations in content or delivery format. Steinberg, Klatt, and Duchemin (2017) reported on a pilot study to explore the feasibility of an MBI for personnel working in a high-stress surgical intensive care setting. Novel aspects of the investigation included the delivery of the MBI during work hours, which relied heavily on the support of the organisational management and administration. This aspect was successful, as the researchers were able to retain all of the participants in the intervention group. Responses to the quantitative online survey also indicated that the participants expressed the view that the intervention was beneficial for dealing with stress at work.

Similar to the study by Steinberg et al. (2017), Christopher et al. (2016) tested the feasibility and preliminary effectiveness of an MBI delivered to a specific professional group, in this case law enforcement officers. The Mindfulness–Based Resilience Training (MBRT) programme had been developed by the authors. MBRT was based on the structure of the MBSR programme but was adapted to suit the needs of the target population by modifying the session structure and by contextualising the exercises through scenarios that the participants would likely encounter during their work. The results from the 43 police officers who completed the intervention indicated significant increases in a variety of relevant outcome measures including perceived stress, burnout, anger, and sleep disturbance. The study by Christopher et al. (2016) did not include a control group, and the results were later replicated by a more robust feasibility and preliminary efficacy trial (Christopher et al., 2018). The feasibility of the intervention was confirmed through data on adherence, attendance, participant feedback, and treatment fidelity. However, treatment effects were no longer present at three-month follow-up, indicating the need for additional post-intervention booster sessions.

Other pilot studies used a mixed-methods approach to test the feasibility of an MBI. Kinser, Braun, Deeb, Carrico, and Dow (2016) developed an eight-week mindfulness curriculum that included mindful movement exercises and was designed for healthcare professional and students. While all of the 38 participants completed the programme, only 27 provided pre- and post-intervention data. Quantitative data as well as written qualitative feedback to open-ended questions confirmed the feasibility of this intervention. Similarly, Reese et al. (2015) employed both quantitative and qualitative methods to test acceptability and feasibility of an MBSR programme for individuals with Tourette syndrome. Among other psychometric instruments, participants completed a treatment satisfaction questionnaire and provided written feedback after each class. The qualitative data were analysed for participants' experience with mindfulness practice as well as the presence of any adverse effects.

Pilot studies that include quantitative data will need to provide a sufficient number of intervention sessions for potential experimental effects to emerge and thus be able to gauge likely effect size of the MBI. However, if the goal of the study is primarily to explore the acceptability of an intervention using a qualitative approach, it may not be necessary to expose the participants to the full intervention. For example, Jani et al. (2018) provided a two-hour taster of MBSR to stroke survivors (n=21) and caregivers (n=7). When asked later whether they would be willing to attend a full eight-session mindfulness course, three quarters of the participants responded positively. Participants described their experiences in a focus group and also provided information on how a full programme might best be adapted to suit their needs, such as having shorter sessions.

In some areas, such as the application of MBIs to adolescents and children, a fair amount of pilot and feasibility work has already been conducted, and the field is now ready for larger-scale robust interventions (Burke, 2010). Feasibility and pilot studies continue to be appropriate for novel interventions such as those that combine various elements to address specific issues or respond to specific needs. Alfonso, Caracuel, Delgado-Pastor, and Verdejo-García (2011), for instance, tested the effects of goal management training for individuals with alcohol and polysubstance abuse. The authors reasoned that mindfulness would likely benefit these individuals for developing decision-making skills and thus provided a combined goal-setting and mindfulness intervention to their study protocol. Participants were allocated to either this combined intervention (n=18) or standard treatment (n=16) based on time availability and geographical proximity. Unlike the standard treatment group, participants in the intervention group showed significant improvements on several relevant neuropsychological measures. The same intervention was later applied to substance users in residential treatment (Valls-Serrano, Caracuel, & Verdejo-Garcia, 2016). This time, the study was not labelled as a pilot study but included a similarly sized sample and demonstrated the positive effects of the intervention on executive-function tasks that mimic daily-living activities.

A different approach to exploring the feasibility of a novel MBI was provided by Minami et al. (2018). Focused on only eight participants with psychiatric disorders and smoking habits, this open-label pilot feasibility study collected detailed data and provided detailed information about a newly developed smartphone-assisted mindfulness smoking cessation intervention. This intervention was provided alongside a contingency-management programme that rewarded objectively-verified smoking abstinence with monetary incentives. As this behavioural contingency approach had previously been demonstrated to induce short-term smoking abstinence, this provided an opportunity to explore the effects of an MBI to ensure longer-term results. Participants were prompted five times a day to complete an ecological momentary assessment report about their smoking behaviour and putative mediators of that behaviour, such as mindfulness or cravings. In addition to that, they were encouraged to practise mindfulness and provide a post-practice report. Despite the intensive time investment required for this intervention, adherence was good, with more than 70% of the daily reports completed, and 97% of those having been completed within 30 minutes after receiving them. The second part of the article presented a study protocol of an RCT to explore the effectiveness of the smartphone-assisted mindfulness intervention more systematically. The feasibility study provided valuable information about intervention adherence, acceptability, and challenges in participant recruitment. In another feasibility and acceptability study comparing MBSR, MBCT, and TAU, Alsubaie et al. (2018) noted a low recruitment rate and a high withdrawal rate between the screening stage and participant randomisation, and the researchers concluded that study recruitment procedures would need to be revised if a decision is made to implement a definitive trial.

It has become increasingly common to find advance publication of study protocols of experimental trials that are to be conducted. The advantages of this approach are recognised to be opportunities to obtain early feedback or the reduction of duplication of effort. Additionally, study protocols provide evidence for the existence of methods and hypotheses that have been formulated *a priori*, which reduces the possibility of type-1 errors. In mindfulness research, study protocols have been published for RCTs comparing the comparative effectiveness of mindfulness meditation with qigong and Taichi practice (Carlson et al., 2017; Ho et al., 2017). Other study protocol examples include RCTs to test the effectiveness of acupuncture and MBSR to address fatigue in patients with multiple sclerosis (Bellmann-Strobl et al., 2018) or RCTs to investigate the effects of specific MBIs with university students (Galante et al., 2016; Rowland, Wenzel, & Kubiak, 2016).

Protocols may also be published about systematic literature reviews and meta-analyses. An example in the mindfulness literature would be a proposed systematic review and meta-analysis on the effects of MBSR for adults with sleep disturbance (Kim, Park, & Seo, 2016). Information about other proposed and completed systematic reviews can be obtained on websites such as those by the Cochrane Database of Systematic Reviews (www.cochranelibrary.com) or Campbell Collaboration (www.campbellcollaboration.org).

Participant characteristics and other potential confounding variables

A number of research design considerations that have been raised or addressed in the mindfulness literature are those that are also commonly found in psychological research or health research more broadly. For example, it is not uncommon to find research reporting on the effects of MBI to include a statistical control for social desirability, or the tendency for respondents to answer questions in a way that will be viewed favourably by others (e.g. Arch & Craske, 2006; Jain et al., 2007). While it is certainly not standard practice to account for social desirability as a potential confounding variable, the regularly reported lack of effects of social desirability may have led to the perception that this is not a confound that researchers need to be much concerned about. Additionally, participant response burden when completing large batteries of self-report instruments may certainly also be a factor limiting the wider uptake of social desirability measures.

Some of the other research design considerations that have been highlighted in the mindfulness literature with a fair amount of detail are those related to the use of appropriate control conditions (Baer, 2003; Davidson & Kaszniak, 2015). Shennan et al. (2011) referred to MBIs as so-called complex interventions as defined by the guidelines of the Medical Research Council of the United Kingdom (Medical Research Council, 2006). According to these guidelines, MBIs would be complex due to characteristics such as difficulty of behaviours required by course facilitators and participants, variability of outcomes, and the fact that interventions typically permit a degree of flexibility to tailor them to the specific needs of the course participants. Waitlist control conditions are seen as inferior to active control groups as the former cannot control for placebo effects (Baer, 2003). Some of the mindfulness research reported on the use of active control groups that appear relevant to the topic of investigation based on face validity (e.g. a coping training programme used as active control by Lindsay et al., 2018). MacCoon et al. (2012), in contrast, reported on specific validation work of an active control condition in studies exploring the efficacy of MBSR. This active control programme includes a variety of topics on behaviours to enhance physical and psychological well-being. In an RCT to dismantle the effects of MBCT (Williams et al., 2014), participants in the active control group received cognitive psychological education, which was modelled on MBCT but did not teach meditation.

Occasionally, studies reporting on the effects of MBIs also arranged an active control that included some mindfulness material. For example, in an RCT testing the effects of an MBI on psychological distress and fatigue in patients with inflammatory rheumatic joint diseases, Zangi et al. (2012) included a TAU control group that also received a CD that could be used for voluntary mindfulness-based home practice. The authors stated that the purpose of this arrangement was to compensate participants for the negative effects of being allocated the routine care only. The use of the CD was not monitored, but the authors speculated that the slight improvement in outcomes for the control group may have been related to voluntary mindfulness practice. Outcomes for the experimental group, however, increased more, thus indicating that the attention and guidance from the group MBI had provided benefits additional to providing awareness of mindfulness and self-practice opportunities.

Further considerations regarding alternative experimental and control conditions in RCTs of MBIs include the need for facilitators of the alternative conditions to be similarly enthusiastic so that each intervention is delivered to maximise its effectiveness (Davidson & Kaszniak, 2015). In a three-arm RCT of the effects of MBCT, Britton et al. (2018) ensured that the facilitators of the groups to be compared (in this case, MBCT, focused attention, and open monitoring) were delivered by a person who was considered an expert in that area. However, to control for therapist effects, a second facilitator was present in both conditions, and in order to control for gender effects, this second facilitator was also of a different gender as the expert facilitators. Lastly, to control for placebo effects, participants in none of the groups were aware that they were receiving a certain treatment as opposed to another since all three active treatments were presented to them as mindfulness training. In another three-arm RCT on the effects of MBSR on fibromyalgia, Schmidt et al. (2011) allocated participants to an MBSR group, an active control for nonspecific aspects of MBSR such as social support and topical educational discussion, or a waitlist control. The two interventions were presented to the participants as novel and innovative treatments in order to equalise participants' expectations regarding any possible outcomes. In most of the RCTs, participants were allocated randomly, which appears appropriate when the sample size is large. Other approaches include propensity matching where group allocation takes place based on a measure of the main outcome, such as depressive symptoms (Dimidjian et al., 2014).

Some further design considerations found in the mindfulness research literature are those that are not particularly defining of the field and thus found in health research in general. This includes the recognition of the need to obtain a measure of treatment fidelity. Kechter, Amaro, and Black (2018) adapted general treatment fidelity guidelines and proposed a tool to monitor and report fidelity of MBIs using a standardised format. Britton et al. (2018) verified the adherence of the actual sessions to the planned content outline through the use of specifically designed checklists as rated by researchers who were present as well as those who listened to audio-recordings of the sessions. Similarly, Ridderinkhof, de Bruin, Blom, and Bögels (2018) reported on the use of published scales to assess the competence of teaching MBIs and adherence to the MBCT programme. Schmidt et al. (2011), in contrast, stated that they had decided against monitoring treatment fidelity due to concerns that this may have been disruptive and discouraged participants to disclose personal emotional issues freely and openly. In terms of treatment adherence or participant attendance to sessions, studies have used different ways to define it (Spijkerman et al., 2016). Especially when sample sizes are small, analysing results separately for those who have attended most sessions as opposed to the entire sample or those who missed classes has led to different effect sizes (Krägeloh et al., 2018). Such so-called intention-to-treat analyses of the entire sample have been recognised as good practice to guard against over-optimistic estimates of treatments efficacy (Gupta, 2011), although it has been argued that they could be more widely used in mindfulness research (Bawa et al., 2012).

Another aspect that has been identified as important for studies reporting on the results of MBIs is the need for a rich description of the intervention so that results can be compared with those of other studies (Davidson & Kaszniak, 2015). For example, when reporting on the effects of a hybrid MBSR/MBCT intervention, Van Dam, Hobkirk, Sheppard, Aviles-Andrews, and Earleywine (2014) provided a detailed outline of the content of each session, with the names of some of the readings or stories discussed with participants. In addition to the intervention itself, the importance of providing sufficient background information about the mindfulness facilitator has also been increasingly recognised. Ruijgrok-Lupton, Crane, and Dorjee (2018) specifically explored to what extent teacher training and experience may be related to MBI outcomes. While the researchers found a positive effect for formal MBI teacher training on stress and well-being, no significant relationship was found for teacher training and changes in mindfulness levels of participants as well as teacher meditation experience and outcomes. In addition to training and experience, therapeutic alliance generated by the therapist with the client has been recognised in the process of providing psychological therapy. Some links have been made by investigating associations between the level of mindfulness of the therapist and the strength of the alliance rated by clients (Escuriex & Labbé, 2011; Leonard, Campbell, & Gonzales, 2018; Ryan, Safran, Doran, & Muran, 2012). Such work, however, has largely occurred in general psychological service delivery. An example of related work that is more specifically about MBIs is the development of the Teaching Mindfulness in Education Observation Scale for the purpose of assessing the extent to which those delivering MBIs are perceived to be embodying the attitudinal foundations of mindfulness (Broderick et al., 2018).

Where MBIs may perhaps be perceived as having fairly unique characteristics is in regards to the additional home practice that participants are typically encouraged to engage in. While home practice has increasingly been recognised as a variable to be considered in statistical analyses of the outcomes of MBIs, such data have also been reported to be difficult to obtain and may thus be prone to being incomplete (Krägeloh et al., 2018). Specific investigations into the effects of home practice have produced rather mixed results. Ribeiro, Atcheley, and Oken (2018) tracked 55 mildly stressed participants recruited for a mindfulness meditation intervention. While the researchers reported high home-practice adherence and increases in self-report measures as a result of the intervention, these improvements were not significantly correlated with practice time. When conducting a systematic review of controlled studies using MBSR or MBCT, Lloyd, White, Eames, and Crane (2018) found that seven studies provided sufficient information about the relationship between home practice and relevant clinical outcomes, of which four studies reported a significant association. However, there was substantial variation across studies in terms of guidance of required length of home practice, the distinction between formal and informal practice, resources to assist this practice, and procedures to monitor this practice. Using broader criteria that also included non-RCT studies, a systematic review and meta-analysis by Parsons, Crane, Parsons, Fjorback, and Kuyken (2017) analysed 43 studies reporting on an MBSR or MBCT intervention. Similar to the findings by Lloyd et al. (2018), there was a substantial amount of heterogeneity in which home practice was assessed. Across 28 studies, a small significant association was detected between home practice and intervention outcomes.

The mixed results in regard to the association between home-practice time and intervention outcomes may be the result of a nonlinear relationship. For example, when Perich, Manicavasagar, Mitchell, and Ball (2013) analysed treatment outcome changes separately for participants who practised at least three times per week, improvements were larger than for those who practised less than three times per week. The role of home practice may also depend on the stage of mindfulness practice of the participants. For example, as reported by Madson et al. (2018), home practice was significantly correlated with mindfulness levels within a two-year period after an MBSR intervention. However, such compliance with and use of mindfulness techniques during and post-intervention has also been shown to depend partly on some personality characteristics of the MBI course participants (Barkan et al., 2016).

The importance of monitoring home practice can be seen from the results by Agee et al. (2009) who found that participants in a mindfulness meditation group practised twice as often as their counterparts in the progressive muscle relaxation group. Shapiro, Schwartz, and Bonner (1998) delivered MBSR to medical and premedical students and measured home-practice compliance in terms of number of minutes that participants had recorded in diary journals, which they submitted at every weekly session. A fairly detailed way of checking compliance in a short-term mindfulness meditation and loving-kindness intervention was reported by Aspy and Proeve (2017): Subjective questions asked participants to rate how well they had followed the instructions in guided audio-recordings, while objective questions required participants to name the specific meditation technique, which they were only able to know if they had listened to the recording until the end.

An aspect that may not have been appreciated sufficiently in analyses of moderating variables and baseline levels of MBI participants is that of the statistical phenomenon of regression towards the mean. Although this may not necessarily be a limitation of mindfulness research, this statistical artefact nevertheless needs to be considered when attempting to identify populations that could benefit the most from an MBI. As outlined by Barnett, van der Pols, and Dobson (2015), when participants are selected based on certain symptomatic characteristics or when participants self-select due to a self-identified need, participant recruitment may then tend to include more of those participants who happened to have been at the lower end of a naturally fluctuating spectrum. If levels of variables indeed fluctuate independently, an increase in an outcome measure could thus simply be a reflection of the fact that scores are more likely to increase if they have been low to start with. This confounding effect of selective recruitment can be controlled for by obtaining multiple measures and through random allocation of participants to comparison groups (Barnett et al., 2015).

A number of studies have asked the research question whether certain participant characteristics such as demographic or personality variables may affect the extent to which an MBI is either more or less effective. When comparing MBSR completers with noncompleters, Petersen and la Cour (2016) found that completers tended to be older and were more likely to be married or have a partner. While it has been noted that description of participant drop-out and withdrawal needs to be presented in more detail in MBIs (Hanley, Abell, Osborn, Roehrig, & Canto, 2016; Spijkerman et al., 2016), such concerns have also been discussed in relation to psychological therapies in general (van Kessel, Krägeloh, Babbage, 2016) and are thus not specific to the mindfulness literature. However, the expectations that new course participants may have regarding MBIs may be very unique. Online survey work has mapped out the reasons why individuals may decide to start practising mindfulness meditation (Pepping, Walters, Davis, & O'Donovan, 2018). These can be relatively varied, although, for the majority of individuals, the main purpose appears to be alleviation of some kind of emotional distress. Popular conceptions of mindfulness no doubt also play an important role in shaping expectations around the effects of MBIs. Hitchcock, Martin, Fischer, Marando-Blanck, and Herbert (2016) investigated lay conceptions of mindfulness by surveying undergraduate university students. In open-ended answers, participants linked mindfulness to awareness factors and being in the present moment. When asked to rate a variety of sentences, participants strongly linked mindfulness to controlling emotions.

In relation to meditation more broadly, an early correlational study about meditators concluded that outcomes are directly related to one's goals and expectations, which Shapiro (1992a) described as "what you get is related to what you want" (p.29). To investigate the role of motivation to practise, a meditation motivation scale has been developed, and research has shown that those with longer meditation experience tended to have stronger spiritual motivation to practise as opposed to short-term motivations such as well-being, which tend to be endorsed more by those with little experience (Schmidt, 2014). Even in the context of mindfulness for very specific benefits such as sport performance enhancement, expectations and goals vary across individuals. While these predict some of the improvements in outcome measures, those without any particular expectation also appear to improve on some outcome measures (Mistretta, Glass, Spears, Perskaudas, Kaufman, & Hoyer, 2017). Other ways of assessing motivational factors have been through physical and psychological engagement with MBIs, which have been found to have different effects on various mindfulness skills that are being developed by MBIs (Banerjee, Cavanagh, & Strauss, 2018). Lastly, Beattie, Hankonen, Salo, Knittle, and Volanen (2018) applied theory of planned behaviour (Ajzen, 1991) to explain engagement of adolescents in mindfulness practice, which was largely predicted by the extent to which participants perceived that their peers were also practising mindfulness.

Related to expectation of outcomes of MBI participation is the issue of self-selection, which has increasingly been raised as a topic for further research (Krägeloh et al., 2018; Van Dam et al. 2018b). Individuals seeking complementary and alternative treatments for various medical conditions have been found to differ in some personality variables from those who seek out traditional medical treatments (Honda & Jacobson, 2005), and such differences in uptake also appear to be present for MBIs. In a study with non-randomised assignment of medical students to an MBSR group or a control group, participants who self-selected to participate in the MBSR programme reported higher overall mood (Rosenzweig, Reibel, Greeson, Brainard, & Hojat, 2003). Although demographic discrepancies in MBIs have been noted such as by Blanck et al. (2018) who reported in their meta-analysis that 76% of participants in the studies they analysed were female, only a few studies explicitly discussed and explored demographic biases. Waldron, Hong, Moskowitz, and Burnett-Zeigler (2018) conducted a systematic review of the demographic characteristics of participants in RCTs of MBSR and MBCT courses conducted in the United States and confirmed that males were heavily under-represented (30%). Additionally, participants were more likely to be Caucasian and have higher average educational attainment. In a Danish study, Juul et al. (2018) evaluated the effectiveness of MBSR in a community sample of individuals who self-selected and self-paid as opposed to participating as a result of a clinical referral. Females and socioeconomically advantaged individuals were also over-represented in that sample. Such observations of socioeconomic bias in MBIs have prompted explicit research investigations such as a feasibility study by Jiga, Kaunhoven, and Dorjee (2018) who explored to what extent adaptations to MBI training are necessary for delivery of this type of intervention for adults experiencing psychosocial stress due to poverty.

Demographic variables and other characteristics have also been recognised as important variables to consider as potential moderators of the effectiveness of MBIs and have thus been discussed in the context of the research question of whether MBIs are more effective for certain individuals than for others. Much of the MBI research has explored such moderator effects in relation to diagnostic characteristics. For example, Williams et al. (2014) conducted a dismantling trial comparing MBCT with TAU as well as an active control condition and found that MBCT was not superior than the two comparison groups for recurrent depression overall. However, there was significantly more improvement for people suffering from depression due to childhood trauma. Other research has also investigated to what extent MBCT might also be applied to individuals with current episodes of depression as opposed to recurrent depression, for which MBCT was originally designed. According to results from a meta-analysis of RCTs, there is evidence to suggest that MBCT could also be recommended for current depressive disorder (Strauss, Cavanagh, Oliver, & Pettman, 2014).

Other studies did not compare the effects of MBIs on individuals with different diagnostic characteristics but in terms of baseline characteristics relevant to the intended treatment outcome. For example, Arch and Ayers (2013) examined the role of baseline symptoms in a clinical RCT comparing MBSR with cognitive behavioural therapy. Effectiveness for the two interventions was different depending on type of psychological issue (depression or anxiety) and whether comparisons were made post-treatment only or at follow-up. As mentioned in an earlier section of this chapter, Juul et al. (2018) considered baseline stress levels as a moderator and found that effect sizes for outcome measures were largest for a sub-group of participants with the highest initial levels of perceived stress.

In addition to the importance of considering baseline levels in relevant clinical symptoms, MBI have also been examined in reference to the role of demographic characteristics. In the context of MBIs for adolescents in educational settings, moderation effects by gender have been explored, and it was found that female participants in MBIs experience larger gains in positive affect than males (Kang et al., 2018). When comparing course engagement and post-intervention use of mindfulness skills after an MBI with adolescents, Bluth, Roberson, and Girdler (2017) found females to be more engaged and to have lower stress levels after the intervention. However, these findings are based on a small sample of 15 individuals, and also Kang et al. (2018) acknowledged that their sample size as well as the small effect size for some of the outcomes limited any conclusions derived from the reported gender-specific effects. In clinical situations, studies have also specifically investigated the effects of demographic variables. In a mixed-methods study with

58 patients with chronic pain, Petersen and la Cour (2016) found no differences in effects of MBSR by sociodemographic variables except for the fact that older age tended to predict better outcomes. In an open MBSR trial with 322 adult community members, Greeson et al. (2015) also found the intervention to be effective in reducing depressive symptoms irrespective of religious affiliation, sense of spirituality, trait mindfulness at the start of the intervention, sex, and age. Another study explored the role of attachment style as a personality variable: Cordon, Brown, and Gibson (2009) classified MBSR course participants as securely and insecurely attached and found that the latter presented with significantly higher levels of stress prior to commencing the MBSR course. While both groups benefitted from MBSR, findings indicated that the intervention may have been slightly more effective for those with insecure attachment styles.

Any discussion of between-participant variation of effectiveness of MBIs would be incomplete if only positive change was considered and not the possibility of contraindication. The potential for adverse effects of meditation practice has been acknowledged already before the development of MBSR. Deatherage (1975), for example, cautioned against the use of insight meditation practice for participants with psychosis, although subsequent empirical research indicated that MBIs appear to be safe interventions for people with distressing psychosis (Chadwick, Hughes, Russell, Russell, & Dagnan, 2009). However, evidence from a study of 27 participants in an intensive 10-day Vipassana meditation retreat revealed that most participants had experienced one adverse effect, while two participants suffered profound adverse effects (Shapiro, 1992b). Future research will need to explore to what extent this may have been a reflection of self-selection biases or whether it might have been due to the fact that Vipassana retreats include a more restricted range of meditation and mindfulness techniques than MBIs. Another possibility may have been the absence of a discussion-based format and guidance such as found in MBIs, which may protect against the emergence of adverse effects.

Apart from general conclusions about the safety of MBIs for individuals with certain conditions, the literature has also started to address the issue of participant monitoring during the intervention, although reviews by Dobkin, Irving, and Amar (2012) as well as Hanley et al. (2016) indicated that such monitoring is still very sporadic. On the other hand, there may not be any particular pattern that could be used to identify at-risk individuals as indicated by a study that explicitly investigated the progression of emotional responding in an MBI (Harel, Hadash, Levi-Belz, & Bernstein, 2018). In order to investigate to what extent the experience of positive and negative affect may predict drop-out, Harel et al. (2018) modelled the effects of emotional responding on a weekly basis during a four-week MBI. There was no evidence that early emotional reactions to the intervention were associated with subsequent treatment outcomes, nor were there any indications that those that reported experiencing more negative emotions were more likely to drop out.

A very different approach in regard to tracking trajectories of change is taken in the literature on single-subject designs (also referred to as single-case or small-*n* designs) where the effects of experimental manipulations are demonstrated within the participant. Although not qualifying as an MBI, Jouper and Johansson (2013) reported on a single-case report of a participant who had to leave work due to burnout. The aim of the study was described as being achieved if the participant recovered her mood to a functional level. Over a period of 12 weeks, the participant engaged in qigong and mindfulness exercises, while noting exercise behaviours, stress levels, and wellness daily, and mindfulness at three time points. In another single-case study, Demarzo et al. (2014) offered an adapted MBSR programme to a male high-performance athlete. Over a period of 23 weeks, the participant was taught various mindfulness exercises and related psychoeducation face to face by an MBI instructor. The session-to-session outline was presented in detail in a table, and the length of the programme was a result of the fact that the participant was unavailable for several weeks for reasons such attendance at sports competitions. Based on pre-post comparisons as well as weekly tracking of various physiological and psychological measures, the authors concluded that the intervention could present a feasible and useful approach for high-performance athletes. Other related single-case design studies for mindfulness interventions focused on the teaching of a mindfulness-based self-control strategy to assist an adult with intellectual disability in dealing with his aggression (Singh, Wahler, Adkins, Myers, & The Mindfulness Research Group, 2003) or mindfulness training as part of one of the intervention phases in a changing-criterion ABCD design study to address issues related to hyperphagia in an adolescent with Prader-Willi Syndrome (Singh et al., 2008b).

Summary and conclusion

Since the first publications reporting on the results from MBSR programme in the early 1980s, the MBI literature has expanded substantially. In addition to clinical applications such as MBCT for recurring depression, a large variety of specific MBIs has been developed and tested, which also extended the use of mindfulness to broader, nonclinical, contexts. An increasing number of systematic literature reviews and meta-analyses point to the growing evidence base for the effectiveness of MBIs, although a number of methodological shortcomings of MBI studies continue to be identified. This includes selection of adequate control conditions in RCTs, sufficiently large sample sizes, information on treatment fidelity, or adherence to home practice. Research has also started to collect information on the cost effectiveness of MBIs and investigated the effects of moderating variables such as participant characteristics and expectations. The popularity of MBIs has also led to the development of alternative delivery formats to reach a larger range of participants such as through smartphones or other eHealth platforms.

The empirical evidence for the effectiveness of MBIs is also able to inform further theoretical development through testing models of action. While initial work generally confirmed the theoretical understanding of the mechanism by which MBIs exert their therapeutic benefits, dismantling studies have also attempted isolate specific aspects that may be associated with various psychological outcomes variables. Due to the variety of techniques employed in MBIs and the subtle and transformative elements of mindfulness practice, MBIs have to be understood as complex interventions. Additionally, MBIs cannot be understood as uniform as there are substantial differences in the content of the various interventions (Chiesa & Malinowski, 2011). At the same time, the effects of various aspects of mindfulness practice that are commonly found in MBIs are also tested using laboratory designs that focus their investigations on fundamental psychological processes.

References

Agee, J. D., Danoff-Burg, S., & Grant, C. A. (2009). Comparing brief stress management courses in a community sample: mindfulness skills and progressive muscle relaxation. *Explore*, 5(2), 104–109. doi:10.1016/j.explore.2008.1doi:2.004

Ajzen, I. (1991). The theory of planned behavior. *Organizational Behavior and Human Decision Processes*, 50(2), 179–211. doi:10.1016/0749-5978(91)90020-T

Alberts, H. J. E. M., & Thewissen, R. (2011). The effect of a brief mindfulness intervention on memory for positively and negatively valenced stimuli. *Mindfulness*, 2(2), 73–77. doi:10.1007/s12671-011-0044-7

Alfonso, J. P., Caracuel, A., Delgado-Pastor, L. C., & Verdejo-García, A. (2011). Combined goal management training and mindfulness meditation improve executive functions and decision-making performance in abstinent polysubstance abusers. *Drug and Alcohol Dependence*, 117(1), 78–81. doi:10.1016/j.drugalcdep.2010.12.0doi:25

Alsubaie, M., Dickens, C., Dunn, B. D., Gibson, A., Ukoumunne, O. C., Evans, A., ..., & Kuyken, W. (2018). Feasibility and acceptability of Mindfulness-based Cognitive Therapy with Mindfulness-based Stress Reduction and treatment as usual in people with depression and cardiovascular disorders: a three-arm randomised controlled trial. *Mindfulness*. Online First. doi:10.1007/s12671-018-0999-8

Arain, M., Campbell, M. J., Cooper, C. L., & Lancaster, G. A. (2010). What is a pilot or feasibility study? A review of current practice and editorial policy. *BMC Medical Research Methodology*, 10, 67. doi:10.1186/1471-2288-10-67

Arch, J. J. & Ayers, C. R. (2013). Which treatment worked better for whom? Moderators of group cognitive behavioural therapy versus adapted mindfulness based stress reduction for anxiety disorders. *Behaviour Research and Therapy*, 51(8), 434–442. doi:10.1016/j. brat.2013.04doi:004

Arch, J. J. & Craske, M. G. (2006). Mechanisms of mindfulness: emotion regulation following a focused breathing induction. *Behaviour Research and Therapy*, 44(12), 1849–1858. doi:10.1016/j.brat.2005doi:12.007

Aspy, D. J. & Proeve, M. (2017). Mindfulness and loving-kindness meditation: effects on connectedness to humanity and to the natural world. *Psychological Reports*, 120(1), 102–117. doi:10.1177/0033294116685867

Aust, J. & Bradshaw, T. (2017). Mindfulness interventions for psychosis: a systematic review of the literature. *Journal of Psychiatric and Mental Health Nursing*, 24(1), 69–83. doi:10.1111/jpm.12357

Baer, R. A. (2003). Mindfulness training as a clinical intervention: a conceptual and empirical review. *Clinical Psychology: Science and Practice*, 10(2), 125–143. doi:10.1093/clipsy/bpg015

Baer, R. A., Smith, G. T., Hopkins, J., Krietemeyer, J., & Toney, L. (2006). Using self-report assessment methods to explore facets of mindfulness. *Assessment*, 13(1), 27–45. doi:10.1177/1073191105283504

Banerjee, M., Cavanagh, K., & Strauss, C. (2018). Barriers to mindfulness: a path analytic model exploring the role of rumination and worry in predicting psychological and physical engagement in an online mindfulness-based intervention. *Mindfulness*, 9(3), 980–992. doi:10.1007/s12671-017-0837-4

Barkan, T., Hoerger, M., Gallegos, A. M., Turiano, N. A., Duberstein, P. R., & Moynihan, J. A. (2016). Personality predicts utilization of Mindfulness-Based Stress Reduction during and post-intervention in a community sample of older adults. *Journal of Alternative and Complementary Medicine*, 22(5), 390–395. doi:10.1089/acm.2015.0177

Barnett, A. G., van der Pols, J. C., & Dobson, A. J. (2015). Regression to the mean: what it is and how to deal with it. *International Journal of Epidemiology*, 34(1), 215–220. doi:10.1093/ije/dyh299

Bawa, F. L. M., Mercer, S. W., Atherton, R. J., Clague, F., Keen, A., Scott, N. W., & Bond, C.M. (2012). Does mindfulness improve outcomes in patients with chronic pain? Systematic review and meta-analysis. *British Journal of General Practice*, 65(635), e387–e400. doi:10.3399/bjgp15X685297

Bayot, M., Vermeulen, N., Kever, A., & Mikolajczak, M. (2018). Mindfulness and empathy: differential effects of explicit and implicit Buddhist teachings. *Mindfulness*. Online First. doi:10.1007/s12671-018-0966-4

Bazarko, D., Cate, R. A., Azocar, F., & Kreitzer, M. J. (2013). The impact of an innovative Mindfulness-Based Stress Reduction program on the health and well-being of nurses employed in a corporate setting. *Journal of Workplace Behavioral Health*, 28(2), 107–133. doi:10.1080/15555240.2013.779518

Beattie, M., Hankonen, N., Salo, G., Knittle, K., & Volanen, S.-M. (2018). Applying behavioral theory to increase mindfulness practice among adolescents: an exploratory intervention study using a within-trial RCT design. *Mindfulness*. Online First. doi:10.1007/s12671-018-0976-2

Bellmann-Strobl, J., Pach, D., Chang, Y., Pasura, L., Liu, B., Jäger, S. F., ..., & Shi, X. (2018). The effectiveness of acupuncture and mindfulness-based stress reduction (MBSR) for patients with multiple sclerosis associated fatigue: a study protocol and its rationale for a randomized controlled trial. *European Journal of Integrative Medicine*, 20, 6–15. doi:10.1016/j.eujim.2018doi:04.001

Bergen-Cico, D., Possemato, K., & Cheon, S. (2013). Examining the efficacy of a brief Mindfulness-Based Stress Reduction (Brief MBSR) program on psychological health. *Journal of American College Health*, 61(6), 348–360. doi:10.1080/07448481.2013.813853

Beshara, M., Hutchinson, A. D., & Wilson, C. (2013). Does mindfulness matter? Everyday mindfulness, mindful eating and self-reported serving size of energy dense foods among a sample of South Australian adults. *Appetite*, 67, 25–29. doi:10.1016/j.appet.2013.03.doi:012

Blanck, P., Perleth, S., Heidenreich, T., Kröger, P., Ditzen, B., Bents, H., & Mander, J. (2018). Effects of mindfulness exercises as stand-alone intervention on symptoms of anxiety and depression: systematic review and meta-analysis. *Behaviour Research and Therapy*, 102, 25–35. doi:10.1016/j.brat.2017.1doi:2.002

Bluth, K., Roberson, P. N. E., & Girdler, S. S. (2017). Adolescent sex differences in response to a mindfulness intervention: a call for research. *Journal of Child and Family Studies*, 26(7), 1900–1914. doi:10.1007/s11896-015-9161-x

Bohlmeijer, E., Prenger, R., Taal, E., & Cuijpers, P. (2010). The effects of mindfulness-based stress reduction therapy on mental health of adults with chronic medical disease: a meta-analysis. *Journal of Psychosomatic Research*, 68(6), 539–544. doi:10.1016/j.jpsychores.2009.10.0doi:05

Britton, W. B., Davis, J. H., Loucks, E. B., Peterson, B., Cullen, B. H., Reuter, L., ..., & Lindahl, J. R. (2018). Dismantling Mindfulness-Based Cognitive Therapy: creation and validation of 8-week focused attention and open monitoring interventions within a 3-armed randomized controlled trial. *Behaviour Research and Therapy*, 101, 92–107. doi:10.1016/j.brat.2017.09.doi:010

Broderick, P. C., Frank, J. L., Berrena, E., Schussler, D. L., Kohler, K., Mitra, J., …, & Greenberg, M. T. (2018). Evaluating the quality of mindfulness instruction delivered in school settings: development and validation of a teacher quality observational rating scale. *Mindfulness*. Online First. doi:10.1007/s12671-018-0944-x

Burke, C. A. (2010). Mindfulness-based approaches with children and adolescents: a preliminary review of current research in an emergent field. *Journal of Child and Family Studies*, 19(2), 133–144. doi:10.1007/s10826-009-9282-x

Büssing, A., Hedtstück, A., Khalsa, S. B. S., Ostermann, T., & Heusser, P. (2012). Development of specific aspects of spirituality during a 6-month intensive yoga practice. *Evidence-Based Complementary and Alternative Medicine*, Article ID 981523. doi:10.1155/2012/981523

Carlson, L. E., Zelinski, E. L., Speca, M., Balneaves, L. G., Jones, J. M., Mina, D. S., …, & Vohra, S. (2017). Protocol for the MATCH study (mindfulness and tai chi for cancer health): a preference-based multi-site randomized comparative effectiveness trial (CET) of mindfulness-based cancer recovery (MBCR) vs. tai chi/qigong (TCQ) for cancer survivors. *Contemporary Clinical Trials*, 59, 64–76. doi:10.1016/j.cct.2017.0doi:5.015

Carmody, J., & Baer, R. A. (2009). How long does a mindfulness-based stress reduction program need to be? A review of class contact hours and effects sizes for psychological distress. *Journal of Clinical Psychology*, 65(6), 627–638. doi:10.1002/jclp.20555

Carmody, J., Baer, R. A., Lykins, E. L. B., & Olendzki, N. (2009). An empirical study of the mechanisms of mindfulness in a Mindfulness-Based Stress Reduction program. *Journal of Clinical Psychology*, 65(6), 613–626. doi:10.1002/jclp.20579

Carson, J. W., Carson, K. M., Gil, K. M., & Baucom, D. H. (2004). Mindfulness-based relationship enhancement. *Behavior Therapy*, 35(3), 471–494. doi:10.1016/S0005-7894(04)80028-5

Chadwick, P., Hughes, S., Russell, D., Russell, I., & Dagnan, D. (2009). Mindfulness groups for distressing voices and paranoia: a replication and randomized feasibility trial. *Behavioural and Cognitive Psychotherapy*, 37(4), 403–412. doi:10.1017/S1352465809990166

Chiesa, A., Anselmi, R., & Serretti, A. (2014). Psychological mechanisms of mindfulness-based interventions. *Holistic Nursing Practice*, 28(2), 124–148. doi:10.1097/HNP.0000000000000017

Chiesa, A. & Malinowski, P. (2011). Mindfulness-based approaches: are they all the same? *Journal of Clinical Psychology*, 67(4), 404–424. doi:10.1002/jclp.20776

Chiesa, A. & Serretti, A. (2009). Mindfulness-Based Stress Reduction for stress management in healthy people: a review and meta-analysis. *Journal of Alternative and Complementary Medicine*, 15(5), 593–600. doi:10.1089/acm.2008.0495

Chiesa, A. & Serretti, A. (2014). Are mindfulness-based interventions effective for substance use disorders? A systematic review of the evidence. *Substance Use & Misuse*, 49(5), 492–512. doi:10.3109/10826084.2013.770027

Christopher, M. S., Goerling, R. J., Rogers, B. S., Hunsinger, M., Baron, G., Bergman, A. L., & Zava, D. T. (2016). A pilot study evaluating the effectiveness of a mindfulness-based intervention on cortisol awakening response and health outcomes among law enforcement officers. *Journal of Police and Criminal Psychology*, 31(1), 15–28. doi:10.1007/s11896-015-9161-x

Christopher, M. S., Hunsinger, M., Goerling, R. J., Bowen, S., Rogers, B. S., Gross, C. R., …, & Pruessner, J. C. (2018). Mindfulness-based resilience training to reduce health risk, stress reactivity, and aggression among law enforcement officers: a feasibility and preliminary efficacy trial. *Psychiatry Research*, 264, 104–115. doi:10.1016/j.psychres.2018.03.doi:059

Cordon, S. L., Brown, K. W., & Gibson, P. R. (2009). The role of mindfulness-based stress reduction on perceived stress: preliminary evidence for the moderating role of attachment style. *Journal of Cognitive Psychotherapy*, 23(3), 258–269. doi:10.1891/0889-8391.23.3.258

Crane, R. S., Brewer, J., Feldman, C., Kabat-Zinn, J., Santorelli, S., Williams, J. M. G., & Kuyken, W. (2017). What defines mindfulness-based programs? The warp and the weft. *Psychological Medicine*, 47(6), 990–999. doi:10.1017/S0033291716003317

Crockett, J. E., Cashwell, C. S., Tangen, J. L.Hall, K. H., & Young, J. S. (2016). Breathing characteristics and symptoms of psychological distress: an exploratory study. *Counseling and Values*, 61(1), 10–27. doi:10.1002/cvj.12023

Davidson, R. J., Kabat-Zinn, J., Schumacher, J., Rosenkranz, M., Muller, D., Santorelli, S. F., …, & Sheridan, J. F. (2003). Alterations in brain and immune function produced by mindfulness meditation. *Psychosomatic Medicine*, 65(4), 564–570. doi:10.1097/01. PSY.0000077505.67574.E3

Davidson, R. J., & Kaszniak, A. W. (2015). Conceptual and methodological issues in research on mindfulness and meditation. *American Psychologist*, 70(7), 581–592. doi:10.1037/a0039512

Demarzo, M. M. P., de Oliveira, R. M. J., Silva, D. F. A., Lessa-Moreno, I., de Abreu, L. C., Barceló, A., & Garcia-Campayo, J. (2014). Mindfulness applied to high performance athletes: a case report. *Actas Españolas de Psiquiatría*, 43(Supl. 1), 84–90.

Demarzo, M., Montero-Marin, J., Puebla-Guedea, M., Navarro-Gil, M., Herrera-Mercadal, P., Moreno-González, S., …, & Garcia-Campayo, J. (2017). Efficacy of 8- and 4-session mindfulness-based interventions in non-clinical populations: a controlled study. *Frontiers in Psychology*, 8, 1343. doi:10.3389/fpsyg.2017.01343

Dhillon, A., Sparkes, E., & Duarte, R. V. (2017). Mindfulness-based interventions during pregnancy: a systematic review and meta-analysis. *Mindfulness*, 8(6), 1421–1437. doi:10.1007/s12671-017-0726-x

Dimidjian, S., Beck, A., Felder, J. N., Boggs, J. M., Gallop, R., & Segal, Z. V. (2014). Web-based Mindfulness-based Cognitive Therapy for reducing residual depressive symptoms: an open trial and quasi-experimental comparison to propensity score matched controls. *Behaviour Research and Therapy*, 63, 83–89. doi:10.1016/j.brat.2014.09.004

Dimidjian, S., & Segal, Z. V. (2015). Prospects for a clinical science of mindfulness-based intervention. *American Psychologist*, 70(7), 593–620. doi:10.1037/a0039589

Dobkin, P. L., Irving, J. A., & Amar, S. (2012). For whom may participation in a mindfulness-based stress reduction program be contraindicated? *Mindfulness*, 3(1), 44–50. doi:10.1007/s12671-011-0079-9

Dobkin, P. L., Hickman, S., & Monshat, K. (2014). Holding the heart of Mindfulness-Based Stress Reduction: balancing fidelity and imagination when adapting MBSR. *Mindfulness*, 5(6), 710–718. doi:10.1007/s12671-013-0225-7

Doyle, S. L., Brown, J. L., Rasheed, D., Jones, D. E., & Jennings, P. A. (2018). Cost analysis of ingredients for successful implementation of a mindfulness-based professional development program for teachers. *Mindfulness*. Online First. doi:10.1007/s12671-018-0958-4

Eisenbeck, N., Luciano, C., & Valdivia-Salas, S. (2018). Effects of a focused breathing mindfulness exercise on attention, memory, and mood: the importance of task characteristics. *Behaviour Change*, 35(1), 54–70. doi:10.1017/bec.2018.9

Escuriex, B. F. & Labbé, E. E. (2011). Health care providers' mindfulness and treatment outcomes: a critical review of the research literature. *Mindfulness*, 2(4), 242–253. doi:10.1007/s12671-011-0068-z

Falcone, G. & Jerram, M. (2018). Brain activity in mindfulness depends on experience: a meta-analysis of fMRI studies. *Mindfulness*. Online First. doi:10.1007/s12671-018-0884-5

Feldman, G., Greeson, J., & Senville, J. (2010). Differential effects of mindful breathing, progressive muscle relaxation, and loving-kindness meditation on decentering and negative reactions to repetitive thoughts. *Behaviour Research and Therapy*, 48(10), 1002–1011. doi:10.1016/j.brat.2010.0doi:6.006

Fisher, C., Hauck, Y., Bayes, S., & Byrne, J. (2012). Participants experiences of mindfulness-based childbirth education: a qualitative study. *BMC Pregnancy and Childbirth*, 12, 126. doi:10.1186/1471-2393-12-126

Fjorback, L. O., Arendt, M., Ørnbøl, E., Fink, P., & Walach, H. (2011). Mindfulness-Based Stress Reduction and Mindfulness-Based Cognitive Therapy: a systematic review of randomized controlled trials. *Acta Psychiatrica Scandinavica*, 124(2), 102–119. doi:10.1111/j.1600-0447.2011.01704.x

Fox, K. C. R., Nijeboer, S., Dixon, M. L., Floman, J. L., Ellamil, M., Rumak, S. P., ..., & Christoff, K. (2014). Is meditation associated with altered brain structure? A systematic review and meta-analysis of morphometric neuroimaging in meditation practitioners. *Neuroscience and Biobehavioral Reviews*, 43, 48–73. doi:10.1016/j.neubiorev.2014.03.016

Fresco, D. M., Segal, Z. V., Buis, T., & Kennedy, S. (2007). Relationship of posttreatment decentering and cognitive reactivity to relapse in major depression. *Journal of Consulting and Clinical Psychology*, 75(3), 447–455. doi:10.1037/0022-006X.75.3.447

Galante, J., Dufour, G., Benton, A., Howarth, E., Vainre, M., Croudace, T. J., ..., & Jones, P. B. (2016). Protocol for the Mindful Student Study: a randomised controlled trial of the provision of a mindfulness intervention to support university students' well-being and resilience to stress. *BMJ Open*, 6, e012300. doi:10.1136/bmjopen-2016-012300

Galhardo, A., Moura-Ramos, M., Cunha, M., & Pinto-Gouveia, J. (2018). How does the Mindfulness-Based Program for Infertility (MBPI) work in reducing depressive symptoms? *Mindfulness*, 9(2), 629–635. doi:10.1007/s12671-017-0805-z

Gard, T., Brach, N., Hölzel, B. K., Noggle, J. J., Conboy, L. A., & Lazar, S. W. (2012). Effects of a yoga-based intervention for young adults on quality of life and perceived stress: the potential mediating roles of mindfulness and self-compassion. *Journal of Positive Psychology*, 7(3), 165–175. doi:10.1080/17439760.2012.667144

Gotink, R. A., Chu, P., Busschbach, J. J. V., Benson, H., Fricchione, G. L., & Hunink, M. G. M. (2015). Standardised mindfulness-based interventions in healthcare: An overview of systematic reviews and meta-analyses of RCTs. *PLoS ONE*, 10(4), e0124344. doi:10.1371/journal.pone.0124344

Gotink, R. A., Meijboom, R., Vernooij, M. W., Smits, M., & Hunink, M. G. M. (2016). 8-week Mindfulness Based Stress Reduction induces brain changes similar to traditional long-term meditation practice: a systematic review. *Brain and Cognition*, 108, 32–41. doi:10.1016/j.bandc.2016doi:07.001

Greeson, J. M., Smoski, M. J., Suarez, E. C., Brantley, J. G., Ekblad, A. G., Lynch, T. R., & Wolever, R. Q. (2015). Decreased symptoms of depression after mindfulness-based stress reduction: potential moderating effects of religiosity, spirituality, trait mindfulness, sex, and age. *Journal of Alternative and Complementary Medicine*, 21(3), 166–174. doi:10.1089/acm.2014.0285

Grossman, P., Niemann, L., Schmidt, S., & Walach, H. (2004). Mindfulness-based stress reduction and health benefits: a meta-analysis. *Journal of Psychosomatic Research*, 57(1), 35–43. doi:10.1016/S0022-3999(03)00573-7

Gu, J., Strauss, C., Bond, R., & Cavanagh, K. (2015). How do mindfulness-based cognitive therapy and mindfulness-based stress reduction improve mental health and wellbeing? A systematic review and meta-analysis of mediation studies. *Clinical Psychological Review*, 37, 1–12. doi:10.1016/j.cpr.2015.01doi:006

Gupta, S. K. (2011). Intention-to-treat concept: a review. *Perspectives in Clinical Research*, 2 (3), 109–112. doi:10.4103/2229-3485.83221

Hanley, A. W., Abell, N., Osborn, D. S., Roehrig, A. D., & Canto, A. I. (2016). Mind the gaps: are conclusions about mindfulness entirely conclusive? *Journal of Counseling & Development*, 94(1), 103–113. doi:10.1002/jcad.12066

Harel, O., Hadash, Y., Levi-Belz, Y., & Bernstein, A. (2018). Does early emotional responding to initial mindfulness training impact intervention outcomes? *Mindfulness.* Online First. doi:10.1007/s12671-018-1018-9

Harrington, A. & Dunne, J. D. (2015). When mindfulness is therapy: ethical qualms, historical perspectives. *American Psychologist,* 70(7), 621–631. doi:10.1037/a0039460

Hayes, S. C., Strosahl, K. D., & Wilson, K. G. (2011). *Acceptance and Commitment Therapy: the process and practice of mindful change.* New York, USA: Guilford Press.

Henning, M. A., Krägeloh, C. U., Dryer, R., Moir, F., Billington, R., & Hill, A. G. (Eds.) (2018). *Wellbeing higher education: cultivating a healthy lifestyle among faculty and students.* Oxon, United Kingdom: Routledge.

Hertzog, M. A. (2008). Considerations in determining sample size for pilot studies. *Research in Nursing & Health,* 31(2), 180–191. doi:10.1002/nur.20247

Hitchcock, P. F., Martin, L. M., Fischer, L., Marando-Blanck, S., & Herbert, J. D. (2016). Popular conceptions of mindfulness: awareness and emotional control. *Mindfulness,* 7(4), 940–949. doi:10.1007/s12671-016-0533-9

Ho, R. T. H., Wan, A. H. Y., Chan, J. S. M., Ng, S. M., Chung, K. F., & Chan, C. L. W. (2017). Study protocol on comparative effectiveness of mindfulness meditation and qigong on psychophysiological outcomes for patients with colorectal cancer: a randomized controlled trial. *BMC Complementary and Alternative Medicine,* 17, 390. doi:10.1186/s12906-017-1898-6

Hofmann, S. G., Sawyer, A. T., Witt, A. A., & Oh, D. (2010). The effect of mindfulness-based therapy on anxiety and depression: a meta-analytic review. *Journal of Consulting and Clinical Psychology,* 78(2), 169–183. doi:10.1037/a0018555

Holmes, E. M., Craske, M. G., & Graybiel, A. M. (2014). A call for mental health science. *Nature,* 511(7509), 287–289. doi:10.1038/511287a

Hölzel, B. K., Ott, U., Gard, T., Hempel, H., Weygandt, M., Morgen, K., & Vaitl, D. (2008). Investigation of mindfulness meditation practitioners with voxel-based morphometry. *Social Cognitive and Affective Neuroscience,* 3(1), 55–61. doi:10.1093/scan/nsm038

Hölzel, B. K., Carmody, J., Vangel, M., Congleton, C., Yerramsetti, S. M., Garda, T., & Lazara, S. W. (2011). Mindfulness practice leads to increases in regional brain gray matter density. *Psychiatry Research: Neuroimaging,* 191(1), 36–43. doi:10.1016/j.psycychresns.2010.08doi:006

Honda, K., & Jacobson, J. S. (2005). Use of complementary and alternative medicine among United States adults: the influences of personality, coping strategies, and social support. *Preventive Medicine,* 40(1), 46–53. doi:10.1016/j.ypmed.2004doi:05.001

Hunt, M., Al-Braiki, F., Dailey, S., Russell, R., & Simon, K. (2018). Mindfulness training, yoga, or both? Dismantling the active components of a mindfulness-based stress reduction intervention. *Mindfulness.* Online First. doi:10.1007/s12671-017-0793-z

Hussein, M., Egan, H., & Mantzios, M. (2017). Mindful construal diaries: a less anxious, more mindful, and more self-compassionate method of eating. *Sage Open.* Online First. doi:10.1177/2158244017704685

Ietsugu, T., Crane, C., Hackmann, A., Brennan, K., Gross, M., Crane, R. S., ..., & Barnhofer, T. (2015). Gradually getting better: trajectories of change in rumination and anxious worry in Mindfulness-Based Cognitive Therapy for prevention of relapse to recurrent depression. *Mindfulness,* 6(5), 1088–1094. doi:10.1007/s12671-014-0358-3

Jager, J., Putnick, D. L., & Bornstein, M. H. (2017). II. More than just convenient: the scientific merits of homogeneous convenience samples. *Monographs of the Society for Research in Child Development,* 82(2), 13–30. doi:10.1111/mono.12296

Jain, S., Shapiro, S. L., Swanick, S., Roesch, S. C., Mills, P. J., Bell, I., & Schwartz, G. E. R. (2007). A randomized controlled trial of mindfulness meditation versus relaxation training:

effects on distress, positive states of mind, rumination, and distraction. *Annals of Behavioral Medicine*, 33(1), 11–21. doi:10.1207/s15324796abm3301_2

Jani, B. D., Simpson, R., Lawrence, M., Simpson, S., & Mercer, S. W. (2018). Acceptability of mindfulness from the perspective of stroke survivors and caregivers: a qualitative study. *Pilot and Feasibility Studies*, 4, 57. doi:10.1186/s40814-018-0244-1

Jarry, J. L., Chang, F. M., & La Civita, L. (2018). Ashtanga yoga for psychological well-being: initial effectiveness study. *Mindfulness*. Online First. doi:10.1007/s12671-017-0703-4

Jiga, K., Kaunhoven, R. J., & Dorjee, D. (2018). Feasibility and efficacy of an adapted mindfulness-based intervention (MBI) in areas of socioeconomic deprivation (SED). *Mindfulness*. Online First. doi:10.1007/s12671-018-0977-1

Jouper, J. & Johansson, M. (2013). Qigong and mindfulness-based mood recovery: exercise experiences from a single case. *Journal of Bodywork & Movement Therapies*, 17(1), 69–76. doi:10.1016/j.jbmt.2012.06.0doi:04

Juul, L., Pallesen, K. J., Piet, J., Parsons, C., & Fjorback, L. O. (2018). Effectiveness of mindfulness-based stress reduction in a self-selecting and self-paying community setting. *Mindfulness*, 9(4), 1288–1298. doi:10.1007/s12671-017-0873-0

Kabat-Zinn, J. (1982). An outpatient program in behavioral medicine for chronic pain patients based on the practice of mindfulness meditation: theoretical considerations and preliminary results. *General Hospital Psychiatry*, 4(1), 33–47. doi:10.1016/0163-8343(82)90026-3

Kabat-Zinn, J., Lipworth, L., & Burney, R. (1985). The clinical use of mindfulness meditation for the self-regulation of chronic pain. *Journal of Behavioral Medicine*, 8(2), 163–190. doi:10.1007/BF00845519

Kabat-Zinn, J., Lipworth, L., Burney, R., & Sellers, W. (1986). Four-year follow-up of a meditation-based program for the self-regulation of chronic pain: treatment outcomes and compliance. *Clinical Journal of Pain*, 2(3), 159–173. doi:10.1097/00002508-198602030-00004

Kabat-Zinn, J. (1990). *Full catastrophe living: using the wisdom of your body and mind to face stress, pain, and illness*. New York, USA: Delacourt.

Kabat-Zinn, J. (1994). *Wherever you go, there you are*. New York, USA: Hyperion Books.

Kabat-Zinn, J., Wheeler, E., Light, T., Skillings, A., Scharf, M. J., Cropley, T. G., Hosmer, D., & Bernhard, J. D. (1998). Influence of a mindfulness meditation-based stress reduction intervention on rates of skin clearing in patients with moderate to severe psoriasis undergoing phototherapy (UVB) and photochemotherapy (PUVA). *Psychosomatic Medicine*, 60(5), 625–632. doi:10.1097/00006842-199809000-00020

Kang, Y., Rahrig, H., Eichel, K., Niles, H. F., Rocha, T., Lepp, N. E., …, & Britton, W. B. (2018). Gender differences in response to a school-based mindfulness training intervention for early adolescents. *Journal of School Psychology*, 68, 163–176. doi:10.1016/j.jsp.2018.doi:03.004

Kechter, A., Amaro, H., & Black, D. S. (2018). Reporting of treatment fidelity in mindfulness-based intervention trials: a review and new tool using NIH Behavior Change Consortium guidelines. *Mindfulness*. Online First. doi:10.1007/s12671-018-0974-4

Keng, S.-L., Smoski, M. J., Robins, C. J., Ekblad, A. G., & Brantley, J. G. (2012). Mechanisms of change in Mindfulness-Based Stress Reduction: self-compassion and mindfulness as mediators of intervention outcomes. *Journal of Cognitive Psychotherapy*, 26 (3), 270–280. doi:10.1891/0889-8391.26.doi:3.270

Keng, S.-L., Seah, S. T. H., Tong, E. M. W., & Smoski, M. (2016). Effects of brief mindful acceptance induction on implicit dysfunctional attitudes and concordance between implicit and explicit dysfunctional attitudes. *Behaviour Research and Therapy*, 83, 1–10. doi:10.1016/j.brat.2016.0doi:5.004

Khoury, B., Lecomte, T., Fortin, G., Masse, M., Therien, P., Bouchard, V., …, & Hofmann, S. G. (2013). Mindfulness-based therapy: a comprehensive meta-analysis. *Clinical Psychology Review*, 33(6), 763–771. doi:10.1016/j.cpr.2013.05doi:005

Khoury, B., Sharma, M., Rush, S. E., & Fournier, C. (2015). Mindfulness-based stress reduction for healthy individuals: a meta-analysis. *Journal of Psychosomatic Research*, 78(6), 519–528. doi:10.1016/j.jpsychores.2015. 03. 00doi:9

Kim, S. M., Park, J. M., & Seo, H.-J. (2016). Effects of mindfulness-based stress reduction for adults with sleep disturbance: a protocol for an update of a systematic review and meta-analysis. *Systematic Reviews*, 5, 51. doi:10.1186/s13643-016-0228-2

Kinser, P.Braun, S., Deeb, G., Carrico, C., & Dow, A. (2016). "Awareness is the first step": an interprofessional course on mindfulness & mindful-movement for healthcare professionals and students. *Complementary Therapies in Clinical Practice*, 25, 18–25. doi:10.1016/j.ctcp.2016.08.003

Klingbeil, D. A., Renshaw, T. L., Willenbrink, J. B., Copek, R. A., Chan, K. T., Haddock, A., ..., & Clifton, J. (2017). Mindfulness-based interventions with youth: a comprehensive meta-analysis of group-design studies. *Journal of School Psychology*, 63, 77–103. doi:10.1016/j.jsp.2017.03.doi:006

Krägeloh, C. U., Medvedev, O. N., Taylor, T., Wrapson, W., Rix, G., Sumich, A., ..., & Siegert, R. J. (2018). A pilot randomized controlled trial for a videoconference-delivered mindfulness-based group intervention in a nonclinical setting. *Mindfulness*. Online First. doi:10.1007/s12671-018-1024-y

Kristeller, J. L., Baer, R. A., & Quillian-Wolever, R. (2006). Mindfulness-based approaches to eating disorders. In R. Baer (Ed.), *Mindfulness and acceptance-based interventions: conceptualization, application, and empirical support* (pp.75–91). San Diego, CA: Elsevier.

Kuyken, W., Watkins, E., Holden, E., White, K., Taylor, R. S., Byford, S., ..., & Dalgleish, T. (2010). How does mindfulness-based cognitive therapy work? *Behaviour Research and Therapy*, 48(11), 1105–1112. doi:10.1016/j.brat.2010. 08. 00doi:3

Kuyken, W., Hayes, R., Barrett, B., Byng, R., Dalgleish, T., Kessler, D., ..., & Byford, S. (2015). Effectiveness and cost-effectiveness of mindfulness-based cognitive therapy compared with maintenance antidepressant treatment in the prevention of depressive relapse or recurrence (PREVENT): a randomised controlled trial. *Lancet*, 386(9988), 63–73. doi:10.1016/S0140-6736(14)62222-4

Lancaster, S. L., Klein, K. P., & Knightly, W. (2016). Mindfulness and relaxation: a comparison of brief, laboratory-based interventions. *Mindfulness*, 7(3), 614–621. doi:10.1007/s12671-016-0496-x

Langer, Á., Cangas, A. J., Salcedo, E., & Fuentes, B. (2012). Applying mindfulness therapy in a group of psychotic individuals: a controlled study. *Behavioural and Cognitive Psychotherapy*, 40(1), 105–109. doi:10.1017/S1352465811000464

Lauche, R., Cramer, H., Dobos, G., Langhorst, J., & Schmidt, S. (2013). A systematic review and meta-analysis of mindfulness-based stress reduction for the fibromyalgia syndrome. *Journal of Psychosomatic Research*, 75(6), 500–510. doi:10.1016/j.jpsychores.2013.10.0doi:10

Lee, A. C., Harvey, W. F., Price, L. L., Morgan, L. P. K., Morgan, N. L., & Wang, C. (2017a). Mindfulness is associated with psychological health and moderates pain in knee osteoarthritis. *Osteoarthritis and Cartilage*, 25(6), 824–831. doi:10.1016/j.joca.2016.06.0doi:17

Lee, S., Kim, M. W., McDonough, I. M., Mendoza, J. S., & Kim, M. S. (2017b). The effects of cell phone use and emotion-regulation style on college students' learning. *Applied Cognitive Psychology*, 31(3), 360–366. doi:10.1002/acp.3323

Lengacher, C. A., Reich, R. R., Kip, K. E., Barta, M., Ramesar, S., Paterson, C. L., ..., & Park, J. Y. (2014). Influence of Mindfulness-Based Stress Reduction (MBSR) on telomerase activity in women with breast cancer (BC). *Biological Research for Nursing*, 16(4), 438–447. doi:10.1177/1099800413519495

Leonard, N. R., Jha, A. P., Casarjian, B., Goolsarran, M., Garcia, C., Cleland, C. M., ..., & Massey, Z. (2013). Mindfulness training improves attentional task performance in incarcerated youth: a group randomized controlled intervention trial. *Frontiers in Psychology*, 4, 792. doi:10.3389/fpsyg.2013.00792

Leonard, H. D., Campbell, K., & Gonzales, V. M. (2018). The relationships among clinician self-report of empathy, mindfulness, and therapeutic alliance. *Mindfulness*. Online First. doi:10.1007/s12671-018-0926-z

Li, G., Yuan, H., & Zhang, W. (2016). The effects of Mindfulness-Based Stress Reduction for family caregivers: systematic review. *Archives of Psychiatric Nursing*, 30(2), 292–299. doi:10.1016/j.apnu.2015.08.doi:014

Lim, X. & Qu, L. (2017). The effect of single-session mindfulness training on preschool children's attentional control. *Mindfulness*, 8(2), 300–310. doi:10.1007/s12671-016-0600-2

Lindsay, E. K., Young, S., Smyth, J. M., Brown, K. W., & Creswell, J. D. (2018). Acceptance lowers stress reactivity: dismantling mindfulness training in a randomized controlled trial. *Psychoneuroendocrinology*, 87, 63–73. doi:10.1016/j.psyneuen.2017.0doi:9.015

Lloyd, A., White, R., Eames, C., & Crane, R. (2018). The utility of home-practice in mindfulness-based group interventions: a systematic review. *Mindfulness*, 9(3), 673–692. doi:10.1007/s12671-017-0813-z

MacCoon, D. G., Imel, Z. E., Rosenkranz, M. A., Sheftel, J. G., Weng, H. Y., Sullivan, J. C., …, & Lutz, A. (2012). The validation of an active control intervention for Mindfulness Based Stress Reduction (MBSR). *Behaviour Research and Therapy*, 50, 3–12. doi:10.1016/j.brat.2011.doi:10.011

MacDonald, D. A., & Friedman, H. L. (2009). Measures of spiritual and transpersonal constructs for use in yoga research. *International Journal of Yoga*, 2(1), 2–12. doi:10.4103/0973-6131.53837

Madson, L., Klug, B., Madson, L., Stimatze, T., Eness-Potter, K. & MacDonald, J. (2018). Effectiveness of mindfulness-based stress reduction in a community sample over 2 years. *Annals of Clinical Psychiatry*, 30(1), 52–60.

Mahmood, L., Hopthrow, T., & Randsley de Moura, G. R. (2016). A moment of mindfulness: computer-mediated mindfulness practice increases state mindfulness. *PLoS ONE*, 11(4), e0153923. doi:10.1371/journal.pone.0153923

Mak, C., Whittingham, K., Cunnington, R., & Boyd, R. N. (2018). Efficacy of mindfulness-based interventions for attention and executive function in children and adolescents: a systematic review. *Mindfulness*, 9(1), 59–78. doi:10.1007/s12671-017-0770-6

Massion, A. O., Teas, J., Herbert, J. R., Wetheimer, M. D., & Kabat-Zinn, J. (1995). Meditation, melatonin and breast/prostate cancer: hypothesis and preliminary data. *Medical Hypotheses*, 44(1), 39–46. doi:10.1016/0306-9877(95)90299-6

Matiz, A., Fabbro, F., & Crescentini, C. (2018). Single vs. group mindfulness meditation: effects on personality, religiousness/spirituality, and mindfulness skills. *Mindfulness*, 9(4), 1236–1244. doi:10.1007/s12671-017-0865-0

McLean, G., Lawrence, M., Simpson, R., & Mercer, S. W. (2017). Mindfulness-based stress reduction in Parkinson's disease: a systematic review. *BMC Neurology*, 17, 92. doi:10.1186/s12883-017-0876-4

Medical Research Council (2006). *Developing and evaluating complex interventions: new guidance*. Retrieved from www.mrc.ac.uk/complexinterventionsguidance

Minami, H., Brinkmann, H. R., Nahvi, S., Arnsten, J. H., Rivera-Mindt, M., Wetter, D. W., …, & Brown, R. A. (2018). Rationale, design and pilot feasibility results of a smartphone-assisted, mindfulness-based intervention for smokers with mood disorders: project mSMART MIND. *Contemporary Clinical Trials*, 66, 36–44. doi:10.1016/j.cct.2017.1doi:2.014

Mistretta, E. G., Glass, C. R., Spears, C. A., Perskaudas, R., Kaufman, K. A., & Hoyer, D. (2017). Collegiate athletes' expectations and experiences with mindful sport performance enhancement. *Journal of Clinical Sport Psychology*, 11(3), 201–221. doi:10.1123/jcsp.2016-0043

Moore, P. (2008). Introducing mindfulness to clinical psychologists in training: an experiential course of brief exercises. *Journal of Clinical Psychology in Medical Settings*, 15(4), 331–337. doi:10.1007/s10880-008-9134-7

Morrison, A. B., Goolsarran, M., Rogers, S. L., & Jha, A. P. (2014). Taming a wandering attention: short-term mindfulness training in student cohorts. *Frontiers in Human Neuroscience*, 7, 897. doi:10.3389/fnhum.2013.00897

Nila, K., Holt, D. V., Ditzen, B., & Aguilar-Raab, C. (2016). Mindfulness-based stress reduction (MBSR) enhances distress tolerance and resilience through changes in mindfulness. *Mental Health & Prevention*, 4(1), 36–42. doi:10.1016/j.mhp.2016. 01. 00doi:1

Noone, C. & Hogan, M. J. (2018). Improvements in critical thinking performance following mindfulness meditation depend on thinking dispositions. *Mindfulness*, 9(2), 461–473. doi:10.1007/s12671-017-0789-8

Nyklíček, I. & Kuijpers, K. F. K. (2008). Effects of mindfulness-based stress reduction intervention on psychological well-being and quality of life: is increased mindfulness indeed the mechanism? *Annals of Behavioral Medicine*, 35(3), 331–340. doi:10.1007/s12160-008-9030-2

O'Connor, M., Munnelly, A., Whelan, R., & McHugh, L. (2018). The efficacy and acceptability of third-wave behavioural and cognitive eHealth treatments: a systematic review and meta-analysis of randomized controlled trials. *Behavior Therapy*, 49(3), 459–475. doi:10.1016/j.beth.2017.07.doi:007

O'Leary, K., O'Neill, S., & Dockray, S. (2016). A systematic review of the effects of mindfulness interventions on cortisol. *Journal of Health Psychology*, 21(9), 2108–2121. doi:10.1177/1359105315569095

Ostafin, B. D. & Kassman, K. T. (2012). Stepping out of history: mindfulness improves insight problem solving. *Consciousness and Cognition*, 21(2), 1031–1036. doi:10.1016/j.concog.2012.02.doi:014

Parsons, C. E., Crane, C., Parsons, L. J., Fjorback, L. O., & Kuyken, W. (2017). Home practice in Mindfulness-Based Cognitive Therapy and Mindfulness-Based Stress Reduction: a systematic review and meta-analysis of participants' mindfulness practice and its association with outcomes. *Behaviour Research and Therapy*, 95, 29–41. doi:10.1016/j.brat.2017.0doi:5.004

Pascoe, M. C., Thompson, D. R., & Ski, C. F. (2017). Yoga, mindfulness-based stress reduction and stress-related physiological measures: a meta-analysis. *Psychoneuroendocrinology*, 86, 152–168. doi:10.1016/j.psyneuen.2017.08.008

Pepping, C. A., Walters, B., Davis, P. J., & O'Donovan, A. (2016). Why do people practice mindfulness? An investigation into reasons for practicing mindfulness meditation. *Mindfulness*, 7(2), 542–547. doi:10.1007/s12671-016-0490-3

Perich, T., Manicavasagar, V., Mitchell, P. B., & Ball, J. R. (2013). The association between meditation practice and treatment outcome in Mindfulness-based Cognitive Therapy for bipolar disorder. *Behaviour Research and Therapy*, 51(7), 338–343. doi:10.1016/j.brat.2013.03.0doi:06

Petersen, M. & la Cour, P. (2016). Mindfulness – what works for whom? Referral, feasibility, and user perspectives regarding patients with mixed chronic pain. *Journal of Alternative and Complementary Medicine*, 22(4), 298–305. doi:10.1089/acm.2015.0310

Prioli, K. M., Pizzi, L. T., Kash, K. M., Newberg, A. B., Morlino, A. M., Matthews, M. J., & Monti, D. A. (2017). Costs and effectiveness of Mindfulness-Based Art Therapy versus standard breast cancer support group for women with cancer. *American Health & Drug Benefits*, 10(6), 288–295.

Reese, H. E., Vallejo, Z., Rasmussen, J., Crowe, K., Rosenfield, E., & Wilhelm, S. (2015). Mindfulness-based stress reduction for Tourette syndrome and chronic tic disorder: a pilot study. *Journal of Psychosomatic Research*, 78(3), 293–298. doi:10.1016/j.jpsychores.2014.08doi:001

Reiner, K., Tibi, L., & Lipsitz, J. D. (2013). Do mindfulness-based interventions reduce pain intensity? A critical review of the literature. *Pain Medicine*, 14(2), 230–242. doi:10.1111/pme.12006

Ribeiro, L., Atchley, R. M., & Oken, B. S. (2018). Adherence to practice of mindfulness in novice meditators: practices chosen, amount of time practiced, and long-term effects following a mindfulness-based intervention. *Mindfulness*, 9(2), 401–411. doi:10.1007/s12671-017-0781-3

Ridderinkhof, A., de Bruin, E. I., Blom, R., & Bögels, S. M. (2018). Mindfulness-based program for children with autism spectrum disorder and their parents: direct and long-term improvements. *Mindfulness*, 9(3), 773–791. doi:10.1007/s12671-017-0815-x

Roberts-Wolfe, D., Sacchet, M. D., Hastings, E., Roth, H., & Britton, W. (2012). Mindfulness training alters emotional memory recall compared to active controls: support for an emotional information processing model of mindfulness. *Frontiers in Human Neuroscience*, 6, 15. doi:10.3389/fnhum.2012.00015

Robinson, F. P., Mathews, H. L., & Witek-Janusek, L. (2003). Psycho-endocrine-immune response to Mindfulness-Based Stress Reduction in individuals infected with the human immunodeficiency virus: a quasiexperimental study. *Journal of Alternative and Complementary Medicine*, 9(5), 683–694. doi:10.1089/107555303322524535

Rosenzweig, S., Reibel, D. K., Greeson, J. M, Brainard, G. C., & Hojat, M. (2003). Mindfulness-Based Stress Reduction lowers psychological distress in medical students. *Teaching and Learning in Medicine*, 15(2), 88–92. doi:10.1207/S15328015TLM1502_03

Rowland, Z., Wenzel, M., & Kubiak, T. (2016). The effects of computer-based mindfulness training on Self-control and Mindfulness within Ambulatorily assessed network Systems across Health-related domains in a healthy student population (SMASH): study protocol for a randomized controlled trial. *Trials*, 17, 570. doi:10.1186/s13063-016-1707-4

Ruijgrok-Lupton, P. E., Crane, R. S., & Dorjee, D. (2018). Impact of mindfulness-based teacher training on MBSR participant well-being outcomes and course satisfaction. *Mindfulness*, 9(1), 117–128. doi:10.1007/s12671-017-0750-x

Ruskin, D., Harris, L., Stinson, J., Kohut, S. A., Walker, K., & McCarthy, E. (2017). "I learned to let go of my pain". The effects of mindfulness meditation on adolescents with chronic pain: an analysis of participants' treatment. *Children*, 4(12), 110. doi:10.3390/children4120110

Ryan, A., Safran, J. D., Doran, J. M., & Muran, J. C. (2012). Therapist mindfulness, alliance and treatment outcome. *Psychotherapy Resesarch*, 22(3), 289–297. doi:10.1080/10503307.2011.650653

Sampl, J., Maran, T., & Furtner, M. R. (2017). A randomized controlled pilot intervention study of a Mindfulness-Based Self-Leadership Training (MBSLT) on stress and performance. *Mindfulness*, 8(5), 1393–1407. doi:10.1007/s12671-017-0715-0

Santarnecchi, E., D'Arista, S., Egiziano, E., Gardi, C., Petrosino, R., Vatti, G., …, & Rossi, A. (2014). Interaction between neuroanatomical and psychological changes after mindfulness-based training. *PLoS ONE*, 9(10), e108359. doi:10.1371/journal.pone.0108359

Schmidt, S. (2014). Opening up meditation for science: the development of a meditation classification system. In S. Schmidt & H. Walach (Eds.), *Meditation: neuroscientific approaches and philosophical implications*, pp. 137–152. Switzerland: Springer. doi:10.1007/978-3-319-01634-4_8

Schmidt, S., Grossman, P., Schwarzer, B., Jena, S., Naumann, J., & Walach, H. (2011). Treating fibromyalgia with mindfulness-based stress reduction: results from a 3-armed randomized controlled trial. *Pain*, 152(2), 361–369. doi:10.1016/j.pain.2010.10.0doi:43

Segal, Z. V., Williams, J. M. G., & Teasdale, J. D. (2002). *Mindfulness-based cognitive therapy for depression: a new approach to preventing relapse*. New York, USA: The Guilford Press.

Shapiro, D. H. (1992a). A preliminary study of long-term meditators: goals, effects, religious orientation, cognitions. *Journal of Transpersonal Psychology*, 24(1), 23–39.

Shapiro, D. H. (1992b). Adverse effects of meditation: a preliminary investigation of long-term meditators. *International Journal of Psychosomatics*, 39(1–4), 62–67.

Shapiro, S. L., Schwartz, G. E., & Bonner, G. (1998). Effects of Mindfulness-Based Stress Reduction on medical and premedical students. *Journal of Behavioral Medicine*, 21(6), 581–599. doi:10.1023/A:1018700829825

Shapiro, S. L., Carlson, L. E., Astin, J. A., & Freedman, B. (2006). Mechanisms of mindfulness. *Journal of Clinical Psychology*, 62(3), 373–386. doi:10.1002/jclp.20237

Shennan, C., Payne, S., & Fenlon, D. (2011). What is the evidence for the use if mindfulness-based interventions in cancer care? A review. *Psycho-Oncology*, 20(7), 681–697. doi:10.1002/pon.1819

Shi, Z., & MacBeth, A. (2017). The effectiveness of mindfulness-based interventions on maternal perinatal mental health outcomes: a systematic review. *Mindfulness*, 8(4), 823–847. doi:10.1007/s12671-016-0673-7

Singal, A. G., Higgins, P. D. R., & Waljee, A. K. (2014). A primer on effectiveness and efficacy trials. *Clinical and Translational Gastroenterology*, 5, e45. doi:10.1038/ctg.2013.13

Singh, N. N., Wahler, R. G., Adkins, A. D., Myers, R. E., & The Mindfulness Research Group (2003). Soles of the feet: a mindfulness-based self-control intervention for aggression by an individual with mild mental retardation and mental illness. *Research in Developmental Disabilities*, 24(3), 158–169. doi:10.1016/S0891-4222(03)00026-X

Singh, N. N., Lancioni, G. E., Winton, A. S. W., Singh, A. N., Adkins, A. D., & Singh, J. (2008a). Clinical and benefit-cost outcomes of teaching a mindfulness-based procedure to adult offenders with intellectual disabilities. *Behavior Modification*, 32(5), 622–637. doi:10.1177/0145445508315854

Singh, N. N., Lancioni, G. E., Singh, A. N., Winton, A. S. W., Singh, J., McAleavey, K. M., & Adkins, A. D. (2008b). A mindfulness-based health wellness program for an adolescent with Prader-Willi syndrome. *Behavior Modification*, 32(2), 167–181. doi:10.1177/0145445507308582

Sistig, B., Lambrecht, I., & Friedman, S. H. (2015). Journey back into body and soul: an exploration of mindful yoga with psychosis. *Psychosis*, 7(1), 25–36. doi:10.1080/17522439.2014.885556

Snippe, E., Bos, E. H., van der Ploeg, K. M., Sanderman, R., Fleer, J., & Schroevers, M. J. (2015). Time-series analysis of daily changes in mindfulness, repetitive thinking, and depressive symptoms during mindfulness-based treatment. *Mindfulness*, 6(5), 1053–1062. doi:10.1007/s12671-014-0354-7

Snippe, E., Nyklíček, I., Schroevers, M. J., & Bos, E. H. (2015). The temporal order of change in daily mindfulness and affect during mindfulness-based stress reduction. *Journal of Counseling Psychology*, 62(2), 106–114. doi:10.1037/cou0000057

Snippe, E., Dziak, J. J., Lanza, S. T., Nyklíček, I., & Wichers, M. (2017). The shape of change in perceived stress, negative affect, and stress sensitivity during mindfulness-based stress reduction. *Mindfulness*, 8(3), 728–736. doi:10.1007/s12671-016-0650-5

Spijkerman, M., Pots, W., & Bohlmeijer, E. (2016). Effectiveness of online mindfulness-based interventions in improving mental health: a review and meta-analysis of randomised controlled trials. *Clinical Psychology Review*, 45, 102–114. doi:10.1016/j.cpr.2016.03.doi:009

Steinberg, B. A., Klatt, M., & Duchemin, A.-M. (2017). Feasibility of a mindfulness-based intervention for surgical intensive care unit personnel. *American Journal of Critical Care*, 26(1), 10–18. doi:10.4037/ajcc2017444

Strauss, C., Cavanagh, K., Oliver, A., & Pettman, D. (2014). Mindfulness-based interventions for people diagnosed with a current episode of an anxiety or depressive disorder: a meta-analysis of randomised controlled trials. *PLoS ONE*, 9(4), e96110. doi:10.1371/journal.pone.00961104

Stück, M., Meyer, K., Rigotti, T., Bauer, K., & Sack, U. (2003). Evaluation of a yoga-based stress management training for teachers: effects of immunoglobulin A secretion and subjective relaxation. *Journal of Meditation and Meditation Research*, 3, 59–68.

Thabane, L., Ma, J., Rong, C., Cheng, J., Ismaila, A., Rios, L. P., ..., & Goldsmith, C. H. (2010). A tutorial on pilot studies: the what, why and how. *BMC Medical Research Methodology*, 10, 1. doi:10.1186/1471-2288-10-1

Valls-Serrano, C., Caracuel, A., & Verdejo-Garcia, A. (2016). Goal management training and mindfulness meditation improve executive functions and transfer to ecological tasks of daily life in polysubstance users enrolled in therapeutic community treatment. *Drug and Alcohol Dependence*, 165, 9–14. doi:10.1016/j.drugalcdep.2016doi:04.040

Van Dam, N. T., Hobkirk, A. L., Sheppard, S. C., Aviles-Andrews, R., & Earleywine, M. (2014). How does mindfulness reduce anxiety, depression, and stress? An exploratory examination of change processes in wait-list controlled mindfulness meditation training. *Mindfulness*, 5(5), 88–99. doi:10.1007/s12671-013-0229-3

Van Dam, N. T., van Vugt, M. K., Vago, D. R., Schmalzl, L., Saron, C. D., Olendzki, A., ..., & Meyer, D. E. (2018a). Mind the hype: a critical evaluation and prescriptive agenda for research on mindfulness and meditation. *Perspectives on Psychological Science*, 13(1), 36–61. doi:10.1177/1745691617709589

Van Dam, N. T., van Vugt, M. K., Vago, D. R., Schmalzl, L., Saron, C. D., Olendzki, A., ..., & Meyer, D. E. (2018b). Reiterated concerns and further challenges for mindfulness and meditation research: a reply to Davidson and Dahl. *Perspectives on Psychological Science*, 13(1), 66–69. doi:10.1177/1745691617727529

van der Velden, A. M., Kuyken, W., Wattar, U., Crane, C., Pallesen, K. J., Dahlgaard, J., ..., & Piet, J. (2015). A systematic review of mechanisms of change in mindfulness-based cognitive therapy in the treatment of recurrent major depressive disorder. *Clinical Psychology Review*, 37, 26–39. doi:10.1016/j.cpr.2015.doi:02.001

Van Gordon, W., Shonin, E., & Griffiths, M. D. (2015). Towards a second generation of mindfulness-based interventions. *Australian & New Zealand Journal of Psychiatry*, 49(7), 591–592. doi:10.1177/0004867415577437

van Kessel, K., Krägeloh, C., Babbage, D. (2016). eTherapy and psychological practice. In W. W. Waitoki, J. S. Feather, N. R. Robertson, & J. J. Rucklidge (Eds.), *Professional practice in Aotearoa New Zealand* (3rd ed.), pp. 285–301. Wellington, New Zealand: New Zealand Psychological Society.

Virgili, M. (2015). Mindfulness-based interventions reduce psychological distress in working adults: a meta-analysis of intervention studies. *Mindfulness*, 6(2), 326–337. doi:10.1007/s12671-013-0264-0

Wahbeh, H., Lane, J. B., Goodrich, E., Miller, M., & Oken, B. S. (2014). One-on-one mindfulness meditation trainings in a research setting. *Mindfulness*, 5(1), 88–99. doi:10.1007/s12671-012-0155-9

Waldron, E. M., Hong, S., Moskowitz, J. T., & Burnett-Zeigler, I. (2018). A systematic review of the demographic characteristics of participants in US-based randomized controlled trials of mindfulness-based interventions. *Mindfulness*. Online First. doi:10.1007/s12671-018-0920-5

Williams, J. M. G., Crane, C., Barnhofer, T., Brennan, K., Duggan, D. S., Fennell, M. J., ..., & Russell, I. T. (2014). Mindfulness-based cognitive therapy for preventing relapse in recurrent depression: a randomized dismantling trial. *Journal of Consulting and Clinical Psychology*, 82(2), 275–286. doi:10.1037/a0035036

Winbush, N. Y., Gross, C. R., & Kreitzer, M. J. (2007). The effects of mindfulness-based stress reduction on sleep disturbance: a systematic review. *Explore*, 3(6), 585–591. doi:10.1016/j.explore.2007.08doi:003

Witkiewitz, K., Marlatt, G. A., & Walker, D. (2005). Mindfulness-Based Relapse Prevention for alcohol and substance use disorders. *Journal of Cognitive Psychotherapy*, 19(3), 211–228. doi:10.1891/jcop.2005.19.3.211

Wylde, C. M., Mahrer, N. E., Meyer, R. M. L., & Gold, J. I. (2017). Mindfulness for novice pediatric nurses: smartphone application versus traditional intervention. *Journal of Pediatric Nursing*, 36, 205–212. doi:10.1016/j.pedn.2017doi:06.008

Young, K. S., van der Velden, A. M., Craske, M. G., Pallesen, K. J., Fjorback, L., Roepstorff, A., & Parsons, C. E. (2018). The impact of mindfulness-based interventions on brain activity: a systematic review of functional magnetic resonance imaging studies. *Neuroscience and Biobehavioral Reviews*, 84, 424–433. doi:10.1016/j.neubiorev.2017doi:08.003

Zangi, H. A., Mowinckel, P., Finset, A., Eriksson, L. R., Høystad, T. Ø., Lunde, A. K., & Hagen, K. B. (2012). A mindfulness-based group intervention to reduce psychological distress and fatigue in patients with inflammatory rheumatic joint diseases: a randomised controlled trial. *Annals of the Rheumatic Diseases*, 71(6), 911–917. doi:10.1136/annrheumdis-2011-200351

Zeidan, F., Gordon, N. S., Merchant, J., & Goolkasian, P. (2009). The effects of brief mindfulness meditation training on experimentally induced pain. *Journal of Pain*, 11(3), 199–209. doi:10.1016/j.jpain.2009.07.doi:015

Zenner, C., Herrnleben-Kurz, S., & Walach, H. (2014). Mindfulness-based interventions in schools: a systematic review and meta-analysis. *Frontiers in Psychology*, 5, 603. doi:10.3389/fpsyg.2014.00603

Zimmermann, F. F., Burrell, B., & Jordan, J. (2018). The acceptability and potential benefits of mindfulness-based interventions in improving psychological well-being for adults with advanced cancer: a systematic review. *Complementary Therapies in Clinical Practice*, 30, 68–78. doi:10.1016/j.ctcp.2017.12.0doi:14

5

CULTURAL AND RELIGIOUS FACTORS IN RESEARCH ON MINDFULNESS-BASED INTERVENTIONS

Discussions on cultural and religious factors have emerged in mindfulness research through conceptual arguments as well as empirical work testing the cross-cultural validity of mindfulness-based interventions (MBIs). Because of the history of development of modern MBIs, which have been informed primarily by traditional religious meditative practices from Buddhism (Williams & Kabat-Zinn, 2011), theoretical discussions of the concept of mindfulness regularly include comparisons with conceptualisations of mindfulness from Buddhist traditions (Shonin, Van Gordon, & Singh, 2015a). Such comparative work often has the purpose to reveal to what extent the process of adapting mindfulness and meditation training for secular contexts has changed the intention of the practice. One theme that has been discussed extensively in the comparative literature is the role of ethics and personal transformation in Buddhist mindfulness practice, which is often presented as a point of contrast to the more immediate goal of alleviation of suffering promoted by modern therapeutic applications (Krägeloh, 2016).

Since the emergence of MBIs such as Mindfulness-Based Stress Reduction (MBSR; Kabat-Zinn, 1982) and Mindfulness-Based Cognitive Therapy (MBCT; Teasdale, Segal, & Williams, 1995; Teasdale et al., 2000) in English-speaking contexts, MBIs have been delivered in many parts of the world. This includes countries as diverse as Brazil (Demarzo et al., 2014), China (Zhang et al., 2015), Germany (Majumdar, Grossman, Dietz-Waschkowski, Kersig, & Walach, 2002), Romania (Degi & Szilagy, 2013), South Africa (Whitesman, Hoogenhout, Kantor, Leinberger, & Gevers, 2018), and South Korea (Lee & Bang, 2010), although research has also explicitly explored the cultural relevance of MBIs in other English-speaking contexts such as New Zealand (Mapel & Simpson, 2011). Systematic reviews and meta-analyses often do not report in which country samples have been collected, which could imply that country of origin is not considered an important variable in determining the extent to which an MBI may be effective. Generally, similar positive benefits are found for participants irrespective of geographical location. Some of the relationships between dispositional mindfulness and variables of psychological well-being have also been replicated in samples from other countries, such as Sweden (Bränström, Duncan, & Moskowitz, 2011) or the Philippines (Klainin-Yobas et al., 2016).

From the point of view of other cultures, MBIs are typically either perceived as Western secular programmes or as being fundamentally based on Buddhist practices and philosophy. For that reason, applications of MBIs in new cultural contexts can occur in different ways. When MBIs have been applied to an equivalent secular context in another country, such applications typically did not report the need for detailed explorations of cross-cultural validity. There is generally little mention in the literature of differences in languages or acknowledgement of the different ways in which people interact in such programmes, and replication of positive results from MBIs are typically implied as having established cross-cultural validity. In other cases, cultural differences are more deeply intertwined with differences in religious beliefs and practices. From that perspective, conceptual work explicitly compared the mindfulness practices and theories of MBIs with understandings of the role of similar practices found in other religions, such as the Islamic religious thought of Rumi (Mirdal, 2012), Christian centring prayer (Knabb, 2012), or a religiously accommodative mindfulness programme for evangelist Christians (Ford & Garzon, 2017).

The present chapter outlines the relevance of cultural context in mindfulness practice and theory. The discussion includes links to various philosophical and religious belief systems, commencing with Buddhism and Buddhist psychology. Because of the focus of MBIs on subjective experiences, cross-cultural comparisons inevitably raise questions about how mindfulness relates to self-identity and a person's values. Many of the empirical investigations that explicitly investigated cultural factors in mindfulness were about measurement, such as testing the validity of self-report questionnaires designed for different countries, cultures, and languages. Apart from the use of language in mindfulness questionnaires, increased awareness of the way in which mindfulness is communicated in different countries is also informative. The specific term used to convey the key concept of mindfulness is likely to influence how MBIs are generally perceived and to what extent these interventions may enjoy social acceptability in various local contexts.

Contrasting mindfulness in Buddhism with mindfulness in secular settings

Conceptual discussions

Even though parallels between Buddhist philosophy and psychological therapy had been outlined earlier (e.g. Fromm, Suzuki, & De Martino, 1960), it was not until the increased proliferation of MBIs from the 1980s and 1990s that more interest emerged in so-called Buddhist psychology. What characterises Buddhist psychology is the attention paid to the concepts and theory from Buddhist philosophy that could be adapted or applied into Western psychology or used for comparative analysis (e.g. de Silva, 1990; McIntosh, 1997).

The widespread adoption of Buddhist-inspired meditation and mindfulness practices in psychology has been met with a range of different points of view. A very critical perspective has been forwarded by Panaïoti (2015) who argued that the Western scientific literature has shown parochialism by adapting Buddhist mindfulness practices yet glossing over the associated Buddhist theory and continuing to integrate new findings into its own existing theoretical frameworks. Samuel (2015), in contrast, highlighted the fact that the field is still in its early development and that mindfulness provides opportunities for richer exchanges between Asian traditions and contemporary Western therapeutic approaches. Using an even more optimistic tone, Van Gordon, Shonin, Griffiths, and Singh (2015b) called for scientific and Buddhist communities to work more closely, arguing that there is no logical and empirical basis for any claims that secular or Buddhist practice is somehow more or less robust than the other.

Gethin (2011) categorised the various different perspectives by Buddhist scholars as follows: Firstly, one might view MBIs as a distortion of traditional Buddhism and misalignment with the Buddhist goal to overcome suffering by eliminating greed, hatred, and delusion. Secondly, one might see this is as simply another way to make the Buddhist teachings accessible to a wider range of people. Thirdly, one might argue that the core teachings of Buddhism are still embedded within MBIs and that unnecessary historical and cultural appendages had been removed. Lastly, one might see this new development as a synthesis of Western psychological science and Buddhist practices that produces something unique and eventually supersedes traditional Buddhism.

Since several high-profile MBI developers and teachers have regularly made comments that clearly linked their personal beliefs to Buddhism (Van Gordon, Shonin, & Griffiths, 2016), it is likely that some of these perspectives listed by Gethin (2011) may have an influence on how MBIs are delivered and researched. Irrespective of individual perspectives, however, Van Gordon et al. (2016) issued a caution against misrepresenting MBIs as camouflaged Buddhism and instead recommended clear and transparent description about whether a specific MBI is purely secular or whether it presents Buddhist content. It is not the case that programmes with Buddhist content have been developed because they are seen as more effective. The purpose of mindfulness programmes with explicitly spiritual or Buddhist themes is not to replace or to compete with standard secular MBIs but simply to offer more choice to increasingly diverse populations (Shonin, Van Gordon, & Griffiths, 2015b).

Some of the recent theoretical debates comparing secular and Buddhist mindfulness practice have focused very specifically on certain points of contrast. One of these relates to ethics (Stanley, Purser, & Singh, 2018). In Buddhism, mindfulness is typically discussed in the context of the Noble Eightfold Path that describes how to eliminate suffering (Rahula, 1974). Mindfulness is included as one of the path factors but is described as *right mindfulness* or *wholesome mindfulness*. This acknowledges the fact that certain mind states lead to negative consequences, while other (more positive) mind states are to be encouraged. These ethical aspects of mindfulness practice might appear to be in contradiction with definitions of mindfulness in psychology that emphasise nonjudgmental awareness, which has triggered a substantial amount of theoretical debate, such as outlined in a special issue that had been devoted to that topic in the journal *Contemporary Buddhism* (Williams & Kabat-Zinn, 2011).

However, the issues are complex and related to the fact that ideas from various Buddhist schools of thought have influenced conceptual development in mindfulness research (Dunne, 2011; Krägeloh, 2016). When characteristics of nonjudgmental awareness are seen within the context of nondual awareness as taught in Mahāyāna Buddhism, nonevaluation does not necessarily pose a conceptual and logical conflict with ethical practice. Despite the enormous differences in communicating Buddhist teachings, all schools fundamentally agree on the Noble Eightfold Path and the importance of ethics. Additionally, even though secular mindfulness programmes do not relate mindfulness practice as explicitly to ethics and morality as in Buddhism, ethics and morality are still very likely to play a role as individuals contextualise their own practice (Krägeloh, 2016).

A second major theme emerging from Buddhist scholarship about the modern mindfulness movement relates to personal transformation. Purser and Loy (2013) used the expression *McMindfulness* to lament the trend of commercialisation of mindfulness training in contrast to the original liberative and transformative practice in Buddhism. Brazier (2013) presented a similar argument that the primary goal of Buddhist mindfulness is not palliative or focused on reduction of distress, but is instead about building meaning and developing a wider purpose in life. While such criticism might be justified for some of the wide-spread mindfulness self-help literature, it appears to misrepresent the intention of some of the major MBIs such as MBSR. In his reflections on the development of MBSR, Kabat-Zinn (2011) clearly emphasised the importance of reflective and transformative practice. Additionally, the dividing line between secular and Buddhist mindfulness practice is often blurred for many MBI course participants who are sometimes even explicitly advised to continue their practice at local Buddhist clubs after completion of their course (Cullen, 2011).

With MBIs, an interesting scenario has emerged where traditional practices have been borrowed heavily from the East, re-packaged into structured programmes, systematically applied, and now presented back to Asian countries with a strong body of evidence that points towards the benefits of this Westernised mindfulness practice. Given the status that Western science enjoys in Asian countries (Agger, 2015), there appears to be a tendency for this outcome to be seen as a welcome validation of Asian cultural wisdom rather than perceived as a cultural challenge or form of plagiarism. For countries with a long Buddhist tradition, the modern psychological literature on mindfulness provides a new theoretical platform to explain the effects of local traditional Buddhist practices. Areas such as Buddhist counselling have attracted renewed interest through comparisons with psychological theory and the mindfulness literature (e.g. Srichannial & Prior, 2014). The acceptability of mindfulness as a mainstream practice and intervention approach also provides some sense of legitimacy to introduce Buddhist practice and ideas to wider areas outside psychological therapy, such as management and cognitive performance, as well as ethics (Lovichakorntikul, Vongbunsin, & Palasak, 2016).

Empirical studies

A certain body of literature reported empirical data on the beneficial effects of Buddhist mindfulness practice in predominantly Buddhist countries. For example, several studies from Thailand have explored the role of mindfulness in various health settings. As Buddhism is strongly embedded within Thai culture, such studies often do not relate their intervention to Western secular MBIs but discuss it exclusively in the context of Buddhist practice. Such interventions are generally described as Vipassana and/or based on the *Mahāsatipaṭṭhāna Sutta*. Wiriyasombat, Pothiban, Panuthai, Sucamvang, and Saengthong (2003), for example, published a randomised controlled trial (RCT) to test the effects of Vipassana meditation and chanting for coping and sleep quality of older adults, and Losatiankij, Teangtum, and Punchote (2006) reported on a quasi-experimental study that investigated the effects of meditation on stress and happiness in hospital staff. Other studies reported on the role of mindfulness using nonexperimental methods, such as the study by Kitsripisarn, Fongkaew, Chanprasit, and Rankin (2008) who explored Thai nurses' perspectives on health, wisdom, and mindfulness, or Sowattanangoon, Kochab-hakdi, and Petrie (2008) who investigated associations between Buddhist values and medication self-care in diabetes patients in Thailand. While the authors did not explicitly explore any potential mechanisms underlying the relationship between mindfulness and various health-related variables, they speculated that mindfulness is likely to have played a role in such associations.

Le and Trieu (2016) explored the feasibility of an MBI for adolescents and young adults with physical and mental disability living in Vietnam. Because of the historical role that Buddhism had played in shaping Vietnamese culture, the researchers antici-pated that an MBI would be well received by both participants as well as the teachers of the vocational school who assisted in delivering the programme. The intervention was culturally adapted from an MBI for native American youth (which itself was based on MBSR and other programmes). To contextualise the intervention for use in Vietnam, content was slightly adapted with more emphasis on impermanence and other Buddhist and cultural themes, which was facilitated by the involvement of a Buddhist scholar. Open-ended personal reflection at the end of the programme indi-cated a high degree of acceptability by both participants and teachers.

Other studies attempted to address specific fundamental research questions and therefore only reported on MBIs and cultural contextualisation in passing. Ratanasir-ipong, Ratanasiripong, Park, and Kathalae (2015), for example, investigated the effi-cacy of a biofeedback and mindfulness meditation programme on stress and anxiety management in Thai nursing students. The researchers justified the use of Vipassana meditation by reviewing some of the general evidence for the benefits of MBIs in the international literature. The mindfulness intervention that Ratanasiripong et al. (2015)

offered alongside the biofeedback intervention and control group was described as teaching of Vipassana meditation by a meditation trainer as well as the instruction to apply the taught skills three times a day for four weeks. Mindfulness meditation was associated with reduction in anxiety and perceived stress. However, issues of cultural contextualisation or comparisons between Vipassana meditation and standard MBIs were not discussed.

Even when standard MBIs have been applied in Asian countries with a Buddhist history, authors generally tend not to address cross-cultural issues specifically. Instead, they may present the same kinds of considerations found in MBI studies from Western countries, namely about how format and delivery of MBIs can be modified slightly to meet the requirements of the particular setting or target population. For example, Xu, Jia, Liu, and Hofmann (2016) delivered an MBCT programme in a Chinese prison and made some modifications such as including some MBSR elements or having the group activities monitored by a prison guard who was also a psychological counsellor. The implicit assumption was therefore that such MBIs are valid in a Chinese context.

The popularity of MBIs in the international literature may perhaps be the reason that specifically Buddhist-themed mindfulness-based or mindfulness-related interventions have become more socially acceptable and increasingly offered. Using the terminology introduced by Van Gordon, Shonin, and Griffiths (2015a), such Buddhist-themed MBIs would be referred to as second-generation MBIs in contrast to the original standardised MBSR-style MBIs that tend to focus on nonjudgmental awareness in clinical applications. Second-generation MBIs vary fairly extensively, and further typological work may need to explore which core course elements are required for an intervention to be categorised as a second-generation MBI. An example of a second-generation MBI is a study by Singh et al. (2018) who conducted an RCT to test the effects of Mindfulness-Based Positive Behaviour Support (MBPBS). This programme teaches caregivers of individuals with intellectual and developmental disabilities to engage in mindful self-care as well as how to use positive behaviour support interventions more skilfully. The authors described MBPBS as a second-generation MBI as it contains several aspects adopted from Buddhist teachings, namely the so-called *Four Immeasurables* of loving kindness, compassion, empathetic or appreciative joy, and equanimity.

Zeng, Chio, Oei, Leung, and Liu (2017a) conducted a systematic review of studies reporting on meditation interventions where at least 50% of major practices were based on the *Four Immeasurables*. All of the 22 studies identified in their review either focused on loving kindness or on compassion as primary meditation methods, although a more recent programme based their intervention primarily on appreciative joy (Zeng, Wang, Oei, & Leung, 2018). Despite common methodological issues such as lack of experimental manipulation, there is some evidence for beneficial effects (Zeng et al., 2017a). However, the programmes delivered in these studies are generally fairly heterogeneous, and it might not be justifiable to group these studies into a single intervention approach. As shown by Zeng, Chan, Liu, Oei, and Leung (2017b), appreciative joy and compassion meditation are associated with similar pro-social attitudes as commonly found for loving kindness medita-tion. However, each approach has also been linked to unique emotions, and the effects on the experience of positive and negative affect in response to witnessing other people's suffering may also be slightly different (Zeng et al., 2017b). As the mechanism of action may thus be different for the various meditation techniques, further research is required to explore to what extent it can be justified to continue to class these programmes as *Four Immeasurables Meditations* or whether it is more appropriate to use different classifications. Further conceptual work is also necessary to compare the mechanism of action of the various approaches with those claimed to be underlying standard MBIs. Some of that work has already started such as through outlining the differences between appreciative joy and the concept of positive empathy from psychology (Zeng, Chan, Oei, Leung, & Liu, 2017c).

The effectiveness of such interventions may also only be indirectly comparable to standard MBIs due to differences in primary goals and outcomes. For example, the outcome measures used in the study by Zeng et al. (2018) reflect the intention of the programme and thus include the Self and Other Four Immeasurables scale that inquiries into attitudes towards oneself and others (Kraus & Sears, 2009), the Appreciative Joy Scale (Zeng et al., 2017d), and the Dispositional Envy Scale (Smith, Parrott, Diener, Hoyle, & Kim, 1999). Other scales that have been developed for similar purposes include a modified and shortened version of the Philadelphia Mindfulness Scale (Cardaciotto, Herbert, Forman, Moitra, & Farrow, 2008) to assess changes related to Vipassana meditation (Zeng, Li, Zhang, & Liu, 2015), a quiet ego scale (Wayment, Wiist, Sullivan, & Warren, 2011), and nonattachment scale (Sahdra, Shaver, & Brown, 2010).

Only few studies have collected empirical data to investigate whether mind-fulness may be understood differently by Buddhist practitioners. Christopher, Woodrich, and Tiernan (2014) evaluated the cultural validity of the Five Facet Mindfulness Questionnaire (FFMQ) (Baer, Smith, Hopkins, Krietemeyer, & Toney, 2006) and the Toronto Mindfulness Scale (TMS) (Lau et al., 2006) by using cognitive interviewing with six ordained and eight lay Zen Buddhists. The participants were presented with the two questionnaires and identified areas of congruence and lack of congruence with their understanding of mindfulness. What the participants considered as missing in these two questionnaires were aspects of intention to return awareness to the present moment as well as compassion for others and awareness of aversion and suffering. Another aspect missing from the FFMQ and TMS was extending beyond one's self.

Another study investigating differences in the conceptualisation of mindfulness between Buddhism and Western psychology interviewed five senior ordained Bud-dhists from three branches of Buddhism (Feng, Krägeloh, Billington, & Siegert, 2018). Similar to the study by Christopher et al. (2014), participants were given various mindfulness questionnaires and asked to think out loud. These were the Mindfulness Attention and Awareness Scale (MAAS; Brown & Ryan, 2003), the Kentucky Inventory of Mindfulness Skills (KIMS; Baer, Smith, & Allen, 2004), the FFMQ (Baer et al., 2006), and the Freiburg Mindfulness Inventory-30 (FMI-30; Buchheld,

Grossman, & Walach, 2001). The participants also rated each questionnaire item as if rated by an imagined ideal Buddhist in their tradition. The purpose of this was to provide a stimulus for discussion and to collect additional quantitative data about the relevance and potential ambiguity of items. The themes from the interviews pointed to considerable differences between Buddhist understanding of mindfulness and the conceptualisation implied by the items in the mindfulness questionnaires. In contrast to the aspects of nonjudgmental, present-centred awareness emphasised in the questionnaires, Buddhist mindfulness contains elements of attentional flexibility, skilfulness, purposefulness, wisdom, and ethics. Buddhist mindfulness also involves awareness of the past and future and not only focuses on self but also on others.

Mindfulness in the context of diverse cultures and belief systems

Research on cultural factors in MBIs is not only limited to comparisons with Buddhist culture and philosophy but also includes empirical and conceptual work outlining similarities and differences with many other cultural and religious traditions. Understanding this literature requires an appreciation of the context in which the culturally neutral format of MBIs has originally arisen. Apart from concerns about the potential for reduced social acceptability of MBSR if it had been presented with explicitly Buddhist themes (Kabat-Zinn, 2011), other motivations for presenting MBIs in a secular format include maximising its accessibility to a wide range of people (Crane et al., 2017). The need to de-emphasise culture-specific elements and practices in therapeutic applications of mindfulness is related to the fact that participants and clients often have diverse cultural and religious backgrounds, and the content of MBIs must not teach anything that is in contradiction with those beliefs (Cullen, 2011).

In addition to the intention to provide a respectful and culturally safe forum for MBI participants, other reasons for de-emphasising cultural factors may be related to attempts to understand the mechanism of action by which mindfulness practice leads to psychological health benefits. From that perspective, reduction of any course material to fundamental elements that are shared by people across cultures and nations may be seen as a step towards achieving that goal by helping to identify a core common ingredient of MBIs (Crane et al., 2017). While this could be the cognitive skills developed through mindfulness training such as concentration, it is a topic of debate to what extent it may be possible to isolate such supposedly key variables. In the absence of formal inclusion of religion in course content, spirituality might play an increasingly important role and might even be a contributing factor in the effects of meditation (Wachholtz & Pargament, 2005). Even if no particular religious or spiritual beliefs are mentioned in MBIs, course participants may independently attempt to link mindfulness practice to their existing belief systems (Krägeloh, 2016).

As a result of increased theoretical discussion of the role of ethics in mindfulness practice, empirical studies have started to investigate this topic more specifically. Chen and Jordan (2018), for example, recruited more than 600 participants for a study that investigated the effects of ethical themes in mindfulness practice. Participants were randomly allocated to receive daily audio-guided training in secular mindfulness training over the period of six days, to receive the same exercises with explicit ethical content, or to complete analytic thought exercises over the same time period. While both types of mindfulness exercises resulted in reduced stress and increased life satisfaction, participants in the ethical mindfulness training group were more likely to donate parts of the $15 they received for participation to a charity. However, some unexpected interactions were observed such that individuals with low trait empathy gave significantly less after secular mindfulness training, and those high on trait empathy gave significantly more after ethical mindfulness training.

Apart from ethics, links to other religions have also been increasingly discussed in the mindfulness literature. Trammel (2017) stressed the importance to be careful not to present mindfulness without acknowledgement of its religious roots. Meditation is certainly not an exclusive feature of Buddhism, which is implied by the fact that there is a Latin-derived word that is used to describe the practice. Referring to meditation as a forgotten Western tradition, Schopen and Freeman (1992) drew attention to the history of meditative practices within Christianity, starting from early Christian mysticism. From the end of the 19th century, meditation somehow became less strongly associated with Christian practice but then experienced a revival in the 1960s as a result of increased interest in mindfulness and Eastern philosophy. Stratton (2015) distinguished between the different types of Christian meditations that are being practised, including contemplative prayer, meditative (blended) prayer, and discursive prayer. Contemplative prayer, which is silent and imageless, shares a fair amount of overlap with concentration and insight meditation techniques from Buddhism (Stratton, 2015).

Blanton (2011) lamented the fact that the clinical usefulness of mindfulness practices from religions other than Buddhism has not received sufficient attention and outlined a case study of how centring prayer can be applied in psychotherapy. In an earlier publication, Blanton (2002) also described the process that the author typically applied to determine whether Christian meditation is suitable to be used with a particular client, which involved an assessment of the person's coping style as well as finding out whether their religious orientation reflected an intrinsic interest in the religion or whether it served mainly an extrinsic purpose such as to achieve personal or social goals. A further case study by Hathaway and Tan (2009) illustrated how elements of MBCT had been adapted for use in individual therapy as no MBCT group had been available at the location of the study at that time. Because the client spontaneously mentioned their religiosity, this mindfulness practice was then contextualised within their faith-affiliated practice. Additionally, a phenomenological study of Christian mental health practitioners who use mindfulness-based techniques with their Christian clients indicated that the incorporation of Christian themes was fairly straightforward, with a range of themes that they could draw on that appeared as a natural fit with mindfulness (Trammel, 2018).

Apart from the above-mentioned case-by-case combining of mindfulness techniques with religious practice, there have also been more systematic applications such as through Christian-themed programmes that were specifically developed as alternatives to standard secular MBIs. Symington and Symington (2012) reported on the development of an eight-week mindfulness programme incorporating Christian material. This programme taught several elements using concepts that Christian participants will be more familiar with, such as presenting language and practice around acceptance as spiritual surrender to God. Using an RCT design, Ford and Garzon (2017) compared the effects of a secular mindfulness programme with that of an equivalent religiously accommodative mindfulness programme on psychological distress in evangelical Christian university students. The intervention was three weeks long for both groups and included psychoeducational group sessions and also prescribed daily meditation practice. Compared to the conventional mindfulness training group, participants in the Christian meditation group experienced larger reductions in psychological distress and exhibited greater treatment compliance.

Work relating mindfulness practice and theory to Islam has often identified parallels with Christian practice. While Christianity might express present-moment attention and self-monitoring of behaviour as the instruction to do everything to the glory of God (Gethin, 2011), Islam also teaches remembrance of God in even the smallest actions somebody engages in each day (Aflakseir & Coleman, 2011). Correlational research has shown frequency of offering Muslim prayer to be correlated with higher scores in mindfulness and mental health measures (Ijaz, Khalily, & Ahmad, 2017). Thomas, Raynor, and Bakker (2016) explored the perceptions of 12 female university students in the United Arab Emirates who participated in an MBSR programme. The views expressed by participants in the focus groups were favourable towards the programme and not in any way seen as a threat to the participants' cultural and religious beliefs. As outlined by Mirdal (2012), there are many commonalities between mindfulness and some of the Islamic philosophical ideas and practices, which have the potential to inform more specifically designed Islamic-themed MBIs. One such intervention has been developed by Aslami, Alipour, Najib, and Aghayosefi (2017) and tested in an RCT. The eight-week Islamic-themed MBI included prayer and discussion of spiritual experiences and was tested against the effects of a control group as well as a 12-week group cognitive behavioural therapy intervention. While depression and anxiety scores of the control group increased, outcomes for the other two groups improved, although significantly more in the Islamic-themed mindfulness programme.

Any discussion of meditative practices in religious traditions other than Buddhism must not omit the rich history of Hinduism, from which Buddhism originated. The profound importance of mindfulness and ethical behaviour in Indian philosophy has been highlighted by Nirban (2018) who referred to the *Bhagavadgītā*. In the West, Hindu meditation has typically been associated with transcendental meditation, which has been particularly popular in the 1970s (Harrington & Dunne, 2015). Tomasino, Chiesa, and Fabbro (2014), however, grouped a variety of other mantra-based and breath-observance techniques into a category they referred to as *Hinduism-inspired meditations*. When conducting a meta-analysis of brain imaging studies involving meditating participants, Tomasino et al. (2014) compared the results from studies employing Hinduism-inspired meditations with those inspired by Buddhism. The authors described the focus of the former to be more on reaching an ineffable state of nothingness accompanied by a loss of sense of self, which is more associated with left lateralised networks such as the parietal lobe and hippocampus. Buddhist-inspired meditation, in contrast, was described as emphasising focused and sustained attention, which in turn was linked more to frontal lobe structures.

Secular MBIs appear to enjoy the same level of acceptability in Hindu cultural contexts than elsewhere. Roberts and Montgomery (2015), for example, modified MBSR into a five-week intervention and piloted it with poor rural women living in central India who had experienced stillbirth. Using a mixed-method design, the study identified the main barriers as difficulties freeing up time from work and family duties to attend sessions. The MBI was perceived as a culturally acceptable intervention, as indicated by the fact that the participants appreciated the fact that elements of yoga had been included in the intervention. Despite the roots of yoga in Indian philosophy, many of the studies investigating the effects of yoga do not mention Hinduism or religious beliefs, including work conducted in India (e.g. Narendran, Nagarathna, Narendran, Gunasheela, & Nagendra, 2005). Nevertheless, the spiritually transformative aspects of yoga are also being recognised such as reflected in awareness of the range of standardised outcome measures available for that purpose including Hindu religious coping scales or those inquiring into Hindu beliefs and practices (MacDonald & Friedman, 2009).

Apart from religious factors, research has also increasingly started to explore to what extent findings from MBI studies may be generalisable to populations that may typically be under-represented in such samples. A systematic review of RCTs of MBIs conducted in the United States revealed that Caucasian participants, females, and participants with higher education levels were generally over-represented in participant samples (Waldron, Hong, Moskowitz, Burnett-Zeigler, 2018). While on one hand this could be due to inequality in access to healthcare services including MBIs, this could also be a reflection of variations in cultural acceptability. To investigate perceived barriers of uptake of MBIs in African American women, Watson, Black, and Hunter (2016) recruited 12 participants for focus groups. Participants expressed that mindfulness meditation training can sometimes be seen as incongruent with African American culture where stress-reduction practices such as prayer may be seen as more normal. Mindfulness was seen to be associated with stereotypes such as hippie practice, new age spiritualism, or atheism. This meant that participants sometimes felt reluctant to tell their friends or family that they were practising mindfulness meditation. The use of floor cushions appeared to reinforce any perceptions that mindfulness is linked to another religion, and participants shared the feeling that they might be judged negatively or be stigmatised by significant others. The importance of understanding the specific needs of other cultural groups has been recognised by Proulx et al. (2018) who gave advice on methodological issues to consider in research and development of MBIs for minority communities in the United States.

Adaptations of MBIs to local contexts were not always stated as the primary purpose of some studies but were instead reported as incidental necessary modifications to be able to offer the MBI in the particular context. For example, in an RCT for an MBI offered to Thai youth to reduce anger expression and violent behaviour, Wongtongkam, Ward, Day, and Winefield (2014) adapted the MBSR programme by removing some somatic relaxation techniques, lengthening meditation practice to make it more in line with Thai meditation practices, and having the programme delivered by monks. A pilot trial by McIntyre, Elkonin, de Kookerm and Magidson (2018), in contrast, specifically aimed to examine the feasibility of delivering MBSR for resource-limited individuals living with the human immunodeficiency virus (HIV) in South Africa. Some of the areas of the programme that required adaptation were related to language issues. Even though English-language ability was a requirement to participate in the intervention, the researchers saw the need to reduce material relying on poetry that required an advanced level of knowledge of English. Additionally, more time at the beginning of the course was dedicated to explaining the concept of mindfulness, which did not have a direct equivalent term in most of the other local native languages of the participants. Other adaptations included making food available for the resource-limited participants and placing more emphasis on informal exercises due to the fact that participants' living circumstances did not permit much uninterrupted time for formal home practice.

Cultural differences in self-identity and values

As mindfulness can be an experiential practice that encourages reflection about one's self, thoughts, and behaviour, it is inevitable that the MBI literature is linked to discussions about self-identity. Such questions arise particularly if mindfulness is regarded as a long-term process that fundamentally transforms one's attitudes as well as one's values and perceptions about external stimuli or thoughts and emotions. If the *self* is understood as a concept to explain how internal stimuli such as thoughts arise and how interactions with an external world occur, the next question is how such a self is to be understood and what sort of transformation or self-development is desirable to take place. Within this discussion, cultural and particularly religious perspectives have played an important role.

Theoretical discussions often centred around the implications of meditation for the perception of selfhood and to what extent Buddhist views are implied by meditation practice. Mamberg and Bassarear (2015) identified the apparent contradictions that can emerge when the essentially Buddhist-informed MBIs are researched using Western scientific methods. The influence of Buddhist philosophy on MBIs is undeniable and inevitably requires a comparative analysis of the concepts of mindfulness as seen from Buddhist and Western worldviews. Since MBIs such as MBSR are at times explicitly and other times implicitly related to and informed by Buddhist psychology, Mamberg and Bassarear (2015) argued that MBIs present a hybrid worldview, which they supported by qualitative data from interviewing individuals who have recently completed an MBSR course. On one hand, MBSR practitioners express views about their newly developed insights from mindfulness practice about how the self is a creation of thoughts and perceptions, thus leading to a view of the self as a process (and thus a *selfing*). On the other hand, modern scientific methods used to study mindfulness tend to reify and objectify the self and thus turn it into an entity or even something that can be reduced to brain functioning (Mamberg & Bassarear, 2015).

Buddhist psychology is frequently offered as an alternative to a Western positivist worldview, which is perceived to medicalise psychological distress. Wada and Park (2009) present an attempt to integrate the two approaches in the context of grief counselling. One of the Buddhist concepts introduced and discussed by the authors for that purpose includes that of *no self*. Known to be an aspect of Buddhist teaching that is hard to understand and prone to misunderstandings (Fontana, 1987), *no self* refers to the absence of a personal self as conceived as a permanent entity. As Wada and Park (2009) described it: "Whereas psychology emphasizes consistency of self over time, the concept of no self in Buddhism focuses on the impermanent and changing nature of self" (p.662). However, while Buddhism conceives of the self as a process, body, and mind, this should not be interpreted nihilistically. The self is still experienced as a phenomenon and can still follow a trajectory or path of development (Feng et al., 2018). In context of meditation practice and its relevance to cognitive analytic psychotherapy as well as mindfulness-based therapy, Marx and Marx (2012) discussed different stages of practice, where more advanced stages are characterised by decreased separation (and eventually no separation) between the observer and the observed.

It needs to be mentioned, though, that the Buddhist view of the self is not necessarily at odds with Western approaches in general, and parallels between Buddhism have been drawn with other psychological theories and traditions. This includes psychodynamic theory (Falkenström, 2003) or Gestalt psychology, which also regards the self as emerging from a formless whole that is constantly in state of change (Kerr & Key, 2011). When comparing discussions about Christianity, on the other hand, clear differences with Buddhism have been noted. While Buddhism has been described as encouraging a view of the self as in one with the universe, the teachings of Christianity emphasise building a relationship with God as well as the fact that there is an eternal soul that will be subjected to a final judgement by God (Knabb, 2012). Such differences in the conceptualisations of the self and purpose of spiritual practice may also mean that different measures may be necessary to assess depth of practice. Hohn (2003), for example, reported some conceptual work to pave the way for future questionnaires to assess meditation paths and stages of consciousness in Christian practice. Such work may be useful for similar purposes as equivalent questionnaires that have been developed for Buddhist meditation (Piron, 2001).

Related to self-identity and mindfulness are goals and values of an individual, at least according to research conducted in Western cultural contexts. As reported by Hanley and Garland (2017), self-concept beliefs play an important role in self-knowledge and the consistent involvement of a person in meaningful and fulfilling pursuits and relationships. Using a sample of more than 1,000 university students, the researchers illustrated how clarity of self-concept beliefs mediated the relationship between mindfulness and psychological well-being. In a study of participants recruited for a cross-sectional online survey, Franquesa et al. (2017) found that the relationship between meditation practice and value-related behaviours (the extent to which individuals' behaviour is congruent with their values) was mediated by aspects of mindfulness. The role of values has also been recognised in an MBI adapted for jail inmates (Malouf, Youman, Stuewig, Witt, & Tangney, 2017). This intervention combined elements from various other MBIs and related therapeutic approaches to teach mindfulness skills and to foster the development of personal values identification to increase motivation to participate in the intervention.

Links between goal-directed attitudes and mindfulness have also recently been explored with the positive psychology concept of grit, or the perseverance and passion for pursuing long-term goals. Raphiphatthana, Jose, and Salmon (2018) hypothesised that mindfulness is positively related to grittiness through increased emotional self-regulation. While the researchers found several positive associations in a cross-sectional study of university students, a longitudinal study with a smaller sample revealed that the two FFMQ subscales *Acting with Awareness* and *Nonjudging* were predictors of grit 4½ months later. In a cross-cultural study with university students from New Zealand and Thailand, Raphiphatthana, Jose, and Chobthamkit (2018) found the relationship between *Acting with Awareness* and *Nonjudging* to be stronger in New Zealand than in Thailand. The authors concluded that the relationship between grit and mindfulness may be more robust in individualistic cultures such as New Zealand than in collectivist ones such as Thailand.

Of course, the distinction between individualistic versus collectivist is often confounded by differences in religions, which is difficult to untangle. Tsai, Miao, and Seppala (2007) investigated to what extent religion is related to ideal affect by controlling for national residence. As hypothesised, Asian Americans tended to value low arousal positive (LAP) states such as calmness more than European Americans who tend to encourage high arousal positive (HAP) states such as excitement. Controlling for ethnicity, LAP states were also valued more by Buddhist participants than Christians, which was also confirmed by further analyses of the respective scriptures.

The term *mindfulness* in different languages

The creation of terminology is a complex sociolinguistic phenomenon, with different languages finding different strategies and solutions. For example, the general political climate or tendency towards language purism can determine to what extent new terms are created through the process of transliteration, through loan words, calques (loan translations), generalised use of existing words, or creation of neologisms (Krägeloh & Neha, 2014). A detailed historical analysis regarding the translation of the term mindfulness into other languages is beyond the scope of the present book. However, the specific terms that are currently used in different cultural and language contexts to describe modern mindfulness applications has some relevance for research as choices of terminology affect how participants might perceive mindfulness practice and the direction in which theory and measurement of mindfulness will develop.

Literature about Buddhism became available in Europe from the early 19th century and had a profound influence on philosophical thought in Europe such as through the philosophy of Arthur Schopenhauer who was the first European known to have referred to himself as a Buddhist (Atzert, 2017). More systematic efforts to translate Buddhist texts into European languages, however, did not commence until the second half of the 19th century (Ladner, 1958). Most notable was the work by the Pali Text Society London, which published a translation of the entire Pali Canon in 1883. Thomas William Rhys Davids is credited to have first translated the Buddhist term *sati* (or *smrti*, which is the Sanskrit equivalent of the Pali term) into English as mindfulness (Gethin, 2011). Dictionaries available at the time tended to translate *sati* as remembrance, memory, or recollection, and Davids' translation as mindfulness captures the ethical and conscience-related nuances of *sati* that the term had gradually acquired in the Buddhist literature (Gethin, 2011).

A few years after the work by Davids, the Austrian Karl Eugen Neumann translated a number of Pali texts into German. While the language of the translation was often considered attractive, it was also heavily criticised for some imprecision around technical terms (Ladner, 1958). To translate *sati*, Neumann used words equivalent to insight but subsequent translations eventually settled on the term *Achtsamkeit* (Nyanaponika, 1989; see also www.palikanon.com). The adjective *achtsam* has multiple nuances, but, similar to the English term mindful, has connotations of attentiveness and vigilance. The systematic application of mindfulness in psychological interventions such as MBSR certainly contributed to the more consistent use of the terms mindfulness and *Achtsamkeit* and their inclusion into the jargon of psychological research, often prompting theorists to distinguish between more clinical usage of these term and usage of these term in Buddhist contexts (Atzert, 2017).

In the French-language academic literature, the term *pleine conscience* tends to be used for mindfulness (e.g. Berghmans, Strub, & Tarquino, 2008; Weber, Jermann, Lutz, Bizzini, & Bondolfi, 2012), where *pleine* means full and *conscience* means consciousness. Both Dutch (e.g. Hellemans, 2008) and Spanish (e.g. García-Campayo & Demarzo, 2016) use the English word *mindfulness* in their literature about MBIs. Russian words for mindfulness used in the context of MBIs include *osoznannost* (осознанность), which refers to awareness (Tukaev & Kuznetsov, 2013) and *vnimatelnost* (внимательность), which literally means attentiveness (Kupriyanova, Tuzikov & Gural, 2014). Neither of these words accurately conveys the meaning of the term mindfulness.

In Chinese, the character 念 is used to describe mindfulness, which consists of the radicals 今 (meaning *now*) and 心 (meaning *heart* or *mind*), thus alluding to the idea of present-moment awareness (Chan, Lo, Lin, & Thompson, 2015). However, this character is typically not used on its own, and mindfulness tends to be referred to as 正念 (Mandarin pronunciation: *zhèngniàn*). While this expression is the translation of the Buddhist concept of *sati* or more specifically *sammāsati* (wholesome mindfulness in the Noble Eightfold Path; Feng et al., 2018), this expression has also been used in the context of secular MBIs (e.g. Lai & Su, 2015). Vietnamese uses the word *Chánh Niệm*, which is a loan word from the Chinese 正念 (Le & Trieu, 2016), and when studies from Thailand reported on mindfulness programmes that were based on Buddhist practice such as from the *Mahāsatipaṭṭhāna Sutta*, the word *sati* (Thai: สติ) was used to refer to mindfulness (Kitsripisarn et al., 2008; Wiriyasombat et al., 2003).

In Japanese, which uses Chinese characters alongside its own script (*hiragana* and *katakana*), 正念 (Japanese pronunciation: *shōnen*) generally refers to mindfulness in Buddhist contexts. When referring to mindfulness in the context of MBIs and psychology, the direct transliteration of the English word mindfulness (マインドフルネス) is generally used (e.g. Sugiura, 2008; Usami & Tagami, 2012). Korean, in contrast, uses neither a Chinese-derived word nor a direct transliteration. Here, the term used to refer to mindfulness in the context of both psychometrics (Jeon, Lee, Lee, & Lee, 2007) as well as MBIs (Gim & Jun, 2012) is *ma-eum-chaeng-gim* (마음챙김), which may be translated as *taking care of your mind*.

Future work could provide a comparative sociolinguistic analysis of the use of terms in different countries. There could be a number of motivations for extending the use of a specific Buddhist term for mindfulness to nonreligious therapeutic settings. It could be a reflection of attempts to emphasise the roots of mindfulness within the local culture (e.g. Le & Trieu, 2016), either to enhance acceptability or effectiveness through cultural contextualisation. Drawing on Buddhist jargon offered by languages that relate to cultures with a rich history of mindfulness practices has the potential to inform further work on conceptual clarity and disagreement about definitions of mindfulness. Nuances in practice may be better expressed through a more comprehensive vocabulary, such as through the distinction between mindfulness and heedfulness (Krägeloh, 2018). On the other hand, using a clearly distinct term such as a translation of the English word mindfulness has the advantage that secular and religious practices are not conflated. As a result, it may be less likely to invoke implicit assumptions about the direct transferability of knowledge about mindfulness from the religious to the nonreligious literature, and vice versa.

Mindfulness measurement across cultures and languages

Except for some of the less commonly used mindfulness scales, questionnaires are now available in many languages. Occasionally, reports on translation and validation of a new language version was not stated as the primary goal of the study such in the case of a study from Hungary (Simor, Köteles, Sándor, Petke, & Bódizs, 2011) that investigated the relationships between mindfulness with anxiety and sleep disturbance. Another example is the study by Jermann et al. (2009) who examined the relationship between mindfulness and emotion regulation strategies using French-language questionnaires or the study by Araya-Vargas, Gapper-Morrow, Moncada-Jiménez, and Buckworth (2009) who explored the role of mindfulness in exercise psychology using Spanish questionnaires.

With the exception of the Freiburg Mindfulness Inventory (FMI; Buchheld et al., 2001), the Comprehensive Inventory of Mindfulness Experiences (CHIME; Bergomi, Tschacher, & Kupper, 2014), and the Multidimensional State Mindfulness Questionnaire (MSMQ; Blanke & Brose, 2017), which were originally developed in German, mindfulness questionnaires have typically been developed in English and then translated into other languages. While it is preferable to translate questionnaires from the original language so that the originally intended nuances are not missed, translations of the FMI often made references to the English version. Some studies only consulted the English version exclusively, such as when translating into French (Trousselard et al., 2010) or Chinese (Chen & Zhou, 2014). The reason for this was not stated, although it may be presumed to be the result of more convenient availability of translators with sufficient knowledge of English rather than German. While the translation of the FMI into Finnish was also based on the English version, the authors also used the German version to help with the translation (Lehto, Uusitalo-Malmivaara, & Repo, 2015). When translating into Dutch, Bruggeman-Everts, Van der Lee, Van 't Hooft, & Nyklíček (2017) referred to both the English and the German versions.

Of all the mindfulness scales, the popular Mindful Attention Awareness Scale (MAAS; Brown & Ryan, 2003) appears to have been translated into the largest number of languages. Translations and subsequent validation work include versions for Bangla (Islam & Siddique, 2016), Chinese (Deng et al., 2012), Danish (Jensen, Niclasen, Vangkilde, Petersen, & Hasselbalch, 2016), Dutch (Schoevers, Nykliček, & Topman, 2008), Estonian (Seema et al., 2015), French (Jermann et al., 2009), German (Michalak, Heidenreich, Ströhle, & Nachtigal, 2008), Greek (Mantzios, Wilson, & Giannou, 2015), Hungarian (Simor et al., 2011), Italian (Veneziani & Voci, 2015), Malay (Zainal, Nor-Aziyan, & Subramaniam, 2015), Persian (Ghorbani, Watson, & Weathington, 2009), Swedish (Hansen, Lundh, Homman, & Wångby-Lundh, 2009), and Turkish (Catak, 2012a). For use of the MAAS in Korean, research articles (Cho, Heiby, McCracken, Lee, & Moon, 2010; Ju & Lee, 2015; Song, & Lindquist, 2015) refer to different sources for a translated version.

For the various varieties of Spanish, several MAAS versions have also been published, such as for use in Argentina (Montes, Ledesma, García, & Poó, 2014), Costa Rica (Araya-Vargas et al., 2009), Mexico (López-Maya et al., 2015), Spain (Soler et al., 2012), and Spanish-speaking populations living in the United States (Johnson, Wiebe, & Morera, 2014). Barajas and Garra (2014) later also translated and validated another Spanish version with several clinical and nonclinical samples from Spain. Of the above-mentioned studies, López-Maya et al. (2015) was the only study that presented more detailed discussion justifying the need for another version based on dialect-related differences. For the other versions, it is unclear to what extent the new versions reflect country- or dialect-specific differences or whether variations in item wording were the consequence of different teams of translators independently translating the MAAS from the original English. Some changes were more related to addressing a perceived inadequacy of the original wording, such as when re-wording item 12 from "I drive places on 'automatic pilot' and then wonder why I went there" to the Spanish equivalent of "I go someplace and then wonder why I went there" so that respondents who do not drive are also able to answer this question (Montes et al., 2014).

Mindfulness questionnaires were typically translated into different languages using the method of forward-backward translation, although there are some exceptions such as the Mexican version of the MAAS (López-Maya et al., 2015) or the Turkish version of the MAAS (Catak, 2012a) that did not involve the back-translation stage. Forward translation refers to translating the original scale into the intended language. Then, the newly translated scale is translated back to the original language by one or more independent translators (Islam & Siddique, 2016). A committee of experts in language and psychology can be involved during both forward- and back-translation stages (e.g. Islam & Siddique, 2016). Comparing the back-translated version of the scale to the original scale can help identify how closely the translated scale conveys the intended meaning of the original scale. Revisions will be made to the scale in the intended language until a consensus on conceptual equivalence between the scales in original language and intended language is achieved. The back-translated version is sometimes sent to the scale developer for comments and approval to finalise the new version of the scale (e.g. Jensen et al., 2016). Some authors referred to specific translation guidelines that they had followed (e.g. Heeren, Douilliez, Peschard, Debrauwere, & Philippot, 2011; Johnson, Wiebe, & Morera, 2014), but many studies did not.

Some authors acknowledged the issues and challenges in translating mindfulness questionnaires. Some difficulties encountered during translation are due to unique characteristics of one language. For example, Seema et al. (2015) developed the Estonian version of the MAAS and reported how Estonian does not have a term for mindfulness. More importantly, since the Estonian language does not distinguish clearly present and future tense, it was challenging to translate mindfulness scales that measure present-moment awareness. Several expert philologists were invited to deal with the issue of these important linguistic differences in order to retain the original intended meaning of the items. In other instances, authors reported only very briefly on translation issues, such as Lilja et al. (2011) who commented that one FFMQ item was discarded "because it did not translate well into Swedish" (p.294).

Accuracy of translation is critical to ensure cross-language equivalence, and there has been no consensus on whether translators at all stages of the translation process should be familiar with mindfulness. Initial forward translations tend to involve the researchers themselves or translators with mindfulness experience. When back-translating the MAAS from Chinese to English, however, Deng et al. (2012) employed a translator who was not familiar with the concept of mindfulness. In other studies, such as translations of the Cognitive and Affective Mindfulness Scale – Revised (CAMS-R) into Chinese (Chan et al., 2015) and Turkish (Catak, 2012b), some of the translations at later stages involved translators not familiar with mindfulness, although their translations were closely assessed by those with mindfulness experience. Given the known issues with comprehensibility of mindfulness items with those unfamiliar with the practice, some involvement of nonmeditators appears sensible, although no formal translation protocol has so far been proposed.

Translation and cross-cultural validation was also commonly used as an opportunity to add to the ongoing debate about suitable factor structure and general psychometric properties of some of the commonly used questionnaires. Similar to the reports of the original study of the FFMQ (Baer et al., 2006), results of hierarchical confirmatory factor analyses (CFA) with other language versions showed that the *Observing* subscale was less related to the overarching mindfulness construct compared to the other four subscales (Heeren et al., 2011; Lilja et al., 2011; Sugiura, Sato, Ito, & Murakami, 2012). Likewise, in line with the original study (Baer et al., 2006), the *Observing* subscale in other languages did not have statistically significant associations with variables of psychological distress and well-being. For instance, *Observing* was not correlated with measures of depression and anxiety in the French version (Heeren et al., 2011), and in the Japanese version it was positively correlated with alexithymia, depression, and some aspects of maladaptive metacognitive self-awareness (Sugiura et al., 2012).

The above-mentioned studies used CFA to assess the factor structure of their language versions, which appears to be the most commonly used approach in studies reporting on the translation or cross-cultural validity of mindfulness questionnaires. Some studies used an exploratory factor analysis, such as for the Costa Rican Spanish version of the MAAS (Araya-Vargas et al., 2009) or when testing the cross-cultural validity of the FFMQ for use with a demographically diverse sample in Australia (Taylor & Millear, 2016). Occasionally, studies did not use a factor analytic method but presented other type of evidence. Hansen et al. (2009), for example, reported data about internal consistency and construct validity for the Swedish versions of both the MAAS and KIMS. Of the so-called classical test theory approaches to investigate cross-cultural validity, multi-group invariance tests are among the most comprehensive. Ghorbani et al. (2009), for example, identified some structural complexities of the MAAS with datasets from Iran and the United States. However, using a subset of items, the authors were able to demonstrate structural invariance and thus cross-cultural generalisability of the instrument. Christopher, Charoensuk, Gilbert, Neary, and Pearce (2009) similarly confirmed cross-cultural equivalence of the MAAS when comparing samples of Thai and US university students. When comparing the KIMS across these two countries, however, Christopher et al. (2009) found the KIMS to lack the basic criterion of configural invariance, indicating a cross-cultural difference of the fundamental factor structure of the instrument.

When using classical test theory approaches, only the approach of invariance testing permits conclusions to be made about the equivalence of mean scores across cultures, countries, or demographic groups. Although it is not a study of cross-cultural validity but instead of invariance of mindfulness scores across time, the study by Krägeloh, Bergomi, Siegert, and Medvedev (2018a) nevertheless serves to demonstrate how mean scores can be adjusted when so-called scalar invariance has not been achieved. Such adjustments can avoid premature conclusions that populations from some countries have overall higher mindfulness levels than those in other countries (Arthur, Dizon, Jooste, Li, Salvador, & Yao, 2018), particularly when it is reasonably well documented that participants from collectivist cultures may have a tendency to endorse middle ratings more than participants from more individualistic cultures (Harzin, 2006). In Rasch analysis, this would be referred to as differences in item difficulty across the two language versions. For example, Japanese individuals with an average level of mindfulness may generally rate a particular item in the Japanese version lower than a US respondent to the English-language version. Such differences in item difficulty can also be found across samples answering the questionnaire in the same language, as indicated by differential item functioning by age (Feng et al., 2016) or country (Krägeloh et al., 2018b). Similar to invariance testing, Rasch analysis permits researchers to make the necessary adjustments in subscale scores to ensure that cross-cultural comparisons are less likely to be affected by such response biases. Even in the absence of explicit cross-country comparisons such as by Krägeloh et al. (2018b), the use of ordinal-to-interval conversion tables produced from single-country studies are able to adjust for some response bias.

Studies reporting on cross-cultural translations of mindfulness questionnaires tend to follow an implicit assumption that it is desirable (or at least appropriate) to have one universally applicable mindfulness instrument and that the main challenge is translation accuracy. As a result, such studies are generally very closely guided by interpretations drawn from attempts to confirm established factor structures through psychometric testing, and they tend not to consider the possibility of culture-specific adaptations. For example, when Christopher et al. (2009) failed to obtain evidence for cross-cultural equivalence of the KIMS, the results were discussed in terms of questioning the adequacy of the original scale or the statistical methods to inform the development of the original factor structure. A different approach would be to argue that the content of the items is overall very similar across cultures, but that there may be differences across cultures in terms of how they may be grouped as factors. For example, in a study reporting on the translation of a mindful parenting instrument into Korean, the translated items did not fit any of the factor structures that have been reported for the various languages for which the questionnaire was available (Kim, Krägeloh, Medvedev, Duncan, & Singh, 2018). As a result, Kim et al. (2018) proposed a shorter version of the instrument for use in Korea, in which the items were also grouped differently into factors. While this means that scores from the instruments cannot be directly compared to those from other countries, it has the advantage that the psychometric properties of the tool are optimised for use in that particular country and can be used for meaningful between-group comparisons within that population. Arguments such as these have been the topic of debate in health outcomes research even before the first mindfulness questionnaires had been developed (Bullinger, 1997). In quality of life research, for example, it is not uncommon to consider country-specific items or modules to enhance conceptual equivalence and measurement precision (Krägeloh et al., 2016). So far, such an approach has not been used widely in mindfulness measurement. One example that may approximate this approach is that used to inform the Srithanya Sati Scale (Silpakit & Silpakit, 2014). After noticing that some of the items of the Thai version of the Philadelphia Mindfulness Scale (Silpakit, Silpakit, & Wisajun, 2011) were difficult to comprehend, the authors retained five of those items and developed six more to capture mindfulness in the context of Thai culture and the Buddhist practice found in Thailand.

Summary and conclusion

Because of the predominantly secular nature of psychotherapeutic approaches in the West, it has been argued that MBIs would not have enjoyed the same extent of rapid success if they had not undergone prior de-contextualisation from Buddhist traditions (Lomas, Etcoff, Van Gordon, & Shonin, 2017). The literature has started to recognise the potential value in re-contextualising mindfulness back to Buddhist theories and practices (Lomas et al., 2017), and links to Buddhist psychology are increasingly found in the MBI literature. While most of the comparative work between mindfulness in secular and in Buddhist settings has been conceptual, more studies with empirical data have been published. This includes reports of applications of MBIs in diverse cultures including those with a Buddhist history and tradition, data from MBIs with explicit Buddhist themes, and empirical investigations that provide specific information about differences between mindfulness conceptualisations and practices.

In addition to linking mindfulness with Buddhism, comparisons with other religious traditions have become to be perceived as equally legitimate (e.g. Mirdal, 2012; Schopen & Freeman, 1992). As a result, Christian and Muslim perspectives are increasingly expressed, and the mindfulness literature may have provided religious theorists with a new framework and jargon to express aspects of their contemplative practice. Cross-cultural comparisons of mindfulness practice also have the potential to inform further development of secular MBIs such as so-called second-generation MBIs (Van Gordon et al., 2015a) that recognise the value of spirituality and religiosity in mindfulness practice.

While much of the conceptual discussion on cultural factors in MBIs has centred on the secular nature of such programmes and the question of how to deliver a culturally neutral health intervention, these MBIs themselves will eventually also become the topic for cultural investigations. Certainly, it could be argued that apparent attempts by MBI research to achieve cultural de-contextualisation have been unrealistic in first place (Misra & Gergen, 1993; van Oers, 1998) and that secularity itself is a particular type of culture (Roof, 2007). References in the MBI literature to mindfulness as a movement (Cullen, 2011; Kabat-Zinn, 2017) also point to the emergence of a new culture of its own.

References

Aflakseir, A., & Coleman, P. G. (2011). Initial development of the Iranian Religious Coping Scale. *Journal of Muslim Mental Health*, 6(1), 44–61. doi:10.3998/jmmh.10381607.0006.104

Agger, I. (2015). Calming the mind: healing after mass atrocity in Cambodia. *Transcultural Psychiatry*, 52(4), 543–560. doi:10.1177/1363461514568336

Araya-Vargas, G. A., Gapper-Morrow, S., Moncada-Jiménez, J., & Buckworth, J. (2009). Translation and cross-cultural validation of the Spanish version of the Mindful Awareness Attention Scale (MAAS): an exploratory analysis and potential applications to exercise psychology, sport and health. *International Journal of Applied Sports Sciences*, 21(1), 94–114.

Arthur, D., Dizon, D., Jooste, K., Li, Z., Salvador, M., & Yao, X. (2018). Mindfulness in nursing students: the five facet mindfulness questionnaire in samples of nursing students in China, the Philippines, and South Africa. *International Journal of Mental Health Nursing*, 27 (3), 975–986. doi:10.1111/inm.12405

Aslami, E., Alipour, A., Najib, F. S., & Aghayosefi, A. (2017). A comparative study of mindfulness efficiency based on Islamic-spiritual schemes and group cognitive behavioral therapy on reduction of anxiety and depression in pregnant women. *International Journal of Community Based Nursing and Midwifery*, 5(2), 144–152.

Atzert, S. (2017). On the "Philosophy of Saintliness": K.E. Neumann's German translations of the Buddha's discourses and Schopenhauer's philosophy. In A. Barua (Ed.), *Schopenhauer on self, world and morality*, pp. 107–118. Singapore: Springer Nature. doi:10.1007/978-981-10-594-4_10

Baer, R. A., Smith, G. T., & Allen, K. B. (2004). Assessment of mindfulness by self-report – the Kentucky Inventory of Mindfulness Skills. *Assessment*, 11(3), 191–206. doi:10.1177/1073191104268029

Baer, R. A., Smith, G. T., Hopkins, J., Krietemeyer, J., & Toney, L. (2006). Using self-report assessment methods to explore facets of mindfulness. *Assessment*, 13(1), 27–45. doi:10.1177/1073191105283504

Barajas, S., & Garra, L. (2014). Mindfulness and psychopathology: adaptation of the Mindful Attention Awareness Scale (MAAS) in a Spanish sample. *Clínica y Salud*, 25(1), 49–56. doi:10.5093/cl2014a4

Berghmans, C., Strub, L., & Tarquino, C. (2008). Mindfulness meditation and psychotherapy: a theoretical overview, measurement and lines of research [French]. *Journal de Thérapie Comportementale et Cognitive*, 18, 62–71. doi:10.1016/j.jtcc.2008.04.0doi:06

Bergomi, C., Tschacher, W., & Kupper, Z. (2014). Construction and initial validation of a questionnaire for the comprehensive investigation of mindfulness [German]. *Diagnostica*, 60(3), 111–125. doi:10.1026/0012–1924/a000109

Blanke, E. S. & Brose, A. (2017). Mindfulness in daily life: a multidimensional approach. *Mindfulness*, 8(3), 737–750. doi:10.1007/s12671-016-0651-4 [Erratum. Blanke, E. S., & Brose, A. (2017). *Mindfulness*, 8(6), 1727–1731. doi:10.1007/s12671-017-0769-z]

Blanton, P. G. (2002). The use of Christian meditation with religious couples: a collaborative language systems perspective. *Journal of Family Psychotherapy*, 13(3/4), 291–307. doi:10.1300/J085v13n03_04

Blanton, P. G. (2011). The other mindful practice: centering prayer & psychotherapy. *Pastoral Psychology*, 60(1), 133–147. doi:10.1007/s11089-010-0292-9

Bränström, R., Duncan, L. G., & Moskowitz, J. T. (2011). The association between dispositional mindfulness, psychological well-being, and perceived health in a Swedish populations-based sample. *British Journal of Health Psychology*, 16(2), 300–316. doi:10.1348/135910710X501683

Brazier, D. (2013). Mindfulness reconsidered. *European Journal of Psychotherapy and Counselling*, 15(2), 116–126. doi:10.1080/13642537.2013.795335

Brown, K. W. & Ryan, R. M. (2003). The benefits of being present: mindfulness and its role in psychological well-being. *Journal of Personality and Social Psychology*, 84(4), 822–848. doi:10.1037/0022-3514doi:84.4.822

Bruggeman-Everts, F. Z., Van der Lee, M. L., Van 't Hooft, E. F. M., & Nyklíček, I. (2017). Validation of the Dutch Freiburg Mindfulness Inventory in patients with medical illness. *SAGE Open*, 7(2) 1–9. doi:10.1177/2158244017705936

Buchheld, N., Grossman, P., & Walach, H. (2001). Measuring mindfulness in insight meditation (Vipassana) and meditation-based psychotherapy: the development of the Freiburg Mindfulness Inventory (FMI). *Journal for Meditation and Meditation Research*, 1, 11–34.

Bullinger, M. (1997). The challenge of cross-cultural quality of life assessment. *Psychology & Health*, 12(6), 815–825. doi:10.1080/08870449708406742

Cardaciotto, L., Herbert, J. D., Forman, E. M., Moitra, E., & Farrow, V. (2008). The assessment of present-moment awareness and acceptance: the Philadelphia Mindfulness Scale. *Assessment*, 15(2), 204–223. doi:10.1177/1073191107311467

Catak, P. D. (2012). The Turkish version of Mindful Attention Awareness Scale: preliminary findings. *Mindfulness*, 3(1), 1–9. doi:10.1007/s12671-011-0072-3

Catak, P. D. (2012b). The Turkish version of the cognitive and affective mindfulness scale-revised. *Europe's Journal of Psychology*, 8(4), 603–619. doi:10.5964/ejop.v8i4.436.

Chan, H.-L., Lo, L.-Y., Lin, M., & Thompson, N. (2015). Revalidation of the Cognitive and Affective Mindfulness Scale – Revised (CAMS-R) with its newly developed Chinese version (Ch-CAMS-R). *Journal of Pacific Rim Psychology*, 10(e1), 1–10. doi:10.1017/prp.2015.4

Christopher, M. S., Charoensuk, S., Gilbert, B. D., Neary, T. J., & Pearce, K. L. (2009). Mindfulness in Thailand and the United States: a case of apples versus oranges? *Journal of Clinical Psychology*, 65(6), 590–612. doi:10.1002/jclp.20580

Chen, S., & Jordan, C. H. (2018). Incorporating ethics into brief mindfulness practice: effects on well-being and prosocial behavior. *Mindfulness*. Online First. doi:10.1007/s12671-018-0915-2

Chen, S.-Y., & Zhou, R.-L. (2014). Validation of a Chinese version of the Freiburg Mindfulness Inventory: short version. *Mindfulness*, 5(5), 529–535. doi:10.1007/s12671-013-0208-8

Cho, S., Heiby, E. M., McCracken, L. M., Lee, S.-M., & Moon, D.-E. (2010). Pain-related anxiety as a mediator of the effects of mindfulness on physical and psychosocial functioning in chronic pain patients in Korea. *Journal of Pain*, 11(8), 789–797. doi:10.1016/j.jpain.2009.12doi:006

Christopher, M. S., Woodrich, L. E., & Tiernan, K. A. (2014). Using cognitive interviews to assess the cultural validity of state and trait measures of mindfulness among Zen Buddhists. *Mindfulness*, 5(2), 145–160. doi:10.1007/s12671-012-0160-z

Crane, R. S., Brewer, J., Feldman, C., Kabat-Zinn, J., Santorelli, S., Williams, J. M. G., & Kuyken, W. (2017). What defines mindfulness-based programs? The warp and the weft. *Psychological Medicine*, 47(6), 990–999. doi:10.1017/S0033291716003317

Cullen, M. (2011). Mindfulness-based interventions: an emerging phenomenon. *Mindfulness*, 2(3), 186–193. doi:10.1007/s12671-011-0058-1

Degi, C. L., & Szilagy, T. (2013). Mindfulness-based stress reduction intervention in Romanian breast cancer inpatients. *Cognition, Brain, Behavior*, 17(2), 135–148.

Demarzo, M. M. P., Andreoni, S., Sanches, N., Perez, S., Fortes, S., & Garcia-Campayo, J. (2014). Mindfulness-Based Stress Reduction (MBSR) in perceived stress and quality of life: an open, uncontrolled study in a Brazilian healthy sample. *Explore*, 10(2), 118–120. doi:10.1016/j.explore.2013.12.0doi:05

Deng, Y.-Q., Li, S., Tang, Y.-Y., Zhu, L.-H., Ryan, R., & Brown, K. (2012). Psychometric properties of the Chinese translation of the Mindful Attention Awareness Scale (MAAS). *Mindfulness*, 3(1), 10–14. doi:10.1007/s12671-011-0074-1

de Silva, P. (1990). Buddhist psychology: a review of theory and practice. *Current Psychology: Research & Reviews*, 9(3), 236–254. doi:10.1007/BF02686862

Dunne, J. (2011). Toward an understanding of non-dual mindfulness. *Contemporary Buddhism*, 12(1), 71–88. doi:10.1080/14639947.2011.564820

Falkenström, F. (2003). A Buddhist contribution to the psychoanalytic psychology of self. *International Journal of Psychoanalysis*, 84(6), 1551–1568. doi:10.1516/XH6D-2YLY-P2JV-9VRC

Feng, X. J., Krägeloh, C. U., Medvedev, O. N., Billington, D. R., Jang, J. Y., & Siegert, R. J. (2016). Assessing mechanisms of mindfulness: improving the precision of the Non-attachment Scale using a Rasch model. *Mindfulness*, 7(5), 1082–1091. doi:10.1007/s12671-016-0546-4

Feng, X. J., Krägeloh, C. U., Billington, D. R., & Siegert, R. J. (2018). To what extent is mindfulness as presented in commonly used mindfulness questionnaires different from how it is conceptualized by senior ordained Buddhists? *Mindfulness*, 9(2), 441–460. doi:10.1007/s12671-017-0788-9

Fontana, D. (1987). Self-assertion and self-negation in Buddhist psychology. *Journal of Humanistic Psychology*, 27(2), 175–195. doi:10.1177/0022167887272005

Ford, K., & Garzon, F. (2017). A randomized investigation of evangelical Christian accommodative mindfulness. *Spirituality in Clinical Practice*, 4(2), 92–99. doi:10.1037/scp0000137

Franquesa, A., Cebolla, A., García-Campayo, J., Demarzo, M., Elices, M., …, & Soler, J. (2017). Meditation practice is associated with a values-oriented life: the mediating role of decentering and mindfulness. *Mindfulness*, 8(5), 1259–1268. doi:10.1007/s12671-017-0702-5

Fromm, E., Suzuki, D. T., & De Martino, R. (1960). *Zen Buddhism and psychoanalysis*. Oxford, UK: Harper.

García-Campayo, J. & Demarzo, M. (2016). Mindfulness and compassion: a Latin American perspective [Spanish]. *Mindfulness & Compassion*, 1(1), 1. doi:10.1016/j.mincom.2016doi:09.001

Gethin, R. (2011). On some definitions of mindfulness. *Contemporary Buddhism*, 12(1), 263–279. doi:10.1080/14639947.2011.564843

Ghorbani, N., Watson, P. J., & Weathington, B. L. (2009). Mindfulness in Iran and the United States: cross-cultural structural complexity and parallel relationships with psychological adjustment. *Current Psychology*, 28(4), 211–224. doi:10.1007/s12144-009-9060-3.

Gim, W.-S. & Jun, J. S. (2012). Effects of K-MBSR program on levels of mindfulness, psychological symptoms, and quality of life: the role of home practice and motive of participation [Korean]. *Korean Journal of Health Psychology*, 17(1), 79–98.

Hanley, A. W. & Garland, E. L. (2017). Clarity of mind: structural equation modeling of associations between dispositional mindfulness, self-concept clarity and psychological well-being. *Personality and Individual Differences*, 106, 334–339. doi:10.1016/j.paid.2016.10doi:028

Hansen, E., Lundh, L.-G., Homman, A., & Wångby-Lundh, M. (2009). Measuring mindfulness: pilot studies with the Swedish versions of the Mindful Attention Awareness Scale and the Kentucky Inventory of Mindfulness Skills. *Cognitive Behaviour Therapy*, 38(1), 2–15. doi:10.1080/16506070802383230

Harrington, A., & Dunne, J. D. (2015). When mindfulness is therapy: ethical qualms, historical perspectives. *American Psychologist*, 70(7), 621–631. doi:10.1037/a0039460

Harzing, A.-W. (2006). Response styles in cross-national survey research: a 26-country study. *International Journal of Cross Cultural Management*, 6(2), 243–266. doi:1177/1470595806066332

Hathaway, W. & Tan, E. (2009). Religiously oriented Mindfulness-Based Cognitive Therapy. *Journal of Clinical Psychology*, 65(2), 158–171. doi:10.1002/jclp.20569

Heeren, A., Douilliez, C., Peschard, V., Debrauwere, L., & Philippot, P. (2011). Cross-cultural validity of the Five Facets Mindfulness Questionnaire: adaptation and validation in a French-speaking sample. *Revue européenne de psychologie appliquée*, 61(3), 147–151. doi:10.1016/j.erap.2011.02.0doi:01

Hellemans, J. (2008). Mindfulness, cognitive psychology and religion [Dutch]. *Psyche & Geloof*, 19(3), 107–111.

Hohn, T. (2003). Christian Meditation paths?: development of a questionnaire for Christian contemplation based on descriptions of Master Eckhart and Teresa of Avila. *Journal for Meditation and Meditation Research*, 3, 7–20.

Ijaz, S., Khalily, M. T., & Ahmad, I. (2017). Mindfulness in Salah prayer and its association with mental health. *Journal of Religion and Health*, 56(6), 2297–2307. doi:10.1007/s10943-017-0413-1

Islam, M. A. & Siddique, S. (2016). Validation of the Bangla Mindful Attention Awareness Scale. *Asian Journal of Psychiatry*, 24, 10–16. doi:10.1016/j.ajp.2016.0doi:8.011

Jensen, C. G., Niclasen, J., Vangkilde, S. A., Petersen, A., & Hasselbalch, S. G. (2016). General inattentiveness is a long-term reliable trait independently predictive of psychological health: Danish validation studies of the Mindful Attention Awareness Scale. *Psychological Assessment*, 28(5), e70–87. doi:10.1037/pas0000196

Jeon, J.-H., Lee, W.-K., Lee, S.-J., & Lee, W.-H. (2007). A pilot study of reliability and validity of the Korean version of Mindfulness Attention Awareness Scale [Korean]. *Korean Journal of Clinical Psychology*, 26(1), 201–212.

Jermann, F., Billieux, J., Larøi, F., D'Argembeau, A., Bondolfi, G., & Zermatten, A. (2009). Mindful Attention Awareness Scale (MAAS): psychometric properties of the French translation and exploration of its relations with emotion regulation strategies. *Psychological Assessment*, 21(4), 506–514.

Johnson, C. J., Wiebe, J. S., & Morera, O. F. (2014). The Spanish version of the Mindful Attention Awareness Scale (MAAS): measurement invariance and psychometric properties. *Mindfulness*, 5(5), 552–565. doi:10.1007/s12671-013-0210-1

Ju, S. J. & Lee, W. K. (2015). Mindfulness, non-attachment, and emotional well-being in Korean adults. *Advanced Science and Technology Letters*, 87, 68–72. doi:10.14257/astl.2015. 87. 15

Kabat-Zinn, J. (1982). An outpatient program in behavioral medicine for chronic pain patients based on the practice of mindfulness meditation: theoretical considerations and preliminary results. *General Hospital Psychiatry*, 4(1), 33–47. doi:10.1016/0163-8343(82)90026-3

Kabat-Zinn, J. (2011). Some reflections on the origins of MBSR, skillful means, and the trouble with maps. *Contemporary Buddhism*, 12(1), 281–306. doi:10.1080/14639947.2011.564844

Kabat-Zinn, J. (2017). Too early to tell: the potential impact and challenges – ethical and otherwise – inherent in the mainstreaming of Dharma in an increasingly dystopian world. *Mindfulness*, 8(5), 1125–1135. doi:10.1007/s12671-017-0758-2

Kerr, M.. & Key, D. (2011). The Ouroboros (Part 1): towards an ontology of connectedness in ecopsychology research. *European Journal of Ecopsychology*, 2, 48–60.

Kim, E., Krägeloh, C. U., Medvedev, O. N., Duncan, L. G., & Singh, N. N. (2018). Interpersonal Mindfulness in Parenting scale: testing the psychometric properties of a Korean version. *Mindfulness*. Online First. doi:10.1007/s12671-12018-0993-0991

Kitsripisarn, S., Fongkaew, W., Chanprasit, C., & Rankin, S. H. (2008). Perspectives on wisdom-health of Thai Buddhist nurses through meditation. *Thai Journal of Nursing*, 12(4), 297–309.

Klainin-Yobas, P., Ramirez, D., Fernandez, Z., Sarmiento, J., Thanoi, W., Ignacio, J., & Lau, Y. (2016). Examining the predicting effect of mindfulness on psychological well-being among undergraduate students: a structural equation modelling approach. *Personality and Individual Differences*, 91, 63–68. doi:10.1016/j.paid.2015.11doi:034

Knabb, J. J. (2012). Centering prayer as an alternative to mindfulness-based cognitive therapy for depression relapse prevention. *Journal of Religion and Health*, 51(3), 908–924. doi:10.1007/s10943-010-9404-1

Krägeloh, C. (2016). Importance of morality in mindfulness practice. *Counseling and Values*, 61(1), 97–110. doi:10.1002/cvj.12028

Krägeloh, C. (2018). Mindfulness, heedfulness, and ethics. In S. Stanley, R. E. Purser, & N. N. Singh (Eds.). *Handbook of ethical foundations of mindfulness*. New York, USA: Springer. doi:10.1007/978-3-319-76538-9_5

Krägeloh, C. & Neha, T. N. (2014). Lexical expansion and terminological planning in indigenous and planned languages: Comparisons between Te Reo Māori and Esperanto. *Language Problems and Language Planning*, 38(1), 59–86. doi:10.1075/lplp.38.1doi:04kra

Krägeloh, C. U., Billington, D. R., Hsu, P. H.-C., Feng, X. J., Medvedev, O. N., Kersten, P., Landon, J., & Siegert, R. J. (2016). Ordinal-to-interval scale conversion tables and national items for the New Zealand version of the WHOQOL-BREF. *PLoS ONE*, 11 (11), e0166065. doi:10.1371/journal.pone.0166065

Krägeloh, C. U., Bergomi, C., Siegert, R. J., & Medvedev, O. N. (2018a). Response shift after a mindfulness-based intervention: measurement invariance testing of the Comprehensive Inventory of Mindfulness Experiences. *Mindfulness*, 9(1), 212–220. doi:10.1007/s12671-017-0764-4

Krägeloh, C. U., Medvedev, O. N., Hill, E. M., Webster, C. S., Booth, R. J., & Henning, M. A. (2018b). Improving measurement of trait competitiveness: a Rasch analysis of the Revised Competitiveness Index with samples from New Zealand and US university students. *Psychological Reports*. Online First. doi:10.1177/0033294118762548

Kraus, S. & Sears, S. (2009). Measuring the immeasurables: Development and initial validation of the self-other four Immeasurables (SOFI) scale based on Buddhist teachings on loving kindness, compassion, joy, and equanimity. *Social Indicators Research*, 92(1), 169–181. doi:10.1007/s11205-008-9300-1

Kupriyanova, S., Tuzikov, E., & Gural, S. (2014). Life quality and mental disorders in cancer patients. *Siberian Journal of Oncology*, 62, 2.

MacDonald, D. A. & Friedman, H. L. (2009). Measures of spiritual and transpersonal constructs for use in yoga research. *International Journal of Yoga*, 2(1), 2–12. doi:10.4103/0973-6131.53837

Marx, R. & Marx, S. (2012). The eye and the "I": the construction and use of the observer in cognitive-analytic psychotherapy and mindfulness-based therapy. *British Journal of Psychotherapy*, 28(4), 496–515. doi:10.1111/j.1752-0118.2012.01308.x

McIntosh, W. D. (1997). East meets west: parallels between Zen Buddhism and social psychology. *International Journal for the Psychology of Religion*, 7(1), 37–52. doi:10.1207/s15327582ijpr0701_5

McIntyre, T.-L., Elkonin, D., de Kooker, M., & Magidson, J. F. (2018). The application of mindfulness for individuals living with HIV in South Africa: a hybrid effectiveness-implementation pilot study. *Mindfulness*, 9(3), 871–883. doi:10.1007/s12671-017-0827-6

Nirban, G. (2018). Mindfulness as an ethical ideal in the Bhagavadgītā. *Mindfulness*. Online First. doi:10.1007/s12671-017-0755-5

Ladner, M. (1958). Buddhistische Mission in Europa. *Zeitschrift für Religions- und Geistesgeschichte*, 10(4), 317–333. doi:10.1163/157007358X00347

Lai, C.-C. & Su, L.-H. (2015). Mindfulness, self-healing and psychological adaptation: the mediating effects of self-compassion and self-disparagement [Chinese]. 中華輔導與諮商學報, 42, 93–124.

Lau, M. A., Bishop, S. R., Segal, Z. V., Buis, T., Anderson, N. D., Carlson, L., …, & Carmody, J. (2006). The Toronto Mindfulness Scale: development and validation. *Journal of Clinical Psychology*, 62(12), 1445–1467. doi:10.1002/jclp.20326

Le, T. N. & Trieu, D. T. (2016). Feasibility of a mindfulness-based intervention to address youth issues in Vietnam. *Health Promotion International*, 31(2), 470–479. doi:10.1093/heapro/dau101

Lee, W. K. & Bang, H. J. T. (2010). The effects of mindfulness-based group intervention on the mental health of middle-aged Korean women in community. *Stress and Health*, 26(4), 341–348. doi:10.1002/smi.1303

Lehto, J. E., Uusitalo-Malmivaara, L., & Repo, S. (2015). Measuring mindfulness and well-being in adults: the role of age and meditation experience. *Journal of Happiness & Well-Being*, 3 (1), 30–40.

Lilja, J. L., Frodi-Lundgren, A., Hanse, J. J., Josefsson, T., Lundh, L.-G., SköldC., …, & Broberg, A. G. (2011). Five Facets Mindfulness Questionnaire – reliability and factor structure: a Swedish version. *Cognitive Behaviour Therapy*, 40(4), 291–303. doi:10.1080/16506073.2011.580367

Lomas, T., Etcoff, N., Van Gordon, W., & Shonin, E. (2017). Zen and the art of living mindfully: the health-enhancing potential of Zen aesthetics. *Journal of Religion and Health*, 56(5), 1720–1739. doi:10.1007/s10943-017-0446-5

López-Maya, E., Hernández-Pozo, M. d. R., Méndez-Segundo, L., Gutiérrez-García, J. J., Araujo-Díaz, D., Nuñez-Gazcón, A., …, Hölzel. B. K. (2015). Psychometric properties of the Mexican version of the Mindful Attention Awareness Scale (MAAS). *Psychologia: avances de la disciplina*, 9(1), 13–27.

Losatiankij, P., Teangtum, S., & Punchote, K. (2006). The effect of mindfulness on stress, happiness and its usage in daily living [Thai]. *Journal of Mental Health of Thailand*, 14(3), 199–206.

Lovichakorntikul, P., Vongbunsin, V., & Palasak, R. (2016). How to practice mindfulness in the era of digital economy? *Journal of the International Association of Buddhist Universities*, 9(2), 4–12.

Majumdar, M., Grossman, P., Dietz-Waschkowski, B., Kersig, S., & Walach, H. (2002). Does mindfulness meditation contribute to health? Outcome evaluation of a German sample. *Journal of Alternative and Complementary Medicine*, 8(6), 719–730. doi:10.1089/10755530260511720

Malouf, E. T., Youman, K., Stuewig, J., Witt, E. A., & Tangney, J. P. (2017). A pilot RCT of a values-based mindfulness group intervention with jail inmates: evidence for reduction in post-release risk behavior. *Mindfulness*, 8(3), 603–614. doi:10.1007/s12671-016-0636-3

Mamberg, M. H. & Bassarear, T. (2015). From reified self to being mindful: a dialogical analysis of the MBSR voice. *International Journal for Dialogical Science*, 9(1), 11–37.

Mantzios, M., & Wilson, J. C., & Giannou, K. (2015). Psychometric properties of the Greek versions of the self-compassion and mindful attention and awareness scales. *Mindfulness*, 6 (1), 123–132. doi:10.1007/s12671-013-0237-3

Mapel, T. & Simpson, J. (2011). Mindfulness-Based Stress Reduction research in Aotearoa New Zealand. *New Zealand Journal of Counselling*, 31(2), 21–34.

Michalak, J., Heidenreich, T., Ströhle, G., & Nachtigall, C. (2008). Die deutsche Version der Mindful Attention Awareness Scale (MAAS). *Zeitschrift für Klinische Psychologie und Psychotherapie*, 37, 200–208. doi:10.1026/1616-3443.37doi:3.200

Mirdal, G. M. (2012). Mevlana Jalāl-ad-Dīn Rumi and mindfulness and mindfulness. *Journal of Religion and Health*, 51(4), 1202–1215. doi:10.1007/s10943-010-9430-z

Misra, G. & Gergen, K. J. (1993). On the place of culture in psychological science. *International Journal of Psychology*, 28(2), 225–243. doi:10.1080/00207599308247186

Montes, S. A., Ledesma, R. D., García, N. M., & Poó, F. M. (2014). The Mindful Attention Awareness Scale (MAAS) in an Argentine population. *Measurement and Evaluation in Counseling and Development*, 47(1), 43–51. doi:10.1177/0748175613513806

Narendran, S., Nagarathna, R., Narendran, V., Gunasheela, S., & Nagendra, H. R. R. (2005). Efficacy of yoga on pregnancy outcome. *Journal of Alternative and Complementary Medicine*, 11(2), 237–244. doi:10.1089/acm.2005.11.2doi:37

Nyanaponika (1989). *Satipatthána – Geistestraining durch Achtsamkeit* (4th Ed.). Konstanz, Germany: Verlag Christiani.

Panaïoti, A. (2015). Mindfulness and personal identity in the Western cultural context: a plea for greater cosmopolitanism. *Transcultural Psychiatry*, 52(4), 501–523. doi:10.1177/1363461515573106

Piron, H. (2001). The Meditation Depth Index (MEDI) and the Meditation Depth Questionnaire (MEDEQ). *Journal for Meditation and Meditation Research*, 1, 50–67.

Proulx, J., Croff, R., Oken, B., Aldwin, C. M., Fleming, C., Bergen-Cio, D., …, & Noorani, M. (2018). Considerations for research and development of culturally relevant mindfulness interventions in American minority communities. *Mindfulness*, 9(2), 361–370. doi:10.1007/s12671-017-0785-z

Purser, R. & Loy, D. (2013). Beyond McMindfulness. *The Huffington Post*. Retrieved from www.huffingtonpost.com/ron-purser/ beyond-mcmindfulness_b_3519289.html

Rahula, W. (1974). *What the Buddha taught*. New York, USA: Grove Press.

Raphiphatthana, B., Jose, P. E., & Salmon, K. (2018a). Does dispositional mindfulness predict the development of grit? *Journal of Individual Differences*, 39(2), 76–87. doi:10.1027/1614-0001/a000252

Raphiphatthana, B., Jose, P. E., & Chobthamkit, P. (2018b). The association between mindfulness and grit: an East vs. West cross-cultural comparison. *Mindfulness*. Online First. doi:10.1007/s12671-018-0961-9

Ratanasiripong, P., Park, J. F., Ratanasiripong, N., & Kathalae, D. (2015). Stress and anxiety management in nursing students: biofeedback and mindfulness meditation. *Journal of Nursing Education*, 54(9), 520–524. doi:10.3928/01484834-20150814-07

Roberts, L. & Montgomery, S. (2015). Mindfulness-based intervention for perinatal grief after stillbirth in rural India. *Issues in Mental Health Nursing*, 36(3), 222–230. doi:10.3109/01612840.2014.962676

Roof, W. C. (2007). Pluralism as a culture: religion and civility in Southern California. *The ANNALS of the American Academy of Political and Social Science*, 612, 82–99. doi:10.1177/0002716207301061

Sahdra, B. K., Shaver, P. R., & Brown, K. W. (2010). A scale to measure nonattachment: a Buddhist complement to Western research on attachment and adaptive functioning. *Journal of Personality Assessment*, 92(2), 116–127. doi:10.1080/00223890903425960

Samuel, G. (2015). The contemporary mindfulness movement and the question of nonself. *Transcultural Psychiatry*, 52(4), 485–500. doi:10.1177/1363461514562061

Schoevers, M., Nykliček, I., & Topman, R. (2008). Validation of the Dutch version of the Mindful Attention Awareness Scale (MAAS) [Dutch]. *Gedragstherapie*, 41(3), 225–240.

Schopen, A. & Freeman, B. (1992). Meditation: the forgotten Western tradition. *Counseling and Values*, 36(2), 123–134. doi:10.1002/j.2161-007X.1991.tb00969.x-

Seema, R., Quaglia, J. T., Brown, K. W., Sircova, A., Konstabel, K., & Baltin, A. (2015). The Estonian Mindful Attention Awareness Scale: Assessing mindfulness without a distinct linguistic present tense. *Mindfulness*, 6(4), 759–766. doi:10.1007/s12671-014-0314-2

Sharf, R. H. (2015). Is mindfulness Buddhist? (and why it matters). *Transcultural Psychiatry*, 52(4), 470–484. doi:10.1177/1363461514557561

Shonin, E., Van Gordon, W., & Singh, N. N. (2015). *Buddhist foundations of mindfulness*. New York, USA: Springer.

Shonin, E., Van Gordon, W., & Griffiths, M. D. (2015). Teaching ethics in mindfulness-based interventions. *Mindfulness*, 6(6), 1491–1493. doi:10.1007/s12671-015-0429-0

Silpakit, C., Silpakit, O., & Wisajun, P. (2011). The validity of Philadelphia Mindfulness Scale Thai version. *Journal of Mental Health in Thailand*, 19, 140–147.

Silpakit, O. & Silpakit, C. (2014). A Thai version of mindfulness questionnaire: Srithanya Sati Scale. *East Asian Archives of Psychiatry*, 24(1), 23–29.

Simor, P., Köteles, F., Sándor, P., Petke, Z., & Bódizs, R. (2011). Mindfulness and dream quality: the inverse relationship between mindfulness and negative dream affect. *Scandinavian Journal of Psychology*, 52(4), 369–375. doi:10.1111/j.1467-9450.2011.00888.x

Singh, N. N., Lancioni, G. E., Medvedev, O. N., Myers, R. E., Chan, J., McPherson, C. L., …, & Kim, E. (2018). Comparative effectiveness of caregiver training in Mindfulness-Based Positive Behavior Support (MBPBS) and Positive Behavior Support (PBS) in a randomized controlled trial. *Mindfulness*. Online First. doi:10.1007/s12671-018-0895-2

Smith, R. H., Parrott, W. G., Diener, E. F., Hoyle, R. H., & Kim, S. H. (1999). Dispositional envy. *Personality and Social Psychology Bulletin*, 25(8), 1007–1020. doi:10.1177/01461672992511008

Soler, J., Tejedor, R., Feliu-Soler, A., Pascual, J. C., Cebolla, A., Soriano, J., …, & Perez, V. (2012). Psychometric proprieties of Spanish version of Mindful Attention Awareness Scale (MAAS). *Actas Españolas De Psiquiatría*, 40(1), 19–26.

Song, Y. & Lindquist, R. (2015). Effects of mindfulness-based stress reduction on depression, anxiety, stress and mindfulness in Korean nursing students. *Nurse Education Today*, 35(1), 86–90. doi:10.1016/j.nedt.2014doi:06.010

Sowattanangoon, N., Kochabhakdi, N., & Petrie, K. J. (2008). Buddhist values are associated with better diabetes control in Thai patients. *International Journal Psychiatry in Medicine*, 38 (4), 481–491. doi:10.2190/PM.38.4.g

Srichannil, C. & Prior, S. (2014). Practise what you preach: counsellors' experience of practising Buddhist counselling in Thailand. *International Journal of Advanced Counselling*, 36 (3), 243–261. doi:10.1007/s10447-013-9204-x

Stanley, S., Purser, R. E., & SinghN. N. (Eds.) (2018). *Handbook of ethical foundations of mindfulness*. New York, USA: Springer.

Stratton, S. P. (2015). Mindfulness and contemplation: secular and religious traditions in Western context. *Counseling and Values*, 60(1), 100–118. doi:10.1002/j.2161-007X.2015.00063.x

Sugiura, Y. (2008). New directions for research of emotion regulation and psychological treatments: potential benefits of mindfulness construct [Japanese]. *Japanese Journal of Research on Emotions*, 16(2), 167–177.

Sugiura, Y., Sato, A., Ito, Y., & Murakami, H. (2012). Development and validation of the Japanese version of the Five Facet Mindfulness Questionnaire. *Mindfulness*, 3(2), 85–94. doi:10.1007/s12671-011-0082-1

Symington, S. H. & Symington, M. F. (2012). A Christian model of mindfulness: using mindfulness principles to support psychological well-being, value-based behavior, and the Christian spiritual journey. *Journal of Psychology and Christianity*, 31(1), 71–77.

Taylor, N. Z. & Millear, P. M. R. (2016). Validity of the Five Facet Mindfulness Questionnaire in an Australian meditating, demographically diverse sample. *Personality and Individual Differences*, 90, 73–77. doi:10.1016/j.paid.201doi:5.10.041

Teasdale, J. D., Segal, Z., & Williams, J. M. G. (1995). How does cognitive therapy prevent depressive relapse and why should attentional control (mindfulness) training help? *Behaviour Research and Therapy*, 33(1), 25–39. doi:10.1016/0005-7967(94)E0011-7

Teasdale, J. D., Segal, Z. V., Williams, J. M. G., Ridgeway, V. A., Soulsby, J. M., & Lau, M. A. (2000). Prevention of relapse/recurrence in major depression by Mindfulness-Based Cognitive Therapy. *Behaviour Research and Therapy*, 68(4), 615–623. doi:10.1037/0022-006X.68.4doi:615

Thomas, J., Raynor, M., & Bakker, M.-C. (2016). Mindfulness-based stress reduction among Emirati Muslim women. *Mental Health, Religion & Culture*, 19(3), 295–304. doi:10.1080/13674676.2016.1168389

Tomasino, B., Chiesa, A., & Fabbro, F. (2014). Disentangling the neural mechanisms involved in Hinduism- and Buddhism-related meditations. *Brain and Cognition*, 90, 32–40. doi:10.1016/j.bandc.2014.doi:03.013

Trammel, R. C. (2017). Tracing the roots of mindfulness: transcendence in Buddhism and Christianity. *Journal of Religions & Spirituality in Social Work: Social Thoughts*, 36(3), 367–383. doi:10.1080/15426432.2017.1295822

Trammel, R. C. (2018). A phenomenological study of Christian practitioners who use mindfulness. *Journal of Spirituality in Mental Health*, 20(3), 199–224. doi:10.1080/193449637.2017.1408445

Trousselard, M., Steiler, D., Raphel, C., Cian, C., Duymedjian, R., Claverie, D., & Canini, F. (2010). Validation of a French version of the Freiburg Mindfulness Inventory – short version: relationships between mindfulness and stress in an adult population. *BioPsychoSocial Medicine*, 4, 8. doi:10.1186/1751-0759-4-8

Tsai, J. L., Miao, F. F., & Seppala, E. (2007). Good feelings in Christianity and Buddhism: religious differences in ideal affect. *Personality and Social Psychology Bulletin*, 33(3), 409–421. doi:10.1177/0146167206296107

Tukaev, R. & Kuznetsov, V. (2013). Universal hypnotherapy and mindfulness-based interventions: similarities and differences, Therapeutic perspectives [Russian]. *Social and Clinical Psychiatry*, 23, 2.

Usami, R. & Tagami, K. (2012). Effortful control mediates the relation between mindfulness and depression [Japanese]. *Bulletin of the Faculty of Education of Hirosaki University*, 107, 131–138.

Van Gordon, W., Shonin, E., & Griffiths, M. D. (2015). Towards a second generation of mindfulness-based interventions. *Australian & New Zealand Journal of Psychiatry*, 49(7), 591–592. doi:10.1177/0004867415577437

Van Gordon, W., Shonin, E., Griffiths, M. D., & Singh, N. N. (2015). There is only one mindfulness: why science and Buddhism need to work together. *Mindfulness*, 6(1), 49–56. doi:10.1007/s12671-014-0379-7

Van Gordon, W., Shonin, E., & Griffiths, M. D. (2016). Are contemporary mindfulness-based interventions unethical? *British Journal of General Practice*, 66(643), 94–94. doi:10.3399/bjgp16X683677

van Oers, B. (1998). The fallacy of decontextualization. *Mind, Culture, and Activity*, 5(2), 135–142. doi:10.1207/s15327884mca0502_7

Veneziani, C. A. & Voci, A. (2015). The Italian adaptation of the Mindful Awareness Attention Scale and its relation with individual differences and quality of life indexes. *Mindfulness*, 6(2), 373–381. doi:10.1007/s12671-013-0270-2

Wachholtz, A. B. & Pargament, K. I. (2005). Is spirituality a critical ingredient of meditation? Comparing the effects of spiritual meditation, secular meditation, and relaxation on spiritual, psychological, cardiac, and pain outcomes. *Journal of Behavioral Medicine*, 28(4), 369–384. doi:10.1007/s10865-005-9008-5

Wada, K.,= & Park, J. (2009). Integrating Buddhist psychology into grief counseling. *Death Studies*, 33(7), 657–683. doi:10.1080/07481180903012006

Waldron, E. M., Hong, S., Moskowitz, J. T., & Burnett-Zeigler, I. (2018). A systematic review of the demographic characteristics of participants in US-based randomized controlled trials of mindfulness-based interventions. *Mindfulness*. Online First. doi:10.1007/s12671-018-0920-5

Watson, N. N., Black, A. R., & Hunter, C. D. (2016). African American women's perceptions of mindfulness meditation training and gendered race-related stress. *Mindfulness*, 7(5), 1034–1043. doi:10.1007/s12671-016-0539-3

Wayment, H. A., Wiist, B., Sullivan, B. M., & Warren, M. A. (2011). Doing and being: mindfulness, health, and quiet ego characteristics among Buddhist practitioners. *Journal of Happiness Studies*, 12(4), 575–589. doi:10.1007/s10902-010-9218-6

Weber, B., Jermann, F., Lutz, A., Bizzini, L., & Bondolfi, G. (2012). Mindfulness-based therapeutic approaches: benefits for individuals suffering from pain [French]. *Revue Médicale Suisse*, 8, 1395–1398.

Whitesman, S. L., Hoogenhout, M., Kantor, L., Leinberger, K. J., & Gevers, A. (2018). Examining the impact of a Mindfulness-Based Stress Reduction intervention on the health of urban South Africans. *African Journal of Primary Health Care & Family Medicine*, 10 (1), a1614. doi:10.4102/phcfm.v10i1.1614

William, J. M. G. & Kabat-Zinn, J. (2011). Mindfulness: diverse perspectives on its meaning, origins, and multiple applications at the intersection of science and dharma. *Contemporary Buddhism*, 12(1), 1–18. doi:10.1080/14639947.2011.564811

Wiriyasombat, R., Pothiban, L., Panuthai, S., Sucamvang, K., & Saengthong, S. (2003). Effectiveness of Buddhist doctrine practice-based programs in enhancing spiritual well-being, coping and sleep quality of Thai elders. *Pacific Rim International Journal of Nursing Research*, 15(3), 203–219.

Wongtongkam, N., Ward, P. R., Day, A., & Winefield, A. H. (2014). A trial of mindfulness meditation to reduce anger and violence in Thai youth. *International Journal of Mental Health and Addiction*, 12(2), 169–180. doi:10.1007/s11469-013-9463-0

Xu, W., Jia, K., Liu, X., & Hofmann, S. G. (2016). The effects of mindfulness training on emotional health in Chinese long-term male prison inmates. *Mindfulness*, 7(5), 1044–1051. doi:10.1007/s12671-016-0540-x

Zainal, N. Z., Nor-Aziyan, Y., & Subramaniam, P. (2015). Psychometric properties of the Malay-translated Mindfulness, Attention and Awareness Scale (MAAS) in a group of nursing students in Malaysia. *Malaysian Journal of Psychiatry*, 24(1), 1–9.

Zeng, X., Li, M., Zhang, B., & Liu, X. (2015). Revision of the Philadelphia Mindfulness Scale for meauring awareness and equanimity in Goenka's Vipassana meditation with Chinese Buddhists. *Journal of Religion and Health*, 54(2), 623–637. doi:10.1007/s10943-014-9870-y

Zeng, X., Chio, F. H. N., Oei, T. P. S., Leung, F. Y. K., & Liu, X. (2017a). A systematic review of associations between amount of meditation practice and outcomes in interventions using the Four Immeasurables Meditations. *Frontiers in Psychology*, 8, 141. doi:10.3389/fpsyg.2017.00141

Zeng, X., Chan, V. Y. L., Liu, X., Oei, T. P. S., & Leung, F. Y. K. (2017b). The Four Immeasurables Meditations: differential effects of appreciative joy and compassion meditations on emotions. *Mindfulness*, 8(4), 949–959. doi:10.1007/s12671-016-0671-0

Zeng, X., Chan, V. Y. L., Oei, T. P. S., Leung, F. Y. K., & Liu, X. (2017c). Appreciative joy in Buddhism and positive empathy in psychology: How do they differ? *Mindfulness*, 8 (5), 1184–1194. doi:10.1007/s12671-017-0690-5

Zeng, X., Liao, R., Zhang, R., Oei, T. P. S., Yao, Z., Leung, F. Y. K., & Liu, X. (2017d). Development of the Appreciative Joy Scale. *Mindfulness*, 8(2), 286–299. doi:10.1007/s12671-016-0599-4

Zeng, X., Wang, R., Oei, T. P. S., & Leung, F. Y. K. (2018). Heart of Joy: a randomized controlled trail [sic] evaluating the effect of an a appreciative joy meditation training on subjective well-being and attitudes. *Mindfulness*. Online First. doi:10.1007/s12671-018-0992-2

Zhang, J.-X., Liu, X.-H., Xie, X.-H., Zhao, D., Shan, M.-S., Zhang, X.-L., ..., & Cui, H. (2015). Mindfulness-Based Stress Reduction for chronic insomnia in adults older than 75 years: a randomized, controlled, single-blind clinical trial. *Explore*, 11(3), 180–185. doi:10.1016/j.explore.2015. 02. 005

INDEX